W9-CIR-112

TINA HOWE was born in New York City. She received her B.A. from Sarah Lawrence College, and did graduate studies at the Sorbonne in Paris, Columbia Teacher's College, N.Y., and Chicago Teachers College. She has been writing plays since her senior year in college, and is presently an instructor of playwriting at New York University. Ms. Howe is married and the mother of two children, and resides in New York City.

THREE PLAYS BY TINA HOWE

MUSEUM
THE ART OF DINING
PAINTING CHURCHES

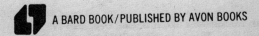 A BARD BOOK/PUBLISHED BY AVON BOOKS

First five lines of "THE SHEEP CHILD," reprinted by permission of Wesleyan University Press. Copyright © 1966 by James Dickey. Reprinted from FALLING, MAY DAY SERMON, AND OTHER POEMS by permission of Wesleyan University Press.

"Le Monocle de Mon Oncle," Copyright © 1923, 1951 by Wallace Stevens. Reprinted by permission of Alfred A. Knopf, Inc. from THE COMPLETE WALLACE STEVENS by Wallace Stevens.

"Dolor" & "I Knew A Woman," by Theodore Roethke. "Dolor" Copyright © 1943 Modern Poetry Association, Inc.; "I Knew A Woman" Copyright © 1954 by Theodore Roethke from THE BOOK OF COLLECTED POEMS by Theodore Roethke. Reprinted by permission of Doubleday & Company, Inc.

Poem "#1593" by Emily Dickinson. Reprinted by permission of the publishers and Trustees of Amherst College from THE POEMS OF EMILY DICKINSON, edited by Thomas H. Johnson, Cambridge, Mass.: The Belknap Press of Harvard University Press, Copyright 1951, © 1955, 1979, 1983 by the President and Fellows of Harvard College.

"Fire and Ice," from the poetry of Robert Frost edited by Edward Connery Lathem. Copyright 1923 © 1969 by Holt, Rinehart and Winston. Copyright © 1951 by Robert Frost. Reprinted by permission of Holt, Rinehart and Winston, Publishers.

The author would like to thank Miss Anne Yeats for permission to reprint "The Song of the Wandering Aengus" by W.B. Yeats.

THREE PLAYS BY TINA HOWE is an original publication of Avon Books. This work has never before appeared in book form. This work is fiction. Any similarity to actual persons or events is purely coincidental.

AVON BOOKS
A division of
The Hearst Corporation
1790 Broadway
New York, New York 10019

Copyright © 1984 by Tina Howe
Published by arrangement with the author
Library of Congress Catalog Card Number: 84-91113
ISBN: 0-380-85001-X

First Bard Printing, September, 1984

BARD TRADEMARK REG. U.S. PAT. OFF. AND IN OTHER COUNTRIES, MARCA REGISTRADA, HECHO EN U.S.A.

Printed in the U.S.A.

OPB 10 9 8 7 6 5 4 3 2 1

Acknowledgments

Plays are like Chinese paper flowers that bloom in water. They don't come to life unless someone fills a glass and then carefully drops them in. The playwright is completely dependent on the good will and dexterity of others. I am blessed in how nimble my collaborators have been. I have many people to thank: the actors, those possessed visionaries, for taking my breath away over and over again; Richard Jordan, for being my most ardent fan, literally arm-wrestling theater owners into doing my early plays; Jane Alexander, for directing my first effort in college and shining as an inspiration ever after; Honor Moore, for producing my first full-length work and constantly reminding me of the strengths of my sex; Joseph Papp, for taking on my most extravagant plays and mounting them with taste and passion; The Second Stage for bringing *Painting Churches* to such stunning life at the South Street Theatre; Carole Rothman, for her luminous and inspired direction; Liz McCann and Nelle Nugent, for their stamina and style in moving it to the Lambs Theatre; Flora Roberts, for her wisdom, buoyancy, and amazing telephone voice; my two children, Eben and Dara, for hanging in with me and not becoming runaways; and finally my husband, Norman, for his abiding integrity and ravishing sense of humor.

Foreword

Ever since the idea of publishing these plays came up, I've been fixated on the brilliant introduction I'd write. Finally I'd be given my say, I'd explain *everything*—compressing each image and nuance into a stunning tour de force like one of those fast-forward nature films that shows a small grey larva erupt into a riotous butterfly in thirty seconds flat.

Four months and 750 drafts later, my typewriter in pieces and the walls spattered with white-out, I realize I can't do it. I've been practicing the art of suggestion too long. I'm unable to make definitive sweeping statements; they just lie there gasping for air—"*Museum* closes with a tableau of a couple silently admiring their son's canvas; in *Painting Churches* the image is pushed to its limit as another set of parents finally steps through that frame and actually *becomes* the work of art." It sounds good, but what does it *mean*? Each of these plays moves according to its own logic and design. I see terrible dangers in insisting on tidy parallels and meaningful departures. It drains away all the mystery.

Clearly these plays inhabit the same aesthetic ground, each attempting to burst the perimeters of the one that went before. They share an absorption with the making and consuming of art, a fascination with food, a tendency to veer off into the primitive and neurotic, and of course a hopeless infatuation with the sight gag. Perhaps their oddest feature is how they shrink in physical dimension as they progress, moving from a crowded museum down to an intimate living room. Writers are supposed to start in their living rooms, not end up there. I did it all backwards and now have nowhere to go unless I jump down my throat and take on a whole new intestinal landscape.

So much for my attempt to turn a larva into a butterfly before your very eyes. I'm afraid I made it disappear altogether.

New York City
January 1984

For Norman

Contents

THREE PLAYS
BY TINA HOWE

MUSEUM

MUSEUM premiered at the Los Angeles Actors Theatre in 1976; artistic director, Ralph Waite

DIRECTORS: Dana Elcar and Richard Jordan
SETTING: Wendy Milner-Calloway
LIGHTING: Stan Bryant
SOUND: John Brasher

CAST

THE GUARD	Philip Baker Hall/Ralph Waite
MICHAEL WALL	David Stafford/Barry Brown
JEAN-CLAUDE	Jean-Francois Ferriol
FRANCOISE	Kerry Shear/Xenia Gratsos
PETER ZIFF	Sean Michael Rice
ANNETTE FROEBEL	Geneva Simmons
LIZ	Alison Coutts
CAROL	Susan Halpern
BLAKEY	Laura Carlson
MR. HOLLINGSFORD	Tom Lawrence
MR. SALT	Michael Shack/Tom Howard
MRS. SALT	Betty Palivoda
MAGGIE SNOW	Manuela Thiess
HANS DURHEIM	Jeff Davis
BOB LAMB	Ron Rickards
WILL WILLARD	Fox Harris
ELIZABETH SORROW	Maxine Borenstein/Jan Burrell

3

TINA HOWE

MR. GREGORY............................. Kamalo Dean
HARRIET POGOL .... Xenia Gratsos/Amy Joyce
BARBARA ZIMMER .... Karen Kondan
BARBARA CASTLE......................Barbara Peacock
CHLOE TRAPP.................... Jacque Lynn Colton/
.... Maxine Borenstein
ADA BILDITSKY .... Viola Kates Stimpson
GILDA NORRIS ....Jan Burrell/Jane Holderman
TINK SOLHEIM .... Francine Lembi/Lisa Richards
KATE SIV .... Mary Farrell/Carol Wyand
BILL PLAID....... Michael MacRae/Philip Baker Hall
MAY.. Sheila Ochs
LILLIAN ....Gwen Van Dam
HARRIET ....Toni Sawyer
1ST LADY & TOUR GROUP ....Gale Vance
2ND LADY & TOUR GROUP............ Judy Armstrong
GIORGIO CALVERRIO .... Barry Michlin/Michael Shack
ZOE CALVERRIO...............................Enid Kent
JULIE JENKINS...........Erin O'Riley/Francine Lembi
MRS. THOFF...................Amy Allen/Zitto Kazann
THE ARTIST .... Donald Moffat/Mitch Ryan
1ST GUARD................................Fred Pinkard
2ND GUARD .... Mel Allen
TOUR GROUP... Helen Berg, Paul Weaver, W.C. Finch
ELDERLY MAN .... George Scott
ELDERLY WOMAN............................. Ina Gould

4

New York Shakespeare Festival Production, 1977; Joseph Papp, Producer.

DIRECTOR: Max Stafford-Clark
SETTING: Robert Yodice
LIGHTING: Jennifer Tipton
COSTUMES: Patricia McGourty

CAST
(in order of appearance)

THE GUARD	Larry Bryggman
MICHAEL WALL	Bruce McGill
JEAN-CLAUDE	Jean-Pierre Stewart
FRANÇOISE	Frederikke Meister
ANNETTE FROEBEL	Kaiulani Lee
LIZ	Robyn Goodman
CAROL	Kathryn Grody
BLAKEY	Kathleen Tolan
MR. HOLLINGSFORD	Gerry Bamman
ELIZABETH SORROW	Dianne Wiest
PETER ZIFF	Dan Hedaya
MR. SALT	Steven Gilborn
MRS. SALT	Jane Hallaren
MAGGIE SNOW	Lynn Milgrim
BOB LAMB	Jeffrey David Pomerantz
WILL WILLARD	Joel Brooks

TINA HOWE

FRED IZUMI ....Calvin Jung
MIRA ZADAL .... Robyn Goodman
FIRST MAN IN PASSING .... Gerry Bamman
SECOND MAN IN PASSING .... Jean-Pierre Stewart
BARBARA CASTLE........................Lynn Milgrim
BARBARA ZIMMER .... Karen Ludwig
MR. GREGORY.....................Jean-Pierre Stewart
CHLOE TRAPP............................Kaiulani Lee
ADA BILDITSKY ....Frederikke Meister
GILDA NORRIS .... Kathryn Grody
TINK SOLHEIM .... Dianne Wiest
KATE SIV .... Robyn Goodman
BILL PLAID...................Jeffrey David Pomerantz
LILLIAN ....Frederikke Meister
HARRIET ....Lynn Milgrim
MAY.. Karen Ludwig
GIORGIO.................................. Gerry Bamman
ZOE his wife ....Jane Hallaren
JULIE JENKINS........................... Kathleen Tolan
FIRST GUARD ....Steven Gilborn
SECOND GUARD...........................Dan Hedaya
STEVE WILLIAMS ....Joel Brooks
AN ELDERLY COUPLE
.... Steven Gilborn, Karen Ludwig

CHARACTERS

THE GUARD, *Guardian of the exhibit*
MICHAEL WALL, *First photographer*
JEAN-CLAUDE, *French visitor*
FRANÇOISE, *French visitor*
ANNETTE FROEBEL, *Lost woman*
LIZ, *College girl*
CAROL, *College girl*
BLAKEY, *College girl*
ELIZABETH SORROW, *Bewildered woman*
PETER ZIFF, *Silent man*
MR. SALT, *Man with recorded tour*

MRS. SALT, *Wife, attached to recorded tour*
MAGGIE SNOW, *Lost woman*
BOB LAMB, *Art enthusiast*
WILL WILLARD, *Art enthusiast*
FRED IZUMI, *Second photographer*
MIRA ZADAL, *Inquiring woman*
FIRST MAN IN PASSING
SECOND MAN IN PASSING
BARBARA CASTLE, *Fashion plate*
BARBARA ZIMMER, *Her mirror image*
MR. GREGORY, *Man with loud recorded tour*
CHLOE TRAPP, *Curator*
ADA BILDITSKY, *Chloe's first guest*
GILDA NORRIS, *Sketcher*
TINK SOLHEIM, *Friend of Agnes Vaag*
KATE SIV, *Friend of Agnes Vaag*
BILL PLAID, *Chloe's second guest*
LILLIAN, *Laughing lady*
HARRIET, *Laughing lady*
MAY, *Laughing lady*
GIORGIO, *Art buff*
ZOE, *His wife*
JULIE JENKINS, *Third photographer, a knockout*
FIRST GUARD, *Guard from another area of the museum*
SECOND GUARD, *Guard from another area of the museum*
STEVE WILLIAMS, *Artist*
MR. AND MRS. MOE, *An elderly couple*

TIME: *The present*
PLACE: *The second floor gallery of a major American museum of modern art on the final day of a group show, titled "The Broken Silence." The artists and works on display are:*

ZACHERY MOE
Born 1945, Fort Wayne, Indiana

Four gigantic white canvases, all identical.

Landscape I, 1984
Acrylic emulsion and wax on canvas
On loan from the Sidney Rubin Gallery

Landscape II, 1984
Acrylic emulsion and wax on canvas
On loan from the Sidney Rubin Gallery

Seascape VII, 1984
Acrylic emulsion and wax on canvas
On loan from the Sidney Rubin Gallery

Starscape XIX, 1984

On loan from the artist

(The dates of completion of the paintings should correspond to the year the play is being read or performed. As the years pass, the dates of the artists' births should also be moved ahead to keep them suitably young.)

9

AGNES VAAG
Born 1960, St. Cloud, Minnesota

Nine small, menacing constructions made of animal teeth, feathers, fur, claws, bone, shell, wings, horn, scales, sponge, and antennae.

Sacred Inquisition, Daylight Savings Time, 1984
On loan from the Minneapolis Institute of Fine Arts

When the Archangels Abandon Their Grace, 1984
On loan from the Minneapolis Institute of Fine Arts

Prometheus, Singed, 1984
On loan from the Minneapolis Institute of Fine Arts

Socratic Dialogue, 1984
On loan from the Corcoran Gallery of Art

The Temptation and Corruption of William Blake, 1984
On loan from the Whitney Museum of American Art

Abraxas, 1984
On loan from the Whitney Museum of American Art

Ode to Emily Dickinson, 1984
On loan from the Rhode Island School of Design

Metaphysics Revisited, 1984
On loan from the private collection of Igmar Vaag

The Holy Wars of Babylon Rage Through the Night, 1984
On loan from the private collection of Igmar Vaag

STEVE WILLIAMS
Born 1938, Santa Rosa, California

A clothesline runs twenty-five feet across the room. On it hang five life-sized cloth figures. They are spookily realistic and are made so they can come apart and be put back together again.

The first figure is a businessman dressed in a pin-striped suit. One of his shoes is missing.

Second is a bride billowing in satin and veils.

Third is a Mexican boy in a tee shirt.

Fourth is a self-portrait of the artist wearing blue jeans and a plaid lumber jacket.

Fifth is a naked Chinese woman with bound feet.

A basket of round-headed clothespins sits under the clothesline. The piece is titled *Wet Dream Left Out to Dry*, 1984. Construction of rope, cloth, papier-mâché, wire, leather, wood, plaster, and fiber glass.
On loan from the Los Angeles County Museum of Art

The audience should be encouraged to walk through the exhibit before the play begins.

The Curtain Rises: *It's morning, several minutes before the museum opens. The gallery is in darkness. Nothing happens; then faraway sounds of footsteps and clanging doors are heard.*

THE GUARD: [*Walks briskly into the room. Turns on the lights, first the Agnes Vaags are illuminated with pinpricks of light, then the Moes are revealed, and finally the clothesline. As* THE GUARD *brings everything to life, a voice sounding something like a combination of God and a newscaster announces:*]

VOICE: Sandro Botticelli's priceless masterpiece *The Birth of Venus* was attacked and virtually destroyed yesterday afternoon by a hooded man armed with a handgun who opened fire on the painting while screaming, "Cursed is the ground for thy sake." Before he was finally overcome by three guards and numerous bystanders, the heavily built assailant pumped more than eighteen bullets into the nude Venus figure, literally shooting her off the face of the canvas. The Acting Director of the Uffizi Gallery, which houses the masterpiece, said in an interview last night that it was the most violent attack ever made against a Renaissance painting. Restoration will be impossible.

THE GUARD: [*Stores this information along with everything else he knows and begins his daily process of*

13

becoming watchful yet as unobtrusive as possible. He rocks on his heels, sucks his breakfast out from between his teeth, picks fuzz off his uniform, hoists up his underwear, and waits.]

MICHAEL WALL: [*Enters carrying an arsenal of photographic equipment including a camera attached to a tripod. He looks around the room, finds the Zachery Moes, and sets his gear down in front of* Landscape I. *He walks up to it, then backs away, walks up close again and then takes out his light meter for a reading. He adjusts his camera and prepares to shoot, all with enormous concentration, energy, and flair.* THE GUARD *is mesmerized by him. After several moments,* WALL *poises his finger on the shutter release.*]

THE GUARD: It's against museum regulations to photograph the art works.

MICHAEL WALL: [*Whirling around, furious.*] You're kidding!

THE GUARD: It's against museum regulations to photograph the art works.

MICHAEL WALL: Thanks a lot for waiting to tell me until I was all set up....

THE GUARD: I'm surprised they even let you in with all that stuff....

MICHAEL WALL: [*Shaking his head.*] Too much!

THE GUARD: The attendant downstairs is supposed to see that all photographic equipment is left in the check room....

MICHAEL WALL: I don't believe this....

THE GUARD: ...and that includes binoculars, telescopes, folding...

MICHAEL WALL: You wait until I'm all set up, tripod locked, camera attached, "f" stop set....

THE GUARD: I've seen the attendant downstairs refuse visitors admittance who were just carrying...film!

MICHAEL WALL: ...AND WHEN ALL OF THAT IS DONE, THEN YOU TELL ME IT'S AGAINST MUSEUM REGULATIONS TO PHOTOGRAPH THE ART WORKS!

THE GUARD: And not just film either, but radios, tape recorders, typewriters and sandwiches...

MICHAEL WALL: Who do I see to get permission?

THE GUARD: I've seen the attendant downstairs stop visitors who had bulging pockets.

MICHAEL WALL: [*Detaching his camera from the tripod.*] The Head of Public Relations? The Administrative Assistant?

THE GUARD: The public has no respect for "place" anymore.

MICHAEL WALL: The Curator? The Chairman of the Board?

THE GUARD: They wear tennis shorts to church. They drink soda at the opera. They bring flash cameras to museums....

MICHAEL WALL: [*His camera in hand, walks up to* THE GUARD *and starts snapping his picture.*] Come on, who do I see for permission to photograph the art works? [*Taking a picture with each guess.*] The Cinematic Representative? The Acting President of the Exhibition? The Liaison for Public Information? [*Pause.*] You have an interesting profile.

THE GUARD: I've caught men exposing their genitals in this room!

MICHAEL WALL: [*Getting involved with* THE GUARD *as a model.*] Good cheek bones!

THE GUARD: Certain shows...inspire that!

MICHAEL WALL: ...strong chin...

THE GUARD: Nineteenth-century French Academy nudes encourage...flashing.

MICHAEL WALL: [*Adjusts* THE GUARD's *head for a shot.*] Hold it....

THE GUARD: [*Voice lowered.*] You'd be surprised, the shortest men have the most swollen genitals....

MICHAEL WALL: Nice...Nice...

THE GUARD: [*Flattered, shyly poses for him.*] And there don't even have to be women in the room in order for these...shorter men to expose their swollen genitals....

15

MICHAEL WALL: [*Still snapping.*] Come on, give me a hint. Do I see the curatorial staff or the administrative staff?

THE GUARD: Very few women expose themselves.

MICHAEL WALL: [*Taking closeups.*] Nice, very nice...

THE GUARD: Though I *have* seen a few younger women lift their skirts and drop their panties.

MICHAEL WALL: Please! Who do I see to get permission to photograph the art works?

[THE GUARD *and* MICHAEL WALL *are still as...*]

JEAN-CLAUDE AND FRANÇOISE: [*Enter, a French couple in their thirties. They are very serious museum-goers. They advance to the Moes.*]

JEAN-CLAUDE: [*Looks at* Landscape I, *then consults his bilingual catalogue.*] Voici, Zachery Moe!

FRANÇOISE: Ah oui, Zachery Moe!

JEAN-CLAUDE: [*Reading from his catalogue.*] "Le publique qui s'intéresse à l'art est tenté de ne voir que chaos dans la profusion des tendances de la peinture contemporaine...."

FRANÇOISE: [*Looking at the painting.*] Il a un style...un style...tout à fait....

JEAN-CLAUDE: [*Reading.*] "Trop près pour distinguer l'authentique du factice, il est le témoin trop passionné de la frénésie d'être divers qui est le propre des artistes de notre temps...."

FRANÇOISE: Tout à fait...tout à fait...FRAGILE!

JEAN-CLAUDE: "Il est troublé par la surproduction de la matière peinte. C'est une des singularités les plus cocasses de notre siècle..."

FRANÇOISE: Mais viens voir, Jean-Claude! Regarde la peinture!

JEAN-CLAUDE: ..."qui abonde pourtant en duperies de toutes sortes...."

FRANÇOISE: C'est une fragilité...mystique...une fragilité...religieuse...une fragilité...

JEAN-CLAUDE: [*Finally looks at the painting.*] PLASTIQUE! Une fragilité plastique, Françoise!

FRANÇOISE: [*Disagreeing.*] Une fragilité...symboliste!

JEAN-CLAUDE: Une fragilité...moderne!

FRANÇOISE: Une fragilité dix-septième siècle!

JEAN-CLAUDE: Une fragilité psychologique!

FRANÇOISE: Une fragilité...fragile!

JEAN-CLAUDE: AH OUI, SURTOUT UNE FRAGILITÉ FRAGILE!

FRANÇOISE: C'est le mot juste....

JEAN-CLAUDE: Fragile...

FRANÇOISE: Un adjectif exact!

JEAN-CLAUDE: Comme...futilé *futile*!

FRANÇOISE: Ou...frivolité *frivole*!

JEAN-CLAUDE: Fraternité *fraternelle*!

FRANÇOISE: Ou même de la...folie *folle*!

JEAN-CLAUDE: [*Kissing her in appreciation.*] Françoise, je t'adore! [*They gaze up at* Landscape I.]

THE GUARD: [*Softly to* MICHAEL WALL.] The Director!

MICHAEL WALL: What?

THE GUARD: The Director.

MICHAEL WALL: What about the Director?

THE GUARD: It's the Director who gives permission to photograph the art works!

MICHAEL WALL: [*Incredulous.*] THE DIRECTOR?

THE GUARD: The Director!

MICHAEL WALL: It just...never occurred to me that...the Director...

THE GUARD: [*In unison, smiling.*] ...the Director.

MICHAEL WALL: [*Amazed, gathers his equipment and hurries out of the room.*] The Director...son of a bitch...

THE GUARD: [*Yelling after him.*] Main floor to the left of the Checkroom.

JEAN-CLAUDE: [*Pointing to his catalogue.*] Regarde Françoise, un photo d'artiste....

FRANÇOISE: [*Looking at it.*] Tiens....

THE GUARD: [*To himself.*] I still don't understand how he got past the attendant downstairs.

FRANÇOISE: Quelle bouche!

JEAN-CLAUDE: [*Looking closely at the picture.*] C'est une bouche...extraordinaire!

THE GUARD: I mean, Raoul is tough on photographers!

FRANÇOISE: Une peu...chimpanzé, n'est-ce-pas?

JEAN-CLAUDE: Chimpanzé!

TINA HOWE

JEAN-CLAUDE: Mais voyons, Françoise, qu'est-ce que tu veux dire? Que c'est artiste extraordinaire resemble... un chimpanzé? Un bête sauvage? [*Looks at the picture, more and more troubled.*] C'est une erreur, une faute de photographe.... [*Looks closer.*] C'est... *incroyable*!

FRANÇOISE: Eh? Eh?

JEAN-CLAUDE: [*Approaches* THE GUARD *with his catalogue opened to the page, speaking in pidgin English.*] Excuse me please. The photograph in my catalogue. Here. This picture of Zachery Moe. There must be some mistake. This is a photo of a chimpanzee!

THE GUARD: Chimpanzee?
[*Takes the catalogue and looks.*]

JEAN-CLAUDE: You see, that is not a photograph of the artist. It's a photograph of a chimpanzee!

FRANÇOISE: [*Leaning over* THE GUARD'S *shoulder.*] C'est toute à fait fantastique!

THE GUARD: [*Looking at the picture very closely.*] It sure looks like a chimpanzee.

FRANÇOISE: [*Delighted, breaks into a light giggle; followed by monkey chattering noise.*]

JEAN-CLAUDE: [*Snatching the catalogue away from* THE GUARD.*] Monsieur, I am shocked. I have never seen such a thing before. Such an insult as this! You should be ashamed!

FRANÇOISE: C'est absolument ridicule!

JEAN-CLAUDE: It's a disgrace....

FRANÇOISE: [*Chatters in his ear, teasing, laughing.*]

JEAN-CLAUDE: [*Realizes how foolish it all is; succumbs and joins her in an answering chatter. Never for a moment do they abandon their French precision or dignity.*]

ANNETTE FROEBEL: [*Enters. She can be any woman of any age. She looks around, confused.*] Where did the Colonial Quilts and Weathervanes go?

THE GUARD: [*Shaking his head.*] No, that was no chimpanzee. I've seen his picture in the papers, and he doesn't look like no chimp!

ANNETTE FROEBEL: [*Remembering them as clear as day.*]

18

Colonial Quilts and Weathervanes used to be in this room...right over there!

THE GUARD: Colonial Quilts and Weathervanes are on the third floor, Miss!

ANNETTE FROEBEL: The *third* floor?

THE GUARD: Third floor.

ANNETTE FROEBEL: Are you sure?

THE GUARD: Colonial Quilts and Weathervanes are on the third floor.

ANNETTE FROEBEL: I could have sworn they were on this floor. [*She exits.*]

LIZ'S VOICE: [*Offstage.*] Did you hear what happened to Botticelli's *Venus* this morning?

CAROL'S VOICE: [*Offstage.*] No, what?

LIZ'S VOICE: Some maniac shot it with a gun.

LIZ, CAROL, AND BLAKEY: [*Enter, enthusiastic college girls who are taking an art course together.*]

CAROL: Someone *shot* it? People don't shoot paintings. They slash them!

LIZ: I heard it on the radio this morning. A hooded man pumped eighteen bullets into the Venus figure at the Uffizi.

CAROL: I've never heard of anyone...shooting a painting.

BLAKEY: You're right! They usually attack them with knives or axes.

CAROL: There's something so...alienated...about shooting a painting.

BLAKEY: ...and then there was the guy that wrote slogans all over *Guernica* with a can of spray paint!

LIZ: [*Laughing.*] That's right: spray paint!

BLAKEY: Red spray paint...and he misspelled everything, remember?

LIZ: [*Leading them to the Moes.*] Carol, Blakey, guys, YOU'RE GOING TO LOVE HIM!

[*They look at his work with reverence.*]

LIZ: [*Softly.*] You know, his parents are deaf mutes...*both* of them...profoundly deaf...

BLAKEY AND CAROL: [*Gasp.*]

LIZ: Can you imagine what it must have been like grow-

19

ing up with parents who couldn't hear you? I mean, when would you figure out that it was *their* affliction and not yours? How could a baby realize there was anything unusual about his parents? [*Pause.*] Since he never heard them utter a word, he must have assumed he couldn't speak either. He could hear his own little baby sounds of course, but he had no idea what they were....

BLAKEY AND CAROL: [*Exhale, impressed with the dilemma.*]

LIZ: When he cried...no one heard him.
[*Pause.*]

BLAKEY: Maybe he never did cry!

LIZ: Of course he cried! All babies cry. Even deaf babies.

CAROL: [*Lost.*] He assumed he couldn't speak either?...

LIZ: Don't forget, his parents could always *see* him cry. Sooner or later he must have realized that in order to get their attention he didn't really *have to cry*, all he had to do was go through the motions....[*She opens her mouth and cries without making a sound.*]

BLAKEY: [*Musing.*] If a deaf, *mute* baby had hearing parents...they couldn't hear *him* cry either....
[*Pause.*]

CAROL: [*Still lost.*] ...go through the motions?

LIZ: [*To* BLAKEY.] The deaf aren't necessarily mute, you know, some of them can make some sort of residual sound....

CAROL: [*She's got it.*] WHEN HE CRIED...NO ONE HEARD HIM!

LIZ: ...but it's not the case with Zachery Moe's parents. They are consigned to absolute and lifelong silence.

BLAKEY: [*Her head spinning from it all, turns her back on the Moes and notices the clothesline.*] OH MY GOD, WILL YOU LOOK AT THAT?! IT'S INCREDIBLE!

LIZ: [*Reaching for* CAROL.] When Moe finally realized that his meandering attempts at speech fell on deaf ears...

BLAKEY: [*Pulling* CAROL *with her.*] THIS IS THE MOST

BEAUTIFUL THING I'VE EVER SEEN IN MY LIFE!

[*Touching it gently.*]

THE GUARD: [*To* BLAKEY.] Please don't handle the art works.

BLAKEY: It's...fantastic!

THE GUARD: DON'T HANDLE THE ART WORKS!

BLAKEY: Oh, I'm sorry. [*To* CAROL.] Imagine thinking of making a clothesline...with the bodies left inside the clothes....

CAROL: [*Torn between her two friends.*] Yeah...

BLAKEY: It's a reality grounded in illusion!...

CAROL: [*Feeling trapped, detaches herself from* BLAKEY.] You know, this is the first time I've ever been in this museum!

BLAKEY: Oh no! There's even a little kid wearing a tee shirt!

THE GUARD: DON'T TOUCH.

BLAKEY: I'm not touching, for Christsakes, I'm just looking!

CAROL: [*Walking around the room.*] I've lived in this city my whole life, and this is the first time I've ever been to this museum!

BLAKEY: It's our bodies that give our clothes meaning, just as without our clothes we...

CAROL: [*Looking out the window.*] You know, you can always tell the quality of a museum by the view out the windows.

BLAKEY: [*Kneels by the basket of clothespins.*] Do you see this? He even left out the basket of clothespins?!

THE GUARD: [*Walks over to her.*] Please don't handle the basket of clothespins.

BLAKEY: [*Rises.*] If you're not supposed to handle the basket of clothespins, how come the artist put them there?

CAROL: [*To* BLAKEY.] The Tate Gallery has just about the shittiest view of any museum in the world!

BLAKEY: [*To* THE GUARD.] He put them there so we *would* touch them!

21

CAROL: The view from the Del Prado isn't so hot either.

LIZ: [*Still enthralled with the Moes.*] He chose painting as his voice! [*Opens her catalogue; stops at a page.*] Look at his early sketches! The drawings he did of his toys when he was only three! Do you believe this technique? Look at his handling of perspective....

JEAN-CLAUDE AND FRANÇOISE: [*Have worked their way to the Agnes Vaag sculptures.*]

FRANÇOISE: Jean-Claude, elle resemble Tougache, tu sais?

JEAN-CLAUDE: Il est beaucoup imité, tu sais, Tougache!

FRANÇOISE: C'est le même esprit que Tougache!

JEAN-CLAUDE: Tougache est trop admiré!

FRANÇOISE: C'est un style un peu comme Kavitsky aussi....

JEAN-CLAUDE: Mon chou, tu sais très bien que je n'aime pas Tougache de tout!

FRANÇOISE: Kavitsky est sombre....

JEAN-CLAUDE: ÉCOUTE, FRANÇOISE, TOUGACHE EST BÊTE!

FRANÇOISE: Elle choisit les objects simples comme Kimoto....

JEAN-CLAUDE: [*Flings down his catalogue in a rage and starts storming around the room.*] TOUGACHE EST DE LA SALOPERIE! JE DÉTESTE TOUGACHE! TOUGACHE EST DE LA MERDE. [*He starts raving in French.*]

FRANÇOISE: [*Upset and embarrassed.*] Jean-Claude ...chéri...

[*They stand at opposite ends of the room, sulking.*]

BLAKEY: The image of people being...laundered... washed...soaking wet...pinned up on the clothesline of life to dry out....

CAROL: [*Standing next to a window.*] If I designed a museum, there would be no art on display...just windows. The public would come *inside* the museum in order to look *outside* the windows. The object of study would be nature itself...as seen through many different types of windows. There'd be...elevated windows, dropped windows, stained glass windows, broken windows, bricked up windows, open windows...all looking out at exactly the same view....

LIZ: [*Still enthralled in front of the Moes.*] I don't know which I like more, his landscapes or seascapes....

CAROL: And then there'd be windows that weren't really windows at all, but *paintings* of windows....

BLAKEY: [*Starts laughing in delight over the clothesline.*]

MR. HOLLINGSFORD: [*Enters. He could be anybody; speaking to* THE GUARD.] Where would I find the...uh...the uh... [*He looks at* BLAKEY *and gets more confused.*]...Colonial Quilts and Weathervanes?

THE GUARD: Third floor.

MR. HOLLINGSFORD: Colonial Quilts and Weathervanes.

THE GUARD: Colonial Quilts and Weathervanes are on the third floor!

MR. HOLLINGSFORD: I was told they were on this floor. [*He consults his catalogue.*]

BLAKEY: [*Can't contain her delight over the clothesline and sways her head back and forth laughing and moaning gently.*]

THE GUARD: "The Broken Silence" is on this floor.

MR. HOLLINGSFORD: What?

THE GUARD: I SAID, "THE BROKEN SILENCE" IS ON THIS FLOOR!

MR. HOLLINGSFORD: Broken...what? [*Looks through his catalogue with rising alarm.*]

EVERYONE: [*Is startled and instantly quiet.*]

MR. HOLLINGSFORD: Broken quilts?

THE GUARD: Colonial Quilts and Weathervanes is on the third floor.

MICHAEL WALL: [*Reenters with all his photographic equipment minus the tripod, drops it to the floor underneath* Landscape I *and waves a paper in his hand.*] I got permission from the Director!

THE GUARD: COLONIAL QUILTS AND WEATHER-VANES IS ON THE THIRD FLOOR!

BLAKEY: [*Still on the floor, sways and croons with renewed feeling.*]

23

MICHAEL WALL: I just got permission from the Director himself. You can see, he signed it!

MR. HOLLINGSFORD: [*Bewildered.*] The broken silence?

MICHAEL WALL: He was very nice about it. He took my tripod, but he invited me back to the next show.

THE GUARD: [*To* MR. HOLLINGSFORD.] This is the last day of the show.

MR. HOLLINGSFORD: Thank you very much, I will. [*He exits.*]

MICHAEL WALL: I know it's the last day of the show, that's why I'm here!

BLAKEY: [*Emits a peal of delighted laughter.*]

LIZ: Just as sound and speech were irrelevant to him, so line and form became irrelevant. [*Pause.*] It makes you wonder where he'll go from here.... [*She dreams in front of the Moes.*]

THE GUARD: [*Takes the permission slip from* MICHAEL WALL.] It's against museum regulations to photograph the art works without permission from the Director.

BLAKEY: [*Advances on the clothesline, wedges in between two of the figures as if she's part of the work.*] Do you know what this makes me want to do? It makes me want to grab some of the clothespins and pin myself right up there alongside the others.... I want to be laundered...hung up to dry...all limp and dripping wet with the sun slowly drying me out....

THE GUARD: [*Going up to her.*] All right Miss, that's enough. I'm going to have to ask you to leave....

BLAKEY: They look so at peace, cleansed...flapping in the sun....

THE GUARD: [*Guiding her out of the room.*] That's it....We've had enough...quietly, quietly...just move it right along....

BLAKEY'S VOICE: [*From Offstage.*] I want to join them! I want to be cleansed! I want to feel the sun on my face....

CAROL: And then at some point, the structure of the museum would...just end...everyone would suddenly be...outside...*in the view*...they'd actually *become the view*, the objects on display. You'll stand in line and pay admission...to see...*yourself*! And then the guards will be hired to watch the people...watching each other...GOD! I'VE GOT TO WRITE THIS DOWN!

[*She exits.*]

LIZ: [*Seated before the Moes, falls into a revery.*] They must be so proud of him, his parents...so very proud. [*A silence descends. It's finally broken by...*]

ELIZABETH SORROW: [*Enters, a highly sensitive woman who has tremendous difficulty orienting herself to the art works. She doesn't know how long it takes to "see" them. She flits from one to the next like a yo-yo spinning on a string that keeps getting shorter and shorter. When she's through looking at something she doesn't trust her impressions, but rushes back to it for another glance, then on to the next one to compare, then back again. In the midst of her confusion...*]

PETER ZIFF: [*Enters. A silent and nervous man who glitters with a strange menace. His moves are stealthy and ambiguous. He should give the impression of having visited this show many times. Like ELIZABETH SORROW, he rarely notices other people.*]

[*Time passes in absolute silence as they alternately explore their hidden worlds. This silence is finally broken by the sound of a lively voice intoning on an acoustiguide.*]

MR. AND MRS. SALT: [*Enter, attached to an acoustiguide and to each other by twin wires they have plugged into their ears. They are not experienced museumgoers and are terrified by the voice babbling into their ears. Furthermore, they've never worn an acoustiguide before, and keep getting hopelessly tangled up in all the wires. The machine hangs around MR. SALT's neck, MRS. SALT follows him timidly. They are eventually overwhelmed by the difficulty of 1) keeping pace, 2) following the instructions of the guide, and 3) maneuvering with all the wires that keep getting in their way...and they collapse on the nearest bench.*]

THIS IS THE TEXT OF THE RECORDED TOUR: On behalf of

25

TINA HOWE

the trustees of the museum, it gives me great pleasure to welcome you to our current exhibition, "The
Broken Silence." Before we start on our tour, let me
say a few words about the operation of the cassette
you are now wearing around your neck. The small
red button on the left allows you to turn me on or
off at your own discretion. When you hear this beep
sound [*Beep sound.*], it is the signal that my com-
mentary about a specific work is finished and that
you may turn the button to the "off" position and
enjoy the painting or sculpture at your own leisure.
When you wish to rejoin me, simply turn the button
back to "on" and our tour will continue. If you in-
advertently miss any of my remarks and would like
to hear them again, switch the red button to "off"
and then turn the adjacent white button to the "re-
play" position. My comments will then be repeated
until you are caught up and ready to proceed. At
that time, just return the white button to "play" and
be sure to remember to flip the red button back to
the "on" position. To raise and lower the volume on
the earphone element, just turn the large black dial
at the center of the cassette clockwise or counter-
clockwise. If the quality of your recorded tour is de-
fective in any way, simply exchange it for another
cassette at the front desk, main floor, to the left of
the checkroom.

JEAN-CLAUDE AND FRANÇOISE: [*Find themselves in front
of the clothesline, and are horrified by it.*]

FRANÇOISE: Mon Dieu, Jean-Claude, regarde!

JEAN-CLAUDE: Quelle horreur!

FRANÇOISE: C'est affreux!

JEAN-CLAUDE: Un insult!

FRANÇOISE: Dégoutant...

JEAN-CLAUDE: Déplorable...

FRANÇOISE: Débraillé...

JEAN-CLAUDE: Décadent...

FRANÇOISE: Déclassé...

[*They get angrier and angrier.*]

JEAN-CLAUDE: Décomposé...

26

FRANÇOISE: Défectif...

JEAN-CLAUDE: Défoncé...

[*And faster and faster.*]

FRANÇOISE: DÉFORMÉ!

JEAN-CLAUDE: DÉGÉNERÉ!

FRANÇOISE: DÉGRADANT!

JEAN-CLAUDE: DÉMODÉ!

FRANÇOISE: [*Weepy.*] Je veux partir, Jean-Claude.

JEAN-CLAUDE: Moi aussi, Françoise.

[*He takes her arm and with the utmost grace and disdain...they exit.*]

[*At this point the following people are in the gallery.* THE GUARD *watching over* LIZ. LIZ *watching the Zachery Moes and thumbing through her catalogue.* ELIZABETH SORROW *resting on one of the benches. The* SALTS *at the mercy of their recorded tour,* MICHAEL WALL *taking pictures, and* PETER ZIFF, *moody and restless.*]

MAGGIE SNOW: [*Enters, a woman in a hurry. To* THE GUARD.] Excuse me, where is the Puritan Pewter and Hooked Rugs?

THE GUARD: You mean, Colonial Quilts and Weathervanes.

MAGGIE SNOW: No! Puritan Pewter and Hooked Rugs!

THE GUARD: We don't have Puritan Pewter or Hooked Rugs on exhibit here, only Colonial Quilts and Weathervanes!

MAGGIE SNOW: [*Exits, running.*] Typical! Typical!

[*Almost bumping into...*]

BOB LAMB AND WILL WILLARD: [*Glide into the room like elegant swans. They are experienced museum-goers, close friends, and arbiters of good taste.*]

WILL WILLARD: Bruce said the show was shit!

BOB LAMB: Bruce says everything is shit!

WILL WILLARD: Well, Bruce said *this* show was especially shit. *Merde de la merde!*

BOB LAMB: [*Looking around the room.*] Pretentious?...

WILL WILLARD: This wasn't my idea!...

BOB LAMB: [*Looking at the Moes.*] Ad Reinhardt was doing those in black twenty years ago!

WILL WILLARD: I would never in a million years...

BOB LAMB: And Yves Klein did them in blue before you were even born!

WILL WILLARD: I'm sorry, my taste is more...

BOB LAMB: It's pure Rauschenberg, but without the emotion.

WILL WILLARD: Wait a minute, I love Rauschenberg!

BOB LAMB: Willard, I love him too, but...*this*...

WILL WILLARD: Rauschenberg is a giant!

BOB LAMB: Rauschenberg is *the* giant!

FRED IZUMI: [*Enters. Another photographer, a second-generation Oriental who's been completely Americanized save for a residue of old world politeness. He starts setting up his equipment in front of one of the Moes.*]

BOB LAMB: [*Looking at the clothesline.*] I like Segal better.

WILL WILLARD: You do?

BOB LAMB: Don't you?

WILL WILLARD: I thought you've said Segal was shallow.

BOB LAMB: I've never said Segal was...shallow. Just a bit...muted for my taste.

WILL WILLARD: Well, what about Duane Hanson?

BOB LAMB: Hanson...[*Laughing with pleasure.*] is divine!

THE GUARD: [*Noticing* FRED IZUMI.] Hey mister, it's against museum regulations to photograph the art works!

WILL WILLARD: Hanson is...insane!

FRED IZUMI: [*To* THE GUARD.] Excuse me, but I notice there is another man here taking photographs.

WILL WILLARD: Of course my all-time favorite is...

WILL WILLARD: Claes Oldenberg!   BOB LAMB: Claes Oldenberg! I know!

FRED IZUMI: [*Going over to* THE GUARD.] I'm sorry for troubling you again, but unless I'm very mistaken, that fellow over there is taking photographs.

THE GUARD: He has permission.

FRED IZUMI: Oh...he has permission.

BOB LAMB: [*Reads the title of the clothesline.*] Wet Dream

Left Out to Dry, 1984 [*He starts to laugh.*]

WILL WILLARD: [*Laughs with him.*]

BOB LAMB: [*Reading in an affected voice.*] "On loan from the Los Angeles County Museum of Art!"

FRED IZUMI: [*To* THE GUARD.] Would there be some way I might get permission as well?

LIZ: [*Comes out of her revery over the Moes. Looks around the room for her friends who have disappeared.*] Carol? Blakey? Guys? Hello? CAROL? GUYS?
[*She exits in a panic.*]

WILL WILLARD: Isn't it terribly loud in here? I can't see a thing!

BOB LAMB: This has always been a noisy museum.

FRED IZUMI: If there is some procedure to follow to get permission, perhaps you'd tell me what it is.

THE GUARD: If you want permission to photograph the art works, you'll have to see the Director.

FRED IZUMI: Oh, the Director?! That's curious, usually it's the Administrative Assistant who authorizes permission to photograph the art works.
[*He exits.*]

BOB LAMB: Oh no, look at that! He put a basket of real clothespins under an imaginary clothesline. Now, that's what I call...*panache*!

WILL WILLARD: You mean, *pastiche*!

BOB LAMB: *Pastiche*?

WILL WILLARD: Real clothespins under an imaginary clothesline!

BOB LAMB: Willard, *pastiche* is collage, I mean, *panache*...dash!

WILL WILLARD: Robert, the word is...*panacea*!

BOB LAMB: *Panacea*?...

WILL WILLARD: No wait, *paradigm*!

BOB LAMB: [*Thinking back, confused.*] *Pastiche*?...

WILL WILLARD: [*Also confused.*] *Placebo*?...

BOB LAMB: PARADIGM?...

FRED IZUMI: [*Reappears; to* THE GUARD, *slightly out of breath.*] Excuse me again, but...uh...where would I...uh...find the Director?

THE GUARD: Main floor, to the left of the Checkroom.

FRED IZUMI: Yes of course! The main floor!
[*He exits again.*]

BOB LAMB: [*Absentmindedly picks up one of the clothespins to help him find the* mot juste.]

THE GUARD: Please don't handle the clothespins!

BOB LAMB: [*Drops it.*] Oh, sorry. [*To* WILLARD, *but also taunting* THE GUARD.] Did you read that the Metropolitan Museum of Art is only going to be open four days a week?

WILL WILLARD: The Metropolitan?

BOB LAMB: [*To* THE GUARD, *pointedly.*] The museum doesn't have enough money to pay its force of two hundred and twenty-seven security guards.

WILL WILLARD: The Metropolitan has two hundred twenty-seven security guards?

BOB LAMB: [*Eyeing* THE GUARD.] The Metropolitan *had* two hundred twenty-seven security guards. They just let eighty-two go.

WILL WILLARD: I had no idea Metropolitan had two hundred twenty-seven guards.

BOB LAMB: They just let eighty-two go.

WILL WILLARD: I thought they had fifty or sixty guards...but *two hundred and twenty-seven*?!

BOB LAMB: All the museums are being forced to cut back.

WILL WILLARD: Two hundred and twenty-seven security guards is a lot of people!

BOB LAMB: They don't have enough money to meet operating costs anymore.

WILL WILLARD: Robert, two hundred and twenty-seven security guards is a crowd!

BOB LAMB: They're all closing down a few days during the week.

WILL WILLARD: Jesus!

BOB LAMB: That's right, "Jesus!" Pretty soon there won't be any fucking culture left!

MIRA ZADAL: [*Enters. She's very pretty and flirtatious. She sidles up to* THE GUARD.] Hello. Where are the museum engagement calendars sold?

THE GUARD: [*Sweating under her gaze.*] In the museum Gift Shop. Main floor, to the left of the Checkroom.

MIRA ZADAL: [*Starts to exit.*] Thank you so much.

FIRST MAN IN PASSING: [*Rushing through the room on the way to somewhere else.*] Did you hear what happened to Botticelli's *Venus* this morning?

SECOND MAN IN PASSING: No.

FIRST MAN IN PASSING: Shot and killed with a gun!

SECOND MAN IN PASSING: Shot and... *killed*?

FIRST MAN IN PASSING: Shot right off the face of the painting!

SECOND MAN IN PASSING: [*As they both exit.*] Son of a bitch!

MIRA ZADAL: [*Reenters, sashays up to* THE GUARD.] Do you also have reproductions of ancient Egyptian jewelry in the museum Gift Shop?

THE GUARD: [*Blushing.*] Books, catalogues, foreign publications, post cards, blown...glass...

MIRA ZADAL: [*With a tremulous sigh.*] ... blown...glass?

THE GUARD: [*With rising ardor.*] Pewter figurines, ceramic reproductions, needlepoint kits, table linens...dried flowers...

MIRA ZADAL: [*Groans.*]

THE GUARD: Silver ladles, cloisonné key rings, solid gold cuff links...rare spices!

MIRA ZADAL: Oooooooh, you're so...helpful!
[*She exits.*]

THE GUARD: Main floor, just a little bit left of the Checkroom!

ELIZABETH SORROW: [*Exits in her fashion, trying to make doubly sure she has taken everything in.*]

PETER ZIFF: [*Starts stalking the same art works* ELIZABETH *has just left. He's bothered by them, but for more destructive and obscure reasons.*]

THE GUARD: [*Watches him like a hawk.*]

PETER ZIFF: [*Frustrated by this scrutiny, sits down on one of the benches.*]
[*A silence into which step...*]

BARBARA ZIMMER AND BARBARA CASTLE: [*Enormously stylish mirror images of each other. They have come to the show to be seen and display themselves with languorous grace.*]

31

BARBARA CASTLE: Gloria said the show was wonderful!

BARBARA ZIMMER: Gloria would!

BARBARA CASTLE: She came to the opening with Misha.

BARBARA ZIMMER: I saw Misha last week!

BARBARA CASTLE: Really?

BARBARA ZIMMER: He was wearing his fur cape!

BARBARA CASTLE: Oh, I love that cape! Did he have on his linen vest with it?

BARBARA ZIMMER: The linen vest...*and* an incredible raw silk shirt!

BARBARA CASTLE: Ooooooooh, what color? *What color?*

BARBARA ZIMMER: Bright...green!

BARBARA CASTLE: Perfect!

BARBARA ZIMMER: ...and his tweed cap...

BARBARA CASTLE: He was wearing his tweed cap?

BARBARA ZIMMER: Yes!

BARBARA CASTLE: But not his tan boots...

BARBARA ZIMMER: ...not his tan boots...

[*Pause.*]

BARBARA ZIMMER: His black ones! [*A groan.*]   BARBARA CASTLE: His black ones! [*A groan.*]

[*Pause.*]

BARBARA CASTLE: What I wouldn't give for that linen vest of his!

BARBARA ZIMMER: Well, you'd have to give a great deal, believe me!

BARBARA CASTLE: Can you see that vest with my gabardine slacks?

BARBARA ZIMMER: Barbara, they don't *make* linen like that anymore!

BARBARA CASTLE: Or, with my Halston skirt...

BARBARA ZIMMER: There's a worldwide shortage of natural fibers. We have quite simply used them all up.

BARBARA CASTLE: And it's reversible too. On the inside, it's a lightweight cream wool!

BARBARA ZIMMER: Drained them...

BARBARA CASTLE: Reversed, I could wear it with practically anything!

BARBARA ZIMMER: Barbara, within the next few years, all our fabric will be synthetic.

BARBARA CASTLE: *Synthetic*? Did you just say, "*synthetic*," Barbara?

BARBARA ZIMMER: Yes, Barbara, I just said, "*synthetic*," Barbara! They hardly grow any cotton in the South anymore, it's just too expensive to harvest.

BARBARA CASTLE: Barbara, I can't wear synthetics!

BARBARA ZIMMER: Who can, Barbara? WHO CAN?!

BARBARA CASTLE: Last week I bought a slip I was told was pure silk, only to read the label two days later and discover it was Cresulon. Do you know what Cresulon does to my skin?

BARBARA ZIMMER: Chinese silk worms are as scarce as hen's teeth!

BARBARA CASTLE: It coats it with a thin layer of petroleum!

BARBARA ZIMMER: ...and as for wool. Because the cost of feeding sheep has skyrocketed, the sheep farmers are going bankrupt. Soon, there will be no more wool, cashmere, or angora!

BARBARA CASTLE: Barbara, I've got a rash. A white rash all over my body!

BARBARA ZIMMER: From now on, it's the man-made substitutes: Orlon, Acrylic, Lycra Spandex, Quiana Nylon, Fortrel Polyester, and Celanese Arnel Triacetate!

BARBARA CASTLE: And it won't go away! I've tried everything. Barbara, I'm desperate!
[*Pause.*]

BOB LAMB: As the costs of running museums keep rising, the price of admission is bound to go up. Museum officials are now talking about ten dollars as a fixed single admission fee.

WILL WILLARD: *Ten dollars to get into the Metropolitan?*

BOB LAMB: Ten dollars for admission into the Metropolitan will be a bargain, Willard, it will be twenty-five before the end of the decade. The only way people will be able to afford visiting museums in the future will be in chartered groups!

WILL WILLARD: Chartered groups?! Robert, I go to the Met by myself, or I don't go at all!

BOB LAMB: The fifty-dollar "Budget" chartered tour will

include admission into the Metropolitan, the Modern, and the Whitney....

WILL WILLARD: I would *pay* fifty dollars to avoid a "Budget" chartered tour....

BOB LAMB: The "Imperial" chartered tour will include those three, and for twenty-five more, admission into the Guggenheim, Cooper-Hewitt, and the Hayden Planetarium!

WILL WILLARD: Stop, stop!

BOB LAMB: And don't think the private galleries aren't hurting either....

WILL WILLARD: I have to be alone with the things I love!

BOB LAMB: The day will come when you'll have to use Master Charge to get into Pace and Castelli!

WILL WILLARD: The Morgan Collection of Renaissance jewels, snuff boxes, and enameled jeweled cups!...

BOB LAMB: Write checks for admittance into second-story Soho galleries!

WILL WILLARD: Do you *know* the Morgan Collection at the Met? Have you ever *seen* the Rospigliosi Cup?

BOB LAMB: Pay cash to...

WILL WILLARD: Robert, when I'm in front of that cup, I can't stand two people within ten feet of me!
[*Pause.*]

BARBARA CASTLE: [*To* BARBARA ZIMMER.] This is the first time I've ever had a...*white* rash!

WILL WILLARD: [*To* BOB LAMB.] The last time I was there, there was a swarm...of screaming children.

BARBARA CASTLE: [*Revealing some bare arm.*] Look! [*She blows on it, a fine white powder rises.*] Did you see that?

WILL WILLARD: I broke out in a sweat....

BARBARA CASTLE: I think I'm on fire....

WILL WILLARD: It's called agoraphobia!

BARBARA CASTLE: It keeps getting worse!

WILL WILLARD: I'm told it's incurable....

BARBARA CASTLE: ...and Barbara, it's spreading!
[*A pause.*]

BARBARA ZIMMER: [*To* BARBARA CASTLE.] The handwriting is on the wall!

BOB LAMB: [*To* WILL WILLARD.] Our troubles have just begun!

BARBARA ZIMMER: [*Agreeing with* BOB LAMB, *but for her own reasons*.] We could lose everything!

BOB LAMB: [*To* BARBARA ZIMMER.] Exactly!

BARBARA ZIMMER: [*To* BOB LAMB.] We're only beginning to wake up...

BOB LAMB: ...and when we finally do, it will be too late!

BARBARA ZIMMER: Of course, this is not the first time.

BOB LAMB: No, we've been through it before.

BARBARA ZIMMER: This is the first time I've ever had a white rash!

WILL WILLARD: I just hope we can retain what's most precious to us.

BARBARA ZIMMER: We've tried so hard!

BOB LAMB: Sacrificed so much...

BARBARA ZIMMER: Given our all...

WILL WILLARD: Gone more than halfway...

BARBARA ZIMMER: Stinted on nothing...

BOB LAMB: Held out for the best.

BARBARA CASTLE: Fought a fair fight...

WILL WILLARD: And stuck to our guns!
[*A pause.*]

BARBARA ZIMMER: He's right!

BOB LAMB: You said it!

BARBARA CASTLE: Well put!

WILL WILLARD: Culture, as we know it...

BOB LAMB: Is on the way out!

BARBARA ZIMMER: On the way out...

BARBARA CASTLE: ...and disappearing round the bend!
[*A pause.*]

THE GUARD: [*Suddenly launches into a tap dance of private protest. It rises in spirit and magnificence. Everyone watches him in amazement. The* SALTS *start to applaud and then check the gauche impulse. The dance suddenly stops and* THE GUARD *returns to his post as if nothing happened. To himself.*] It's the last day of the show.

EVERYONE: [*Resumes their former activities and the room falls into silence.*]

MR. GREGORY: [*Enters, a shy man with a recorded tour that's playing much too loud.*]

THE RECORDED TOUR: ON BEHALF OF THE TRUST-EES AND ADMINISTRATION OF THE MUSEUM, IT GIVES ME GREAT PLEASURE TO WELCOME YOU TO OUR CURRENT EXHIBITION, "THE BROKEN SILENCE." FIRST, LET ME SAY A FEW WORDS ABOUT THE OPERATION OF...

EVERYONE: [*Eyes him with hostility, their hands over their ears.*]

THE GUARD: WILL YOU PLEASE TURN THAT DOWN?

WILL WILLARD: WHAT'S GOING ON IN HERE?

BOB LAMB: I TOLD YOU THIS WAS A NOISY MU-SEUM!

MICHAEL WALL: HEY, MISTER...

THE BARBARAS: [*Shake their heads and cluck.*]

FRED IZUMI: [*Reenters, goes up to* THE GUARD, *hands him a slip.*] My permission slip from the Director! [*He sets his gear down by the Moes.*]

THE GUARD: *WHAT?*

FRED IZUMI: PERMISSION SLIP FROM THE DIREC-TOR!

THE GUARD: I SAID, IT'S AGAINST MUSEUM REG-ULATIONS TO PHOTOGRAPH THE ART WORKS!

FRED IZUMI: MAIN FLOOR TO THE LEFT OF THE CHECKROOM!

THE GUARD: THE GUARD DOWNSTAIRS...

FRED IZUMI: YES, I SAW THE DIRECTOR....

THE RECORDED TOUR: [*Mysteriously regulates itself on, "Yes, I saw the Director."*]

THE GUARD: IT'S AGAINST...

MR. GREGORY: [*Somehow manages to turn the sound completely off.*]

FRED IZUMI: [*Hands* THE GUARD *his slip.*] My permission slip from the Director.

THE GUARD: [*Taking it.*] Wonderful!

FRED IZUMI: Main floor, to the left of the Checkroom!

THE GUARD: ...terrific!

MR. AND MRS. SALT: [*Their recorded tour suddenly goes*

berserk in sympathy with MR. GREGORY's. *It plays insanely loud and then very, very fast.*]

EVERYONE: [*Groans and mutters in angry disbelief.*]

THE GUARD: LOOK...WOULD YOU PLEASE TURN DOWN THE VOLUME....

MR. GREGORY: [*Cowering in a corner.*] THE SAME THING HAPPENED TO MINE, JUST SHAKE IT....[*Etc.*]

MR. AND MRS. SALT: [*Frantic with embarrassment, bang on the controls.*]

| MRS. SALT: TURN THE RED BUTTON, NOT THE WHITE BUTTON....NO, NO.... *THIS* ONE....NOT SO FAR.... | MR. SALT: SOMETHING'S GONE WRONG SOMEWHERE!! I'M TURNING THE WHITE BUTTON, BUT NOTHING HAPPENS...GODDAMNED MACHINE!... |

THE GUARD: LOOK, I'M GOING TO HAVE TO ASK YOU TO LEAVE!

[*Strong-arms* MR. SALT *out of the room.*]

MRS. SALT: [*Is pulled helplessly after him on her attached wire.*]

PETER ZIFF: [*Seizes the moment and quickly rushes over to one of the Moes, takes out a small pencil and scribbles on one corner. With sweat pouring down his face, he looks to see if anyone saw him, and then quietly sneaks out of the room.*]

FRED IZUMI: [*To* THE GUARD.] Both he and his assistant were very courteous. It turns out we have mutual friends in Cincinnati. [*He then paces down the length of all the Moes, reading their titles out loud to himself.*] "Landscape I, 1984. Acrylic emulsion and wax on canvas. On loan from the Sidney Rubin Gallery."

BOB LAMB: [*To* WILL WILLARD.] Not only will it cost ten dollars to get into the Metropolitan, but because of the shortage of guards, certain galleries will be roped off on odd and even days of the month.

FRED IZUMI: "*Landscape II*, 1984. Acrylic emulsion and wax on canvas. On loan from the Sidney Rubin Gallery."

BOB LAMB: Medieval helmets will only be on view even days, from noon 'til one. Renaissance stringed instruments, odd days, from two to three.

FRED IZUMI: "*Seascape VII*, 1984. Acrylic emulsion and wax on canvas. On loan from the Sidney Rubin Gallery."

BOB LAMB: Sooner or later, the less popular exhibits will close altogether: Etruscan bronzes, Mid-Eastern glazed bricks...

FRED IZUMI: "*Starscape XIX*, 1984. Acrylic emulsion and wax on canvas. On loan from the artist."

BOB LAMB: Eventually, entire periods and forms of art will be lost completely as the public is denied access!

FRED IZUMI: [*Amazed.*] "On loan from the...*artist*?!"

BOB LAMB: One by one, all the treasures of Western civilization will be dismantled, put into storage... lowered into fiber glass crates and buried under ground...to be grouped and catalogued by art historians wearing thick, lint-free asbestos gloves. [*Pause.*] We will never again stand face to face with an original painting or sculpture. And if there is no place where that painting or sculpture can be shown, the artist is bound to ask: *Who am I doing it for...and why am I doing it*? The impulse to create will be shattered. Willard, this may be our last day in the presence of live art!

WILL WILLARD: Wait a minute! Yesterday I was standing one foot away from probably *the* most live and stunning object of art made by man in the last four hundred years! Robert, have you ever studied the Rospigliosi Cup? It's a fucking dazzler! [*Pause.*] It's this...incredible scalloped sea shell which rests on the back of an enameled dragon...which in turn rests on the back of an enameled turtle. It's carved out of solid gold and is no more than ten inches high and eight inches across. Instead of a handle, a winged sphinx perches on the rim of the cup, a gigantic baroque pearl hanging between her golden breasts. I mean, the workmanship, the detail...the fantasy! Tiny seed pearl earrings dangle from her ears...and instead of having the traditional legs and paws of a lion...she has flippers! Indigo blue flippers etched in enamel. You can *count* each iridescent scale!

BOB LAMB: Well, you'd better get ready to kiss it goodbye....It won't be there in two weeks. All the museums are closing.

WILL WILLARD: Robert, what on earth are you talking about?

BOB LAMB: The museums...are...shutting...down!

WILL WILLARD: Robert, no museums are shutting down.

BOB LAMB: Willard, we've got to do something!

[*As* BOB LAMB *is tensed for some sort of desperate act, there's a gradual slowing down. The visitors become languid art works themselves.* THE GUARD *paces,* MICHAEL WALL *keeps taking pictures,* FRED IZUMI *prepares to take his,* MR. GREGORY *doggedly follows his tour, the* BARBARAS *pluck at each other's beautiful clothes, and* WILL WILLARD *stares straight ahead. This moment of serenity is broken as...*]

CHLOE TRAPP: [*Enters. She's on the curatorial staff of the museum. Her life and passion center on discovering and explaining the mysteries of modern art.*]

ADA BILDITSKY: [*Enters with her, a patron of the arts who's being given a special private tour.*]

LIZ: [*Suddenly careens into the room*] Carol? Blakey? Guys?

[*She looks around, then exits.*]

CHLOE TRAPP: This is the final day of our group show, "The Broken Silence," and here we have the work of an extraordinary young Post-Conceptual painter, Zachery Moe.

EVERYONE: [*Looks up at the sound of her voice. They are held by her seriousness and authority.*]

CHLOE TRAPP: Most significant painting since Matisse's *Joie de Vivre* has been reductive. Reductivism does not belong to any one style: it is as operative in painting conceived as a gesture...as in painting cut

down to a line or square. The traditional aim of re-
duction has been to push painting to its farthest limits by reducing it to its bare essentials. In slicing
away residues of imagery that have lost their relevance, the artist seeks to transform the apple...into
a diamond.
[*A pause.*]

ADA BILDITSKY: I'm so grateful!

EVERYONE EXCEPT THE GUARD: [*Gathers around* CHLOE
TRAPP *for more.*]

BARBARA CASTLE: Oh, we're all grateful!

WILL WILLARD: *I'm* grateful!

BOB LAMB: No one...is more grateful than me!

MR. GREGORY: I had no idea anyone was going to...

FRED IZUMI: Thank you very much.

CHLOE TRAPP: [*Moves to the next Moe.*] There is left the
void—not Yves Klein's empty sky, but a void that
seeks the cancellation of art as it has been until now
and supplanting it with works from which adulter-
ating impulses have been...purged. It is evident that
Moe saw that a traditional commitment to the the-
oretical picture plane was no longer relevant.

ADA BILDITSKY: Absolutely evident and no longer relevant.

EVERYONE: [*Except* THE GUARD *who's lost in the rhythms
of his own job.*] Absolutely evident and no longer
relevant.

CHLOE TRAPP: For such American artists, the concern
was mainly with the surface of the canvas and the
nature of the pigment applied to it. What states more
plainly the literal character of the picture support
covered by canvas...than a piece of can-
vas...covering that picture support...*painted white*?!
If the first mark on a surface destroys its flatness,
then Moe contradicts this by painting a picture whose
first and *only* mark...is an all-over white one.

ADA BILDITSKY: [*Letting it sink in.*] All-over white!

EVERYONE: [*Understanding, joyous.*] All-over white!

CHLOE TRAPP: White...of course, is the one color carrying in it the potential for all other colors.

[*A pause. These colors should spill out rapid-fire creating a verbal rainbow.*]

ADA BILDITSKY: Red!

MICHAEL WALL: Yellow!

FRED IZUMI: Orange!

BARBARA CASTLE: Violet!

BARBARA ZIMMER: Blue!

BOB LAMB: Green!

WILL WILLARD: Sepia!

MR. GREGORY: Purple!

ADA BILDITSKY: [*Breathing deeply, her favorite color.*] Rose!

MICHAEL WALL: Turquoise!

FRED IZUMI: Umber!

BARBARA CASTLE: Mauve!

BARBARA ZIMMER: Lavender!

BOB LAMB: Cobalt!

WILL WILLARD: Magenta!

MR. GREGORY: Saffron!

CHLOE TRAPP: The difference between historic Dada and the current fundamentalist version lies in the treatment of the spectator....[*With the word "spectator," everyone turns and faces* CHLOE, *suddenly aware that they are the spectators she's talking about.*] Instead of goading you into indignation at the desecration of art, the new Dada converts you into an aesthete.

EVERYONE: [*Flattered, congratulates themselves, murmuring, "aesthete."*]

CHLOE TRAPP: The monotonous shapes and bleak surfaces presented to you as objects wrapped in their own being compel you to embrace a professional sensitivity to contrasts of tone, light, and dimension. The more a work is purged of inessentials, the closer the scrutiny required to see it...and the more precious the sensibility required to respond to it!

[*A reverential silence.*]

ADA BILDITSKY: Oh, you were just...wonderful! Really ...wonderful!

EVERYONE: [*Breaks into applause.*]

CHLOE TRAPP: [*Suddenly made shy by their outpouring, ducks her head to one side, and rushes from the room.*] How kind...you're too kind....

ADA BILDITSKY: I've never heard anything so...lyrical...so inspired...so informative...so apt!
[*She runs after* CHLOE.]

EVERYONE: [*Is stirred by their new vision. They move around the Moes, not daring to speak for fear of breaking the spell.*]

GILDA NORRIS: [*Enters, intense and serious, she carries a folding chair and sketch book. She settles down in front of one of the Moes and starts copying it with as much fury as if she were reproducing a Rembrandt.*]

THE GUARD: I'm sorry, Miss, it's against museum regulations to sketch from the art works!

GILDA NORRIS: I can't sketch without permission from the Director?

THE GUARD: I didn't tell you it was the Director who gave permission to sketch. How did you know the Director gives permission to sketch?

GILDA NORRIS: Because I have sketching permission from the Director.

THE GUARD: You have *sketching* permission from the Director? I've never seen sketching permission from the Director!

GILDA NORRIS: I'm the Director's daughter!

THE GUARD: Oh, you're the Director's *daughter*....

GILDA NORRIS: ...the sketching Director's daughter...

THE GUARD: [*Laughs.*] ...sketching Director's daughter...

GILDA NORRIS: [*Still sketching.*] The...*fetching*, sketching Director's daughter!

THE GUARD: [*Laughs lightheartedly.*]

GILDA NORRIS: The...*letching*, fetching, sketching Director's daughter!

THE GUARD: [*Laughs, with embarrassment.*]

BOB LAMB: Willard, now's the time to make our move. See that basket of clothespins over there, I'm going to steal one dozen of them!

GILDA NORRIS: [*Rises and advances on* THE GUARD.] The...*kvetching*, letching, fetching, sketching Director's daughter!

WILL WILLARD: Robert, you're crazy!

BOB LAMB: [*Checking that* THE GUARD *is engrossed with* GILDA NORRIS, *starts stuffing clothespins in his pocket.*]

WILL WILLARD: Robert, please!

THE GUARD: [*Rushes over to them.*] HEY, WHAT'S GOING ON OVER HERE? I TOLD YOU, YOU ARE NOT TO TOUCH THE CLOTHESPINS! THEY ARE PART OF THE SCULPTURE!

BOB LAMB: For your information, this is not a "sculpture," it's a "construction."

WILL WILLARD: I'm so embarrassed!

THE GUARD: I DON'T CARE WHAT YOU CALL IT, MISTER, IT'S AGAINST MUSEUM REGULATIONS TO TOUCH THE ART WORKS. NOW, PUT THOSE CLOTHESPINS BACK!

BOB LAMB: Are you accusing me of...theft?

THE GUARD: All I said was, put the clothespins back!

BOB LAMB: [*Tossing them back into the basket.*] I hope you realize this is the first time a museum guard has *ever* raised his voice to me....

WILL WILLARD: The poor man is just doing his job!

BOB LAMB: And let me assure you, I've been to every major art museum across the country! The Hirschorn, the Carnegie Institute, the Philadelphia Museum of Art, the Walker Art Center...

THE GUARD: ALL BACK. PUT THEM ALL BACK!

BOB LAMB: Furthermore, this is just about the worst show I've ever seen, anywhere! Real stinko!

WILL WILLARD: Roooooooooooobert...

BOB LAMB: I'd be embarrassed to work here!

THE GUARD: COME ON, HURRY IT UP! [*Clamping his hands on* BOB LAMB.] Each one of those pins is a valuable piece of art!

BOB LAMB: *You touched me*! That does it! [*He throws back the last remaining ones.*] I'm reporting you to the Director of the museum....

BOB LAMB: ... main floor, to the left of the Checkroom!

THE GUARD: ... main floor, to the left of the Checkroom!

BOB LAMB: [*Exiting.*] Bruce said this show was shit!

WILL WILLARD: [*Following him.*] BRUCE IS AN ASS HOLE!

THE GUARD: This is just the beginning, just the beginning....

BARBARA ZIMMER: [*Gazing at* Landscape I.] Barbara, I want one!

BARBARA CASTLE: They are lovely!

BARBARA ZIMMER: *This* one!

BARBARA CASTLE: [*Considering it.*] Mmmmmmmmmmm...

BARBARA ZIMMER: It would be perfect in my bedroom!

BARBARA CASTLE: [*Indicating* Seascape VII.] *That's* the one for your bedroom, Barbara. This one's more for your family room.

BARBARA ZIMMER: Are you crazy, Barbara? It would be terrible in the family room!

BARBARA CASTLE: Well, it would be heaven in *my* family room!

BARBARA ZIMMER: Your family room and my family room are two different places!

BARBARA CASTLE: [*Pointing to* Landscape II.] *That's* the one for your bedroom, Barbara!

BARBARA ZIMMER: You mean, that's the one for *your* bedroom....

BARBARA CASTLE: [*Gazing at* Landscape II, *picturing it in her bedroom.*] No. [*Then looking at the others, settling on* Seascape XIX.] *That's* the one for my bedroom, and... [*After considering, indicating* Landscape I.] ...*this* is the one for your family room!

BARBARA ZIMMER: Well, what about *my* bedroom?

BARBARA CASTLE: Barbara, these aren't easy decisions!

BARBARA ZIMMER: [*Pulling her arm.*] Come on, we've got to get out of here. The cafeteria's probably jammed. We'll be in line forever!

BARBARA CASTLE: [*Exiting with her.*] What are you going to order?

BARBARA ZIMMER: Oh, I don't know, I feel like a quiche....
BARBARA CASTLE: I'm more in the mood for a salad.
BARBARA ZIMMER: Their spinach salads are excellent!
BARBARA CASTLE: [*As they exit.*] Yes, I know....

BARBARA CASTLE: Tarragon and dill dressing...	BARBARA ZIMMER: Tarragon and dill dressing...

MR. GREGORY'S TOUR: [*Suddenly goes berserk again, louder and faster than before. He pounds on it.*]
EVERYONE: [*Looks at him and groans.*]

THE GUARD: HEY, WILL YOU TURN THAT DOWN? LISTEN, I'M AFRAID YOU'RE GOING TO HAVE TO TAKE THAT BACK DOWN TO THE DESK AND GET ANOTHER ONE...MAIN FLOOR....I SAID, MAIN FLOOR...TO THE LEFT OF THE...	MR. GREGORY: IT'S STUCK, THE BUTTON'S STUCK....IT'S JAMMED....I CAN'T...WHAT? I CAN'T TURN IT OFF....YES, I'M TRYING, I'M TRYING, BUT IT'S JAMMED....

THE GUARD: [*Drags* MR. GREGORY *from the room.*]
TINK SOLHEIM AND KATE SIV: [*Enter. They're friends of the artist Agnes Vaag. They're dressed in exotic yet flattering clothes, and both exude a high-strung sensitivity. They've come to the show practically every day.*]
TINK SOLHEIM: ...the last day of the show!
KATE SIV: I can't believe it! The last day!
THE GUARD: [*Has returned, worn out from* MR. GREGORY.] Last day.
TINK SOLHEIM: The last day!
KATE SIV: Ed called this morning, he said Aggie might come.
TINK SOLHEIM: I know....

45

KATE SIV: He thinks she'll come around noon and bring Hilton with her.

TINK SOLHEIM: That's odd, Hilton told me it would be closer to three.

KATE SIV: Ed said Aggie has some appointment later on.

TINK SOLHEIM: Hilton didn't mention anything about it to me.

KATE SIV: Hilton probably hasn't been in touch with Ed.

TINK SOLHEIM: Aggie's busy at noon.

KATE SIV: Not according to Ed.

TINK SOLHEIM: But Aggie would never call Ed!

KATE SIV: You mean, Hilton would never call Ed!

TINK SOLHEIM: Well of course *Hilton* would never call Ed....

KATE SIV: Neither would Aggie.

TINK SOLHEIM: That's true.

KATE SIV: [*Getting depressed.*] She'd never call Hilton, either.

TINK SOLHEIM: But Hilton called *her*!

KATE SIV: She'd never call anyone!

TINK SOLHEIM: ...and then he called *me*!

KATE SIV: She's the problem!

TINK SOLHEIM: Ed's the problem.

KATE SIV: ...and I don't trust Hilton.

TINK SOLHEIM: She'll come.

KATE SIV: What time is it?

TINK SOLHEIM: She'll be here.

KATE SIV: Maybe she already came and left....

TINK SOLHEIM: [*In front of one of her pieces.*] Every time I see her work, it moves me more than the last time.

CHLOE TRAPP: [*Enters again with...*]

BILL PLAID: [*A man who is bewildered by art, and infuriated by modern art. That he is* CHLOE's *guest at all is the result of some horrible mixup.*]

CHLOE TRAPP: [*Advances to the clothesline.*] This is the final day of our group show, "The Broken Silence." [*Pause.*] In his earliest work, Steve Williams experimented with such typically surrealist devices as totemic imagery, often incorporating assemblages of unrelated objects.The idea of indicating a magically demarcated environment... [*She indicates the length of the clothesline.*] for his sculptures, appeared early in his work as did his reliance on cloth and rope for basic materials.

BILL PLAID: [*Confused and depressed.*] Yes. Cloth and rope.

CHLOE TRAPP: A surrealist cast persists in his most recent work, particularly in his use of erotic imagery and in his unexpected variations of color and scale.

TINK SOLHEIM: [*Without knowing what she's doing, picks up one of Agnes Vaag's sculptures and presses it against her cheek.*]

BILL PLAID: Yes, highly erotic.

CHLOE TRAPP: What makes Williams' work of unusual contemporary relevance, however, is his attitude towards the materials he uses and the processes he employs.

BILL PLAID: [*Dimly.*] Cloth and rope.

CHLOE TRAPP: Rather than imposing his will upon materials in order to force them into a preordained form, Williams obeys the inherent capabilities of a given material and follows the suggestions offered by its particular qualities.

BILL PLAID: [*Depressed, sits on one of the benches, head in hands.*]

TINK SOLHEIM: [*Is now rubbing the Vaag statue up and down her face.*]

CHLOE TRAPP: Gesture is a crucial factor in Williams' work, a means of indicating the participation of the artist in the ...

KATE SIV: [*Notices that* TINK *has seized the statue and screams.*]

CHLOE TRAPP: [*Screams because* KATE *screamed.*]

TINK SOLHEIM: [*Screams because their screams have startled her.*]

BILL PLAID: [*Screams because he can't take it anymore.*]

THE GUARD: WHAT'S GOING ON?

KATE SIV: TINK, WHAT ARE YOU DOING WITH AGGIE'S STATUE?

TINK SOLHEIM: [*Lost in her own revery.*] What?

KATE SIV: WHAT...ARE...YOU...DOING?...

CHLOE TRAPP: "The Temptation and Corruption of William Blake!"

KATE SIV: It's "The Temptation and Corruption of William Blake!"

TINK SOLHEIM: [*Clutching it tighter.*] No!

CHLOE TRAPP: On loan from the Whitney Museum of American Art.

THE GUARD: Put that statue down, Miss.

CHLOE TRAPP: Her first attempt to combine porous with nonporous objects.

BILL PLAID: [*Groans.*]

KATE SIV: Tink, put it down!

THE GUARD: Please, Miss....

TINK SOLHEIM: [*Feeling cornered, dashes to the clothesline and stands among the bodies.*]

CHLOE TRAPP:	KATE SIV: Oh	FRED IZUMI: It's
Tink, we'd	Tink, you're	all right. Ev-
all like you	going to drop	erything's
to put the	it, and it will	going to be
statue down	shatter into	all right....
before	a million	
something	pieces....	
terrible		
happens....		

GILDA NORRIS: [*Ready to pounce.*] SURROUND HER!

THE GUARD: Sssssssssh, calm down. Let's everybody just...calm down...take it easy....

MICHAEL WALL: Hey, could I look at it for a minute? [*Holds out his hands to her with great gentleness.*]

TINK SOLHEIM: [*Eyes him, frightened, but then softens and starts to hand him the statue.*]

KATE SIV: Oh Tink, what's happened to you?

THE GUARD: Sssshhhhhh...

MICHAEL WALL: I'll give it right back. It's so beautiful....

GILDA NORRIS: GRAB IT!

TINK SOLHEIM: [*Lifts the statue high over her head.*] DON'T TOUCH ME!

KATE SIV: Oh Tink...

THE GUARD: Miss, you'd better...

CHLOE TRAPP: It's my favorite one, my very...

BILL PLAID: Go ahead...SMASH THE UGLY THING!
[*A silence.*]

TINK SOLHEIM: Yesterday...I was remembering a day
I spent with Agnes Vaag.

KATE SIV: Aggie!

TINK SOLHEIM: ...Aggie...

KATE SIV: We're friends of the artist. *Old* friends...she's
such a wonderful...

TINK SOLHEIM: Agnes Vaag invited me to spend a day
with her in the country. Looking for her things; bones,
wings...teeth...

THE GUARD: [*Reaching up for the statue.*] WATCH IT!

CHLOE TRAPP: ALL OF HER MATERIALS ARE FOUND
MATERIALS!

MICHAEL WALL: I've never seen anything like this....

KATE SIV: She'll be here later, with Hilton.

TINK SOLHEIM: She finds all her objects in Connecticut
state parks.

TINK SOLHEIM: [*Fitfully caressing her face with the
statue.*] At least once a month she gets on a Grey-
hound bus carrying two blue suitcases filled with
soft polyester batting for wrapping her objects
in...and scours one of Connecticut's state parks. The
last time she invited me to go with her. I said I'd
bring along an extra suitcase and a picnic lunch. We
met at the Port Authority Bus Terminal. It was
so...odd. Going with Aggie to look for something. I
mean, whenever you see her in her studio, her hands
are always full: moulding something, gluing something. Her studio is bursting with the exotic: bird
beaks, fish skeletons, turkey down, fox claws....

KATE SIV: I'm Aggie's oldest friend, I've known her for
years!

TINK SOLHEIM: So I just assumed she always *had* these
things, that they were part of her, not something
separate she had to seek out. So it was odd meeting
her at Port Authority carrying those two blue suitcases stuffed with polyester batting.

KATE SIV: She's invited me on her expeditions millions of times...of course I...

TINK SOLHEIM: I don't remember the name of the park we visited, but Aggie seemed to know her way around and before I realized it, we were walking through deep woods. Deep woods is the best place to find small animal skeletons, she told me. While I looked up at the trees and sky, she bent close to the ground, scooping her hands through the underbrush like some human net. In the first hour she found a bat skeleton, several raccoon skulls, a fresh rabbit carcass, patches of fur....

KATE SIV: Aggie's only twenty-four, you know...and so beautiful!...

TINK SOLHEIM: At one moment she was crouched out of view, the next she was holding fragile white bones up to the sun exclaiming over their perfect...

KATE SIV: She has this amazing blond hair. It's as thick as rope and falls down her back in golden cascades....

TINK SOLHEIM: After a while she had filled both her blue suitcases and asked if she could borrow mine. We stopped for lunch and she gave me a long speech about how calcium is formed in the bones of vegetarian animals....

KATE SIV: And her eyes are this deep...green....

TINK SOLHEIM: It wasn't long before my suitcase was filled too and it was starting to get dark. I suggested we walk back along a different route, but she said no, she couldn't stop yet.

KATE SIV: MEN DIE OVER HER!

TINK SOLHEIM: It was then I noticed something... strange. Well, I didn't notice it, I heard it because it was getting too dark to see. As she was combing the underbrush, I heard this soft kind of...licking noise...a slight kind of...slurping...like eating, but not really chewing and swallowing...just licking and tasting. "Is that you, Aggie?" I asked her. But she never answered, and it was such a light muffled sound, she could have been sucking on a mint. [*Deep breath.*] I told her I really thought we should leave before it got any darker and we got lost, and this time with real anger in her voice, she said...NO! And then the nibbling, or kissing...or whatever it was...got louder. We reached a clearing, the trees dropped away, the moon shone down on Aggie's bent form as clear as day, and then I saw...she was holding one of the little skeletons up to her mouth and...was licking it, nibbling on it...running her tongue over it. I screamed. She dropped the little thing and turned white. The next thing I knew, she was hitting me with her fists, socking me hard all over my body, screaming and crying, "I hate you! I hate you! I HATE YOU!"

KATE SIV: [*Near tears.*] I'm not listening to this.

BILL PLAID: Oh boy, oh boy, oh boy, all artists are *crazy!*

CHLOE TRAPP: Her perceptual gifts are extraordinary!

BILL PLAID: NUTS! ALL OF THEM!

KATE SIV: You made it up. You made it all up! That didn't happen! NONE OF IT...HAPPENED!

BILL PLAID: YOU HAVE TO BE NUTS TO MAKE THE STUFF!

TINK SOLHEIM: [*Puts the sculpture back on its pedestal.*] Agnes Vaag's breath reeks!

THE GUARD: Thank you very much.

TINK SOLHEIM: Her breath is...foul!

KATE SIV: You made it up! You've never been invited on one of her expeditions, and you know it. It's your jealousy, Tink...your relentless jealousy...and it's hateful...hateful...hateful....
[*She runs from the room, sobbing.*]

TINK SOLHEIM: [*Giddy.*] I always noticed a certain animal quality about her breath, a certain... rancidness...something sour. You know how certain people have breath that doesn't smell quite ...human?

CHLOE TRAPP: [*Shattered.*] It was at my insistence that Agnes Vaag was invited to exhibit in the show. [*She exits.*]

THE GUARD: For a minute there, you had me worried.

LILLIAN, HARRIET, AND MAY: [*Enter. Their arms are linked and they're on the verge of a belly laugh.* HARRIET *and* MAY *have their eyes covered with their hands as* LILLIAN *leads them to the Moes.*]

LILLIAN: Will you look at that?

HARRIET AND MAY: [*Uncover their eyes and let out a piercing shriek of laughter.*]

LILLIAN: [*Also laughing.*] Modern art!

HARRIET AND MAY: [*Clutching one another.*] I don't believe it...stop...oh stop...please....

LILLIAN: [*Advances to the first Moe and reads the title.*] "Landscape I, 1984. Acrylic emulsion and wax on canvas. On loan from the Sidney Rubin Gallery." [*All three roar.*]

BILL PLAID: ... AND YOU HAVE TO BE NUTS TO LOOK AT IT! [*Rises to exit.*] Sucking on statues...I mean, normal people don't go around sucking statues, do they? [*Going up to* THE GUARD.] I've never seen a *normal* person sucking on a statue, have you? First of all, a *normal* person would never even *think* of sucking on a...

THE GUARD: [*Gently lays his hands on him.*] All right, that's enough, quiet down, it's all right.... [*Leads him off.*]

BILL PLAID: [*Resisting.*] HEY, WHAT ARE YOU DOING? WHAT ARE YOU THROWING *ME* OUT FOR? I DIDN'T DO ANYTHING.... [*Pointing to the laughing ladies.*] They're the ones you ought to throw out...sucking on statues, Jesus! [*And he's gone.*]

HARRIET: [*Looking at the Moes.*] There's...nothing on them!

MAY: They're...blank!

HARRIET: BLANK! [*All three go off into a shower of laughter again, falling against each other, crossing their legs so they don't wet their pants.*]

LILLIAN: "Landscape II, 1984. Acrylic emulsion and wax on canvas. On loan from the Sidney Rubin Gallery!"

HARRIET: It looks just like the first one.

MAY: Blank!

LILLIAN: No, I like the first one better!

HARRIET: Me too, the first one's better!
[*All three go off into gales.*]

THE GUARD: I just wish this day would end.

LILLIAN: [*At* Starscape XIX.] Now...*this* is really special!

HARRIET: You're right, this one's the best!
[*They all stand in front of it.*]

LILLIAN: Guess what the title is?

HARRIET: [*Taking her time.*] Let's see...SNOW STORM!
[*All three laugh like crazy.*]

LILLIAN: "Starscape XIX"!

HARRIET: I don't see any stars!

LILLIAN: I don't see any paint!
[*All three laugh like crazy again.*]

LILLIAN: [*Reading the title.*] "Acrylic emulsion and wax on canvas." They're all acrylic emulsion and wax.

HARRIET: It must be the latest thing.

LILLIAN: I guess they melt the wax right into the acrylic emulsion.

MAY: What is *acrylic emulsion* anyway?

HARRIET: If you ask me, he should have put a wick in with the wax, and lit a match!
[*All three howl.*]

THE GUARD: Ladies, please. You're disturbing the other visitors in the gallery.
[*It's true, with each outbreak of hysteria, the other people in the room are jolted out of their concentration and look at them with annoyance.*]

LILLIAN, HARRIET, AND MAY: [*Work themselves down to the clothesline. They spot* GILDA NORRIS *on the way, furiously sketching from the Moe. They point at her, then at the Moe and collapse with a fresh shower of giggles.*]

LILLIAN: [*Catches sight of the clothesline, lets out her loudest shriek of all.*] OH, NO!

MAY: [*Diving for the basket, enthralled.*] LOOK AT THIS.

HE LEFT OUT THE BASKET OF CLOTHESPINS!

THE GUARD: [*Strides over to them.*] Please don't handle the art works!

MAY: [*Picks up a clothespin.*] Wait a minute, they don't make this kind of round-headed clothespin anymore.

LILLIAN: [*Takes it from her.*] Let me see....

HARRIET: [*Also taking one.*] I HAVEN'T SEEN A ROUND-HEADED CLOTHESPIN WITHOUT A SPRING FOR YEARS!

MAY: My mother used to use round-headed clothespins like these. I still remember her holding a clothespin just like this and leaning down to show it to me, saying, "Masie, line-dried wash hung with round-headed clothespins always hangs better, and don't you ever forget it!"

LILLIAN: I didn't think they made them anymore.

HARRIET: They must be old....

MAY: The round-headed ones grip much better than the flat-headed ones.

LILLIAN: They do, they do!

THE GUARD: [*Trying to get them to put the pins back.*] Ladies...*please!*

MAY: Also, the flat-headed ones tend to split in two.

HARRIET: The springs always rusted on the flat-headed ones.

MAY: That's right, and then they'd come shooting off the line like little rockets....

TINK SOLHEIM: [*Has been gazing at one of the Vaags. To* THE GUARD *with feeling.*] EACH OF HER PIECES IS A SMALL MIRACLE!

THE GUARD: [*Moves to her, trying to keep an eye on the ladies.*] I know, I know....

TINK SOLHEIM: NO YOU DON'T KNOW! NOBODY KNOWS!

LILLIAN, HARRIET, AND MAY: [*Stealthfully stuff clothespins into their handbags and pockets now that* THE GUARD's *busy with* TINK. *They try hard but unsuccessfully to muffle their giggles.*]

THE GUARD: [*To* TINK.] Calm down....

TINK SOLHEIM: There's a secret....

THE GUARD: Yes, Miss, I believe you.

TINK SOLHEIM: Aggie told me that she hid a special surprise inside each piece....

THE GUARD: Yes, I'm sure....

TINK SOLHEIM: It's not visible to the naked eye. You can only find it through vibrations of sound or touch.... [*Laying her hands on the pedestal.*]

THE GUARD: Everything's going to be all right....

TINK SOLHEIM: [*Her movements increasingly manic.*] THAT'S THE THING ABOUT AGNES VAAG. SHE ALWAYS TAKES YOU BY SURPRISE!

LILLIAN, HARRIET, AND MAY: [*Awash with suppressed laughter.*]

THE GUARD: [*Torn in his duty.*] Ladies...*please!*

TINK SOLHEIM: She only reveals the surface.

LILLIAN: I've got twelve. How many do you have?

HARRIET: [*Giggles.*]

MAY: I've got seven.

LILLIAN: Only seven? Take more.

HARRIET: [*Ecstatic.*] I HAVEN'T SEEN A ROUND-HEADED CLOTHESPIN WITHOUT A SPRING ...IN YEARS!

TINK SOLHEIM: She challenged me: FIND THE MIRACLE, TINK! FIND IT ON THE LAST DAY!

THE GUARD: [*Dashes over to the ladies.*] LADIES, LADIES, LADIES! NOW THAT'S ENOUGH. LET'S PUT ALL THE CLOTHESPINS BACK LIKE GOOD GIRLS AND TRY AND REMEMBER THAT YOU'RE IN A MUSEUM! PUT THEM BACK IN THE BASKET...EVERY ONE. HURRY UP....DO AS I SAY....THAT'S IT....THAT'S THE WAY....

LILLIAN, HARRIET, AND MAY: [*Leaking clothespins, lurch out of the room, wobbling with laughter. It's the best time they've had in their lives.*]

[*It's very quiet. Nothing happens for some time.*]

THE GUARD: [*Out of nowhere sings a long, rather mournful note.*]

LIZ: [*Worn out from her search, enters depressed.*] Carol? Blakey? Guys?... Shit!

[*She exits.*]

TINK SOLHEIM: Aggie told me she hid a special surprise in each piece. She challenged me: Find it on the last day.

THE GUARD: [*Dimly.*]...Last day....

GIORGIO AND ZOE: [*Enter, a polished couple in their forties*]

GIORGIO: Today's the last day....

ZOE: The last day?

TINK SOLHEIM: The last day....

ZOE: I didn't realize it was the last day!

THE GUARD: God in heaven...

GIORGIO: Today's the last day!

TINK SOLHEIM: Laaaaaaaaaaaaast day!

JULIE JENKINS: [*Another photographer, enters. A tall, leggy knockout. She carries three times more photographic equipment than the others. She slings it all down in front of the clothesline.*]

THE GUARD: [*Advancing to her.*] NOW WAIT JUST ONE MINUTE, IT'S AGAINST MUSUEM REGULATIONS TO PHOTOGRAPH THE ART WORKS!

GIORGIO: [*Looking at* Landscape I.] Zachery Moe!

ZOE: [*To* GIORGIO.] Look at that girl, [TINK.] she's touching one of the statues....

JULIE JENKINS: But today's the last day!

ZOE: Giorgio, look!

THE GUARD: I'm sorry, Miss. It's against museum regulations.

GIORGIO: His parents are deaf, I believe.

JULIE JENKINS: But I came to photograph Bill Stevens' clothesline!

THE GUARD: You mean, Steve Williams, not Bill Stevens.

JULIE JENKINS: Steve Stevens?

THE GUARD: STEVE WILLIAMS!

JULIE JENKINS: I thought his name was Bill Stevens.

THE GUARD: Steve Stevens?

JULIE JENKINS: [*Desperate.*] *WILLIAM STEVENSON!*

THE GUARD: Stevenson?

JULIE JENKINS: Williamson?

THE GUARD: Stephen Williamson?

JULIE JENKINS: *WILLIAM* Williamson!

THE GUARD: Steve!

JULIE JENKINS: [*Amazed.*] STEVE?

THE GUARD: Williams!

JULIE JENKINS: *Williams*?

THE GUARD: Steve. Williams!

JULIE JENKINS: Artists always have such tricky names....

GIORGIO: Or is it Raoul Io's parents who are deaf?

ZOE: [*Absorbed with* TINK.] She's not supposed to be doing that.

THE GUARD: You have to get permission from the Director to photograph the art work!

JULIE JENKINS: [*Waving a slip.*] I have permission.

THE GUARD: [*Taking it.*] Yes, I see.

JULIE JENKINS: From the Director...

THE GUARD: Oh?

JULIE JENKINS: Daddy!

ZOE: She's going to get into trouble....

JULIE JENKINS: [*Unloading her gear.*] Daddy's the Director!

ZOE: Look at her, Giorgio!

GIORGIO: [*Examining* Landscape I *up close.*] Very interesting!

JULIE JENKINS: GOD, I LOVE STEVE STEVENS' WORK!

THE GUARD: The Director's daughter [*Indicating* GILDA NORRIS.]...your sister's here too!

ZOE: She's touching them....

GIORGIO: Brilliant brushwork!

JULIE JENKINS: All my life I've wanted to photograph a real Bill Stevenson!

GIORGIO: [*Nose against the canvas.*] It's extraordinary how much of the detail you miss when you don't take the time to really examine a canvas!

THE GUARD: [*Going over to him.*] Please sir, don't *smell* the painting!

GIORGIO: I'm not *smelling* the painting, I'm examining the brushwork!

THE GUARD: Zachery Moe doesn't use a brush!

ZOE: Oh, Giorgio!

GIORGIO: He use a roller?

THE GUARD: Nope.

ZOE: Come on, don't start this again.

GIORGIO: Stain technique?

THE GUARD: Nope.

GIORGIO: Spilling?

THE GUARD: No.

[*The* GUARD *and* GIORGIO *faster and faster.*]

GIORGIO: Pooling?

THE GUARD: No.

GIORGIO: Scumbling?

THE GUARD: No.

ZOE: People are staring....

GIORGIO: Blotting?

THE GUARD: No.

GIORGIO: Toweling?

THE GUARD: No.

GIORGIO: Shit!

THE GUARD: No.

GIORGIO: AIR BRUSH?

THE GUARD: You got it!

GIORGIO: [*Laughing.*] I knew it all along!

ZOE: Did not...

GIORGIO: [*To* THE GUARD.] In air brushing successive layers of paint, Moe stresses the actuality of the surface and limits the distances between the...

ZOE: [*Pulling at him.*] Come on, Giorgio, I'm bored. Let's look at something else...I'm tired of this....Come on, let's go to another floor...Giorgio!

GIORGIO: [*To* THE GUARD.] It's the relationship of the figure to the support and the consequent affirmation of the picture plane that makes it difficult to penetrate the atmosphere space behind it....

TINK SOLHEIM: [*Suddenly releases the miracle buried in* The Holy Wars of Babylon Rage Through the Night. *The lights dim. A floodlight pours down on the statue and Bach's* Dorian Toccata and Fugue in D Minor, BWV 538 *for organ swells from a speaker concealed in the pedestal.*] I FOUND IT! I FOUND IT! "The

Holy Wars of Babylon Rage Through the Night"!

EVERYONE: [*Is thunderstruck. They gaze at* TINK *and the statue, chills racing up their backs. There's a hush and a slow realization that the music is* part *of the statue.*]

TINK SOLHEIM: I found the switch. I found it!

GIORGIO: How beautiful...

ZOE: Oh, Giorgio...

GILDA NORRIS: I'm going to die....

EVERYONE: [*Slowly draws near the statue to worship.*]

JULIE JENKINS: It's a wave...cresting!

GIORGIO: It's a stunning Renaissance landscape....

MICHAEL WALL: It's the urban vision of a futurist....

FRED IZUMI: [*Recites some Haiku in Japanese.*]

GILDA NORRIS: "And lo, the angel of the Lord came upon them, and the glory of the Lord shone around about them...."

TINK SOLHEIM: She challenged me: Find it on the last day....

THE GUARD: It's a self-portrait.

ZOE: Growth!

[*As the music pours from its source, each viewer improvises on the unique beauty he sees. Their voices frequently overlap, but rich details of observation come through. This lasts for several minutes. The volume of the music slowly decreases.*]

TINK SOLHEIM: It was worth it....

ZOE: Nothing like this has ever happened to me before....

TINK SOLHEIM: It was all worth it...*everything*!

THE GUARD: The museum had no idea....

GIORGIO: Of course there are precedents for *heard* art....

ZOE: Giorgio, hold me!...

GILDA NORRIS: I'll never forget this day...never!

FRED IZUMI: She must have snuck in after the installation of the show and set it all up....

THE GUARD: None of the security force was told.

TINK SOLHEIM: *She is vindicated*! Through me! Through me!

[*She exits.*]

EVERYONE: [*Takes one last look at the statue and then drifts to other Agnes Vaag works in hopes of finding similar wonders.*]

THE GUARD: [*Watches over The Holy Wars, trying to figure out what triggered the music and lights. He breathes on it in a certain way and the music stops; the lights go back to normal. Baffled, he keeps circling it.*]

FIRST GUARD: [*Dressed just like THE GUARD, enters and joins him.*] Busy?

THE GUARD: [*Caught actually studying an artwork; is embarrassed and feigns indifference. He whistles.*]

FIRST GUARD: You look busy.

THE GUARD: This is the last day of my show.

FIRST GUARD: Oh, a closing.

SECOND GUARD: [*Dressed as the others, joins them.*] Busy?

THE GUARD: Boy!

FIRST GUARD: I've been swamped!

SECOND GUARD: Colonial Quilts and Weathervanes are slow. I only had three people this morning.

FIRST GUARD: I must have sold a hundred and fifty dollars worth of postcards in the last hour.

THE GUARD: It's been very busy here.

SECOND GUARD: My show still has two more weeks. I don't know how I'm going to make it, it's so slow.

FIRST GUARD: Engagement calendars aren't doing well, but they just can't get enough postcards!

SECOND GUARD: Very slow.

THE GUARD: The Director has given three photographers permission to photograph the art works.

FIRST AND SECOND GUARD: THREE?

THE GUARD: ...and a sketcher!

FIRST GUARD: Jesus...

SECOND GUARD: Son of a bitch...

THE GUARD: I don't know where it will end.

FIRST GUARD: [*To the SECOND GUARD.*] You busy this morning? I'm swamped!

SECOND GUARD: Very slow. Only three people. [*Looking*

around.] You look pretty busy.

THE GUARD: This is the last day of my show.

SECOND GUARD: I haven't been busy like this since my American Abstract show last spring.

THE GUARD: They keep stealing my clothespins.

FIRST GUARD: I've just about sold out of your catalogues.

THE GUARD: I'm not surprised.

SECOND GUARD: Thursdays are slow.

FIRST GUARD: Thursdays are slow. But *Tuesdays*...

SECOND GUARD: Tuesdays! [*Silence.*] Saturdays are pretty bad.

FIRST GUARD: I'd rather work on a Saturday than a Sunday, though.

SECOND GUARD: Sundays aren't so bad.

THE GUARD: I don't mind Sundays.

SECOND GUARD: I like Sundays.

THE GUARD: Sundays are   SECOND GUARD: Sunday's
nice....   a good day.

[*Silence.*]

THE GUARD: I just wish people would stop stealing the clothespins.

FIRST GUARD: Hey, did you hear the radio this morning?

SECOND GUARD: THOSE EUROPEAN MUSEUMS HAVE SHIT FOR SECURITY!

EVERYONE: [*Looks up.*]

SECOND GUARD: [*Lowering his voice.*] Any maniac can get away with anything in a European museum. Look what happened to Michelangelo's *Pietà*....

FIRST GUARD: And that Rembrandt last year, slashed with a bread knife.

SECOND GUARD: That's right. It could never happen here.

FIRST GUARD: American security is the best.

THE GUARD: You can't beat American security.

FIRST GUARD: NUMBER ONE!

SECOND GUARD: That's right. WE'RE NUMBER ONE ON SECURITY!

EVERYONE: [*Looks up again.*]

FIRST GUARD: First!

THE GUARD: The best!

FIRST GUARD: American museums have the tightest security of any museum in the whole fucking world!

THE GUARD AND THE SECOND GUARD: Yeah, you said it, that's right, number one. The best. [*Etc.*]

FIRST GUARD: The people over there are nuts!

THE GUARD AND THE SECOND GUARD: You can say that again. Here, here. You ain't just whistling Dixie. [*Etc.*]

FIRST GUARD: Violent bastards. An American would never shoot a painting!

SECOND GUARD: Well, they know they can get away with it over there, so that just encourages them to be violent. [*They get more and more worked up.*]

THE GUARD: That's right, that's right!

FIRST GUARD: The worst that's happened over here is some nut with a can of spray paint that washes right off.

SECOND GUARD: Everyone's nuts these days.

THE GUARD: I just wish they'd stop stealing the clothespins!

FIRST GUARD: Did you hear what the guy kept screaming as he shot the painting? "Cursed is the ground for thy sake."

SECOND GUARD: "Cursed is the *ground* for thy sake?"

THE GUARD: Crazy bastards!

FIRST GUARD: It's what Adam said to Eve after she ate the apple.

SECOND GUARD: Jesus.

THE GUARD: Crazy bastards!

FIRST GUARD: Crazy fuckers always yell out something religious when they attack art works!

SECOND GUARD: You wouldn't find me working over there for shit!

FIRST GUARD: They're all nuts on religion over there....

THE GUARD: Crazy bastards...

FIRST GUARD: He pumped eighteen bullets into the damned painting before he was restrained ...eighteen bullets!

[*Silence.*]

SECOND GUARD: [*Reaches in his pocket.*] Hey, look what I found this morning. Someone must have dropped it.

THE GUARD: Let's see.

FIRST GUARD: What is it?

SECOND GUARD: [*Holding it up to the light.*] A piece of rose quartz.

THE GUARD: [*Takes it and holds it up to the light.*] It looks more like pink tourmaline to me.
[*Hands it to the* FIRST GUARD.]

FIRST GUARD: [*Looking at it.*] This isn't tourmaline, it's rhodochrosite!

SECOND GUARD: [*Snatching it back.*] Rhodochrosite shit, it's rose quartz!

FIRST GUARD: It's too opaque to be rose quartz.

THE GUARD: But it's too dense to be rhodochrosite!

SECOND GUARD: Dense? This isn't dense! It's translucent!

FIRST GUARD: [*Holding it up to the light.*] There *are* semi-translucent varieties of rhodochrosite!

THE GUARD: Pink tourmaline can be dense or translucent. It's pink tourmaline.

SECOND GUARD: This can't be pink tourmaline because tourmaline doesn't come in pink!

FIRST GUARD: How could it be rose quartz? It's closer to pink tourmaline...even if there's no such animal.

THE GUARD: Rhodochrosite is worth a lot more than rose quartz.

FIRST GUARD: ...or pink tourmaline, for that matter.

SECOND GUARD: [*Putting the stone back in his pocket and pulling out some papers.*] All right, you guys, I've got our assignments for lunch hour.
[*The other* GUARDS *groan.*]

SECOND GUARD: It's not too bad. [*To* THE GUARD.] Since Lou and George were let go last week, you'll be needed at the register in the Gift Shop because he's [The FIRST GUARD] got to relieve Otto in the Members' Lounge.

THE GUARD: Son of a...

SECOND GUARD: [*To the* FIRST GUARD.] You go to the Members' Lounge while I cover for Raoul in the Checkroom since no one's been in the Klein retrospective all week. Colonial Quilts and Weathervanes is closed for the rest of the day.

THE GUARD: [*In an urgent whisper.*] But someone has to stay here. It's the last day of the show.

SECOND GUARD: You'll be back in a half hour. I just need you to cover for him in the Gift Shop so he can relieve Otto.

THE GUARD: I don't think it's a good idea to leave the room...unattended....

EVERYONE: [*Looks up and then quickly away.*]

SECOND GUARD: It's orders.

THE GUARD: You know what closings are like. Everyone takes things....

EVERYONE: [*Looks up again.*]

SECOND GUARD: You mean...[*Laughs.*] clothespins?...

THE GUARD: Yes, clothespins!

SECOND GUARD: [*Bursts out laughing.*]

FIRST GUARD: [*Joins him.*] Clothespins!

THE GUARD: [*Picks up a clothespin to show them.*] They can't get enough of them. They're the old-fashioned kind with round heads.

FIRST GUARD: [*Takes it.*] You mean the ones without the spring in the middle?

THE GUARD: That's right.

FIRST GUARD: Jeez, we used to have those....

STEVE WILLIAMS: [*The artist, enters. He radiates charisma. Everyone stares at him; they're not sure who he is, but they know he's someone important and draw back silently. He's come to look at his clothesline and wears the identical clothes as his self-portrait which hangs on the line. He studies the arrangement of the figures from across the room, perplexed.*]
[*A silence.*]

SECOND GUARD: [*Eyes glued to* STEVE WILLIAMS.] You know, I thought my American Abstract show was busy, but I've got to hand it to you, yours is busier!

THE GUARD: [*Also staring at* WILLIAMS.] Huh?! Huh?!

FIRST GUARD: Come on, we've got to get out of here quietly so no one will notice....

THE GUARD: That's right, just slip right out....

SECOND GUARD: Ssssssh-hhhhhh....

[*They exit on tiptoe.*]

FIRST GUARD:	THE GUARD:	SECOND GUARD:
Listen, the Gift Shop isn't as bad as the Members' Lounge, I don't care what you say....[*Etc.*]	Christ, I hate the Gift Shop! The worst shift of all has got to be the goddamned Gift Shop....[*Etc.*]	Otto hasn't had lunch for three weeks now, three weeks. His doctor says he's developing incipient ulcers....[*Etc.*]

GILDA NORRIS: [*The first to realize, her heart in her throat.*] That's...Steve Williams!

GIORGIO: My God, the artist!

ZOE: Oh, Giorgio!

MICHAEL WALL: I thought he looked familiar!

FRED IZUMI: Steve Williams!

ZOE: He's dressed just like his self-portrait!

GILDA NORRIS: [*Swooning.*] Steve...Williams?

JULIE JENKINS: STEVE STEVENS!

[*The three photographers quickly take advantage of this media event, and start snapping pictures of* WILLIAMS *and his amazing performance. At times they work independently, and then suddenly strike group poses.*]

STEVE WILLIAMS: [*Ignores everyone and stands engrossed before his work. Something's wrong, the figures aren't positioned correctly. One by one, he unpins the bodies, laying them carefully on the benches and floor until the clothesline is bare. After careful thought he picks up the Mexican boy, cradles him in his arms, and hangs him first on the line. With considerable dash he adds the bride, then his own figure, which he handles with rough good humor,...and so on until the lineup is complete. He doesn't make a sound and wields the bodies with such grace that everyone is deeply affected. As ...*]

GIORGIO: [*Strides over to the clothesline, and reads Williams' bio from the catalogue.*] Steven Williams was born October 30, 1938, in Santa Rosa, California. He studied at the Leonardo da Vinci School and had his first one-man show at the Dilexi Gallery, San Francisco, in 1947; an exhibition of animal heads in cement, which in their open framework and pitted surfaces, were a powerful refutation of the prevailing modern traditions of neat forms, clean surfaces, and truth to materials. Williams lived in Paris from 1947 through 1953 where he exhibited in a group show at the Galerie Maeght, visited Giacometti's studio, and was exposed to and impressed by the works of Paul Klee, Dada, and Surrealism. His sculpture thereafter presented anguished images of the anonymity of modern man, using cast-off objects assembled according to an indisputably human framework. Since 1965, Williams' sculpture, although still governed by the principles of assemblages, comprise more simply structured monumental components, incorporated with technological precision into quite different icons of modernity."

STEVE WILLIAMS: [*Finished with his works, stands back to survey the new lineup. He smiles.*]

EVERYONE: [*Smiles.*]

THE PHOTOGRAPHERS: [*Pull out all their stops.* JULIE JENKINS *starts using a flash,* MICHAEL WALL *practically crawls inside* WILLIAMS' *clothing,* FRED IZUMI *photographs from daring new angles.*]

THE WOMEN IN THE ROOM: [*Reach out their hands towards* WILLIAMS.]

STEVE WILLIAMS: [*Is pleased and walks energetically out of the room, flashing one final smile.*]

[*A silence. These lines should spill over each other....*]

GILDA NORRIS: I thought I was going to die... just sink down to the floor, shut my eyes, and quietly die....

JULIE JENKINS: Did you see those hands?

MICHAEL WALL: That was pure...once in a lifetime!

FRED IZUMI: Harrison isn't going to believe this!

JULIE JENKINS: ...and his arms...MY GOD, THE TENDERNESS IN HIS ARMS!

GILDA NORRIS: I'll never be the same.

ZOE: But you're not supposed to touch anything once it's been installed, are you?

GIORGIO: His pieces sell for over two hundred thousand dollars! Two hundred thousand dollars!

EVERYONE: [*Is silent again. They gaze at the clothesline for some time.*]

ZOE: Oh, Giorgio, let's take something...as a remembrance.

JULIE JENKINS: Steve Stevens...

ZOE: One of the clothespins...something he touched.

GILDA NORRIS: Something he touched...

JULIE JENKINS: Something he touched...

MICHAEL WALL: A clothespin...

FRED IZUMI: A clothespin...

[*No one moves.*]

ZOE: [*Breaks the spell, walks to the clothesline and brazenly snatches a clothespin.*]

[*One by one each person approaches the basket, and takes one or more pins. It's not a mad scramble, but a communion, enacted with quiet reverence. Once the first theft has been tasted, they become thirsty for more. The bride's arm is pulled off with an awful rending sound.* JULIE JENKINS *rushes up to the* STEVE WILLIAMS *figure and throws her arms around him.* GILDA NORRIS *edges past her and kisses his face; his head falls off in her amazed hands. The others move in for their share: half of the Mexican boy is removed; the businessman's legs are severed; arms, legs, and pieces of clothing are snatched. The lights dim as each person scurries out with his booty. The clothesline is almost picked clean. Only a few stray torsos, heads, and veils are left.*]

MR. AND MRS. MOE: [ZACHERY MOE'S *deaf-mute parents slip in unnoticed during these final moments. Caring only for their son's work, they go directly to his paint-*

ings and stand before them, radiant with pride and happiness.]

THE GUARD: [*Returns from his lunch break, sees the devastation of the clothesline and is horrified. He tries to protect the few scraps that remain and then starts running in terrible confusion. He finally notices the* MOES.] What happened in here? What's been going on? The clothesline! Who did this? Look at it...the clothesline...it's been picked apart...destroyed what...happened? WILL YOU PLEASE TELL ME...WHAT HAPPENED? WHO DID THIS?

[*They don't answer. He realizes they're beyond him and kneels by the basket of clothespins, broken.*]

MR. AND MRS. MOE: [*Keep gazing at the paintings, completely unaware of* THE GUARD. *They move to their favorite one and stand beneath it, riveted.* MRS. MOE *turns to her husband and speaks in sign language.*]

MRS. MOE: Remember the drawings he used to make as a child?

MR. MOE: The sketches he did of all his toys in his nursery...

MRS. MOE: How wonderful they were, bursting with life....

MR. MOE: *Noisy* with life!

MRS. MOE: Remember how he'd make the walls shake when he wanted something?

MR. MOE: And how they shook! He shouted with the voice of a thousand men!

[*The lights fade on their rhapsodic hands as...*]

THE CURTAIN SLOWLY FALLS

THE ART OF DINING

THE ART OF DINING, co-produced by the Kennedy Center and the New York Shakespeare Festival, premiered at the New York Shakespeare Festival in 1979; Joseph Papp, producer.

DIRECTOR: A. J. Antoon
SETTING: David Jenkins
LIGHTING: Ian Calderon
COSTUMES: Hilary Rosenfeld

CAST
(in order of appearance)

ELLEN....................................Suzanne Collins
CAL .... Ron Rifkin
HANNAH GALT............................Jane Hoffman
PAUL GALT .... Robert Gerringer
ELIZABETH BARROW COLT................ Dianne Wiest
HERRICK SIMMONS.........................Kathy Bates
NESSA VOX .... Margaret Whitton
TONY STASSIO ....Jacklyn Maddux
DAVID OSSLOW ....George Guidall

CHARACTERS

ELLEN, *co-owner and chef extraordinaire of The Golden Carrousel, mid-thirties.*

CAL, *co-owner and supple head waiter of The Golden Carrousel, Ellen's husband, mid-thirties.*

HANNAH GALT, *beautifully dressed and hungry, mid-forties.*

PAUL GALT, *beautifully dressed and hungrier, mid-forties.*

ELIZABETH BARROW COLT, *exceedingly shy and near-sighted. A writer in her early thirties, afraid of food.*

HERRICK SIMMONS, *enthusiastic and a good eater, early thirties.*

NESSA VOX, *easily upset and a more neurotic eater, early thirties.*

TONY STASSIO, *perpetually on a diet and miserable, early thirties.*

DAVID OSSLOW, *the head of his own publishing company, successful, at ease, son and husband of good cooks, mid-fifties and in top shape.*

ACT I

Scene 1

TIME: *The present*
PLACE: *The ground floor of a nineteenth-century town-house on the New Jersey shore which has been converted into a restaurant, The Golden Carrousel. The right half of the stage is the dining area, a wonderfully elegant little place with a high tin ceiling, arched windows, hanging plants, and four tables set for dinner. A pair of restored carrousel horses with gleaming gold hardware stand at the entrance of the room. A full working kitchen is on the left half of the stage. A swinging door with a glass window at the top separates the two rooms. It's late November, unusually cold, and a month after the restaurant's grand opening. The doors are about to open for dinner, and the fragrance of the evening's offerings fill the theater.*
ELLEN *and* CAL *are sitting at one of the tables about to sample two different desserts. They should be mistaken for customers.*

ELLEN: [*Tense with expectancy, dips her spoon into her glass of Floating Island, tastes it and holds her breath.*]
CAL: [*Stabs his spoon into his dish of Pears and Cointreau with Frozen Cream and croons with delight.*]
ELLEN: [*Savors her mouthful and exhales with relief.*]
CAL: [*Very rapidly takes another taste, a long sigh.*]
ELLEN: [*Takes a cautious second taste and makes a humming sound.*]
CAL: [*Takes three rapid-fire tastes, making little whimpering sounds after each one.*]

73

ELLEN: [*Licks her lips and pauses.*]

CAL: [*Scraping his spoon against the sides of his dish with fervor, takes a heaping mouthful and groans with pleasure.*]

ELLEN: [*Takes another apprehensive taste. Yes, it's excellent, she purrs.*]

CAL: [*Overcome, drops his head in his hands.*]

ELLEN: [*Puts her spoon down and nods her head yes. Silence. Shoves her dessert over to* CAL *to try. He dips his spoon in, takes a slow loving taste. It's even better than his! He moans helplessly and pushes his dessert over to her.* ELLEN *takes a swift taste of the pears, making little lip-smacking noises.*]

CAL: [*Takes a huge spoonful of Floating Island and is mute.*]

[*A silence.*]

ELLEN: [*Exhales with pleasure. Takes another taste, inhales, stares into space, puts her spoon down, clicks her tongue, exhilarated.*]

CAL: [*Takes a smaller taste, then makes a low sob and takes five very fast spoonfuls, grunting during each one.*]

[*A silence.*]

ELLEN: [*Reaches across the table and takes back her Floating Island and returns the pears to* CAL. *She scrapes the sides of her glass.*]

CAL: [*Fiercely attacks what's left of his pears.*]
[*They finish, breathing heavily.*]

CAL: [*Weakly.*] Pears...

ELLEN: [*Undone.*] Meringues...

CAL: Cointreau...

ELLEN: Vanilla...

CAL: Heavy cream...

ELLEN: Caramel...

CAL: Chilled...

ELLEN: Poached...

CAL: Cool...

ELLEN: Quivering...

CAL: ...to perfection!

ELLEN: In English cream!

CAL: Pure sin!

ELLEN: Real joy.

CAL: A person could die....

ELLEN: Which did you like better?

CAL: What a way to go!

ELLEN: The pears...

CAL: Christ!

ELLEN: ...or the Floating Island?

CAL: [*Frantically scrapes at his dish, nothing is left.*]

ELLEN: I preferred the pears, didn't you?

CAL: [*Reaching for her dish.*] Do you have any left?

ELLEN: They're more challenging.

[*She picks up* CAL's *empty dish and rises. Wipes invisible crumbs from the table, straightens the tablecloth as...*]

CAL: [*Dips his spoon in* ELLEN's *dish for the last bits of Floating Island then plunges his finger in and starts scraping the sides.*]

ELLEN: [*Pushes through the swinging door into the kitchen. She puts* CAL's *dish in the sink and starts stirring the soup on the stove as...*]

CAL: [*Follows* ELLEN *into the kitchen, scraping the sides of his dish with alternate fingers and sucking them clean. He rises and he looks around, finds the saucepan of warm Floating Island and pours more into his empty dish. He gets a new spoon and takes slow loving mouthfuls as he watches* ELLEN *work on her soup.*]

[*These are the various works in progress:*
Belgian Oxtail Soup
Billi Bi on a low flame
Several ducks browning in a heavy frying pan
Veal
Wild rice

Set aside on the counters are the beginnings of:
The stuffing for the veal
The shrimp mousse for the bass
A huge tossed salad
A saucepan full of Floating Island

75

Hidden in the refrigerator are:
The Pears in Cointreau with Frozen Cream
The uncooked bass
Basic ingredients for the sauces, Hollandaise
   and Velouté
Celery
A bowl of grapes for the duck]

ELLEN: [*Stirring and tasting her soup.*] They were firm enough, weren't they?

CAL: [*Involved with his Floating Island.*] Oh...so smooth!

ELLEN: Nothing is worse than limp pears!

CAL: ...so light...

ELLEN: What time is it?

CAL: ...perfect!

ELLEN: They were all right, weren't they?

CAL: [*Referring to the Floating Island.*] You added something.

ELLEN: [*Referring to the pears.*] I added something.

CAL: What is it? I can't tell.

ELLEN: A touch of...ginger.

CAL: [*Smacking his lips.*] It tastes more like... cinnamon....

ELLEN: ...and a hint of almond.

CAL: No, wait, I've got it....

ELLEN: Did you notice?

CAL: NUTMEG!

ELLEN: [*Tasting the soup.*] I'll bet you didn't even notice the almond.

CAL: It's nutmeg.

ELLEN: The ginger flavor is much stronger.

CAL: It's wonderful.

ELLEN: How much time do we have?

CAL: Really delicious.

ELLEN: [*Offering him a taste of soup.*] What do you think? I don't know, the bouquet's a little weak....

CAL: [*Referring to the Floating Island.*] You should make it more often, everyone loves it.

ELLEN: It needs more thyme for one thing.

CAL: [*Gobbling up the rest of the Floating Island.*] I can't stop eating this Floating Island! I don't know what you do to your desserts, this is irresistible!

ELLEN: [*Holding out a spoonful of soup.*] I need you to taste. How is it?

CAL: It tastes like Floating Island.

ELLEN: Come on, Cal, they'll be here soon. Try again.

CAL: Oh, I forgot to tell you, Table Four canceled because of the bad weather.

ELLEN: They'll come back.... [*Holding out a fresh taste of soup.*] Now tell me; how is it?

CAL: [*Takes his time, savors it.*] Good.

ELLEN: *Good*? Is that all?

CAL: [*Helps himself to another spoonful.*] Very good.

ELLEN: Damn!... [*She has another taste.*] The bouquet's still weak....

CAL: [*Strides over to her with his spoon, starts dipping it into the soup and slurping.*]

ELLEN: [*Tastes in a much more exacting way.*] Wait a minute!

CAL: VERY GOOD!

ELLEN: I FORGOT THE WATERCRESS!

CAL: ... and this is without the added touches of smoked ham and Madeira.

ELLEN: [*Laughing, gets the watercress from the refrigerator.*] I forgot the watercress.

CAL: It's perfect, it doesn't need watercress!

ELLEN: What do you mean, it doesn't need watercress?

CAL: It's delicious without watercress.

ELLEN: It's incomplete without watercress! [*She adds some.*]

CAL: Watercress is overrated.

ELLEN: Watercress is *essential*!

CAL: Watercress is a pain in the ass!

ELLEN: Watercress is one of the staples of French and Chinese cuisine!

CAL: It's overrated.

ELLEN: It's piquant....

CAL: It's soggy....

77

ELLEN: It's refreshing....

CAL: It's overpriced....

[*The telephone rings. There are two phones in the kitchen. Depending on where he's standing,* CAL *alternates between them.*]

ELLEN: Oh, God! [*She works faster on her soup.*]

CAL: I've got it! [*On the phone.*] Good evening, The Golden Carrousel, may I help you?

ELLEN: God, God, God!

CAL: Reservations for two this Friday night at eight? ...Hold on a sec, let me check our calendar. [*To* ELLEN.] Reservations for two this Friday at eight.

ELLEN: We're filled for the rest of the week!

CAL: [*Back on the phone, eyeing the calendar.*] Yes, I see a space.

ELLEN: We're filled!

CAL: Could I have your name, please?... I'm sorry, would you mind spelling that for me?

ELLEN: [*In an urgent whisper.*] I'm making apricot brandy soufflés on Friday!

CAL: K.A.S.T.F.S.

ELLEN: I have to prepare a fresh apricot puree for each one.

CAL: [*Slower.*] K.A.S.T.O.F.S.K....WHAT?

ELLEN: It makes all the difference.

CAL: O.F.S.K.*Y*!

ELLEN: That way, the full apricot aroma is retained until the very last.

CAL: *Kas*tofsky.

ELLEN: If you make the puree beforehand and let it sit until the soufflé is ready to pour then...

CAL: Oh, Kas*tof*sky, I'm sorry!

ELLEN: Apricot is very delicate.

CAL: [*Pleased.*] KasTOFsky!

ELLEN: Much more so than lemon or orange, a lemon soufflé...

CAL: Yes, Kas*tof*sky. I've got it now!

ELLEN: Or even a strawberry soufflé would be...

CAL: Well, thank you for calling, Mr. Kastofsky. We'll

see you on Friday night then at eight. Good-bye. [*He hangs up. To* ELLEN, *radiant.*] WHAT DID I TELL YOU?

ELLEN: Apricot is tricky.

CAL: [*Adding the Kastofskys to their calendar which is already black with reservations.*] The word is spreading! We've only been open four weeks and we're already booked into next month!

ELLEN: I can't cook for more than two sittings a night.

CAL: They're breaking down the doors....

ELLEN: We've been over this before.

CAL: Jamming the phones...

ELLEN: If you rush me, the food will suffer.

CAL: [*Goes to the second pot of soup on the stove, the Billi Bi, and helps himself to a huge spoonful. He burns his tongue and yowls in pain, jumping up and down.*]

ELLEN: [*Rushing over to him.*] What happened?

CAL: [*Keeps yowling, his tongue hanging out.*]

ELLEN: I can't understand you....

CAL: [*Completely garbled since his tongue is out.*] I burned my tongue!

ELLEN: Oh, baby!

CAL: [*Jumping up and down.*] Get me the boric acid! [*The telephone starts to ring.*]

ELLEN: [*Rushes to the refrigerator.*] I'm getting the butter!

[*She returns with a stick of butter.*]

CAL: [*Garbled.*] I SAID, *BORIC ACID*!

ELLEN: Hold still, this will numb the pain....

CAL: Answer the phone!

ELLEN: What?

CAL: [*Waving towards the ringing phone.*] The phone, the phone, the phone!

ELLEN: Hold still, or I can't get it on.

CAL: [*Garbled.*] Will you answer the god-damned phone???!

ELLEN: I know it hurts, honey, just hang on one minute! [*She starts smearing butter on his flapping tongue.*]

CAL: [*More garbled than ever.*] I DON'T WANT BUT-

TER! I WANT BORIC ACID, BORIC ACID!

ELLEN: [*Imitates the way he says it to try and understand him.*] Boric acid?

CAL: Will you please answer the phone before they hang up.

ELLEN: [*Says "boric acid" again as before, completely confused.*] Boric acid??

CAL: [*Lunges for the phone, tongue still out and incomprehensible.*] Good evening, The Golden Carrousel, may I help you?

ELLEN: [*Takes the phone from him.*] Oh! The telephone!

CAL: [*Puts his tongue back in his mouth, as clear as day.*] The telephone.

ELLEN: Well, why didn't you say so? [*Into the phone.*] Good evening, The Golden Carrousel, could you hold on for just a moment please? [*She puts the receiver aside. To* CAL.] Now, what is it that you want?

CAL: [*His tongue in his mouth, clearly.*] Boric acid.

ELLEN: [*Amazed.*] Ohhhh! Boric acid! You mean, *baking soda!*

CAL: [*Sticks out his tongue and says it all queer again.*]

ELLEN: [*Copies him. Keeping her tongue out, garbled.*] Coming right up.
[*She gets it from a cupboard.*]

CAL: [*His tongue out.*] I think I burned off all the skin.

ELLEN: [*Laughing, imitates him again.*] I think I burned off all the skin!

CAL: [*His tongue back in, clear.*] I burned off all the skin.

ELLEN: [*Gently fingering his tongue.*] No, you didn't. It's just a bit red. Now hold still so I can get this butter off.

CAL: [*Garbled again.*] At least you could have used sweet butter!

ELLEN: [*Tongue out, imitates what he said.*]

CAL: [*Tongue back in.*] Sweet butter.

ELLEN: Sweet butter! [*Puts some baking soda on his tongue.*] How does that feel?

CAL: It hurts.

ELLEN: I'm sorry. Did you enjoy the soup at least?

CAL: I couldn't taste it.

ELLEN: I haven't added the egg yolks yet.

CAL: [*In pain.*] Son of a bitch.

ELLEN: They make all the difference....

CAL: [*Touching his tongue.*] I burned off all my damned taste buds!

ELLEN: [*Gently blowing on his tongue.*] No, you didn't, it's just red.

CAL: That feels good.

ELLEN: [*Keeps blowing on it.*] Poor baby.

CAL: They're so fragile.

ELLEN: What are?

CAL: Taste buds.

ELLEN: That's because they're nerves.

CAL: ...millions of tiny fragile pink dots. They have roots, you know. Long roots that extend all the way through your tongue...they're like the fingers on a hand...long sensitive fingers, touching and feeling...and now I've burned them all off...OH JESUS, THE TELEPHONE! [*He rushes to the telephone.*] Hello? Are you still there? Hello? Hello? [*He slams the receiver down.*] They hung up! [ELLEN *laughs.*] It's not funny.

ELLEN: They'll call back.

CAL: How do you know?
[*He goes to the refrigerator and starts looking for something to eat.*]

ELLEN: We've got to hurry!

CAL: [*Making a racket moving things about.*] We might have lost a customer just now.

ELLEN: It's getting late.

CAL: They probably won't call back.

ELLEN: [*Holding out a spoonful of soup to him.*] Come on, open.

CAL: [*Pulls out a bowl of green grapes set aside to garnish the duckling in wine, fitfully starts eating them.*] Ellen, we've borrowed seventy-five thousand dollars to open this place, and if we don't come up with twenty thousand next month, the whole thing will go under. Good-bye. Gone. We can't afford to lose any phone calls.

81

ELLEN: [*The spoon still extended.*] Please.

CAL: [*Wolfing down the grapes.*] We've got to clear nine hundred dollars a night!

ELLEN: . . . taste!

CAL: . . . and if we don't serve a minimum of thirty-six customers a night . . .

ELLEN: No!

CAL: . . . at approximately thirty-five dollars each . . .

ELLEN: Cal!

CAL: We won't clear that nine hundred dollars!

ELLEN: Please . . .

CAL: We're so close!

ELLEN: [*Offers him a fresh spoonful, blows on it.*] Taste . . .

CAL: [*Eating the grapes with more relish.*] We could really do it!

ELLEN: Do you like it?

CAL: Serve outstanding food *and* make money at the same time!

ELLEN: Is it all right?

[*The telephone rings.*]

CAL: [*Pushes past her and grabs the phone.*] There they are!

ELLEN: [*Working on her soup.*] I'm falling behind.

CAL: [*On the phone while popping grapes in his mouth.*] Good evening, The Golden Carrousel. Did you just call us? [*To* ELLEN.] It's them! [*On the phone.*] I'm sorry, we had a slight . . . may I help you? Three for next Tuesday? Let me check our calendar.

ELLEN: We're filled.

CAL: [*Looking at the calendar.*] What time was that again? Nine o'clock? Just one moment, please.

ELLEN: We're filled for the entire week. Hey, don't eat all those grapes. I need them for the Duckling in Wine with Green Grapes!

CAL: Yes, I see a space. We could fit you in at nine.

ELLEN: I'm never going to make it.

CAL: Your name, please?

ELLEN: Never!

CAL: Canelli? . . . Thank you very much for calling, Mr. Canelli.

CAL: We'll be expecting you next Tuesday at nine, then.

ELLEN: Cal, we're booked!

CAL: Your friends said it was the best restaurant in the United States? [*To* ELLEN.]...the best restaurant in the United States! [*Back on the phone.*] And you've eaten everywhere? [*To* ELLEN.] They've eaten *everywhere*!

ELLEN: I haven't even started the celery or begun the Sauce Velouté....

CAL: [*On the phone.*] You've already sent five couples here?... [*To* ELLEN.] *Five* couples!

ELLEN: [*Snapping off the tops of the celery.*] Don't panic.

CAL: They loved it!

ELLEN: You see, they loved it!

CAL: [*On the phone.*] Thank you very much for your kind words. I hope we'll be able to live up to them for you next Tuesday. Good-bye. [*He hangs up, pops more grapes in his mouth.*] They can't get enough!

ELLEN: [*Feeling overwhelmed.*] Oh boy!

CAL: They're coming back! A second time, a third time!

ELLEN: Oh boy, oh boy!

CAL: They're telling their friends!

ELLEN: [*Frantically washing, scraping, and cutting the celery.*] Oh boy oh boy oh boy *oh boy*!

CAL: And those friends are telling other friends!

ELLEN: [*Faster and faster.*] OH BOY OH BOY OH BOY!

CAL: [*Lunges back into the bowl of grapes.*] This is just the beginning!

ELLEN: [*Makes a small strangled sound.*]

CAL: We can't lose!

ELLEN: [*Another sound.*]

CAL: The chance of a lifetime!
[*The doorbell rings.*]

ELLEN: [*Whispered.*]   CAL: [*Whispered.*] The
They're here!   door!

ELLEN: [*Grabs an onion, starts chopping it.*] Help!

CAL: Relax! [*He reaches for a black bow tie and starts putting it on.*]

ELLEN: They're here.

CAL: [*Sings his favorite show tune under his breath.*]

ELLEN: I'm not ready.... Nowhere *near* ready! There's still the wine sauce for the duck and the Hollandaise, not to mention the shrimp mousse for the bass....

CAL: [*Sings on, preening.*]

ELLEN: Oh well, it's just par for the course, right? RIGHT???! [*Notices the empty bowl.*] Where did all the Floating Island go?

[*The doorbell rings again.*]

CAL: Just a minute....

ELLEN: You ate all the Floating Island!

CAL: [*Still singing, bolts upstairs to get his tuxedo jacket.*]

ELLEN: [*Gazing into the empty bowl.*] He ate all the Floating Island. Our first customers of the evening have arrived ... and he's eaten half the desserts....

CAL: [*Bounds back into the kitchen, splendid in his tuxedo. He salutes* ELLEN.] We're off! [*Out the door.*] Coming....

ELLEN: [*Goes to the sink, angrily turns on the faucet to wash the celery.*] I don't believe this!

[*The lights fade on her and rise on* CAL *advancing to the front door.*]

Scene 2

CAL *is a transformed person in his tuxedo jacket. He glitters with charm, elegance, and the desire to please. He opens the door.*

PAUL AND HANNAH GALT: [*Are literally blown in. They're in their middle-forties and are sumptuously dressed: he in a hand-tailored suit under a cashmere coat, she in a floating crepe dress under a mink coat.*]

HANNAH: [*Shivering so violently she totters.*] Ooooooooooh, it's soooooooooo cold!

PAUL: [*Slapping his gloved hands together.*] That wind is ...

HANNAH: I've never been so ...

PAUL: WICKED!

CAL: [*Reach for* HANNAH's *coat.*] May I?

HANNAH: Cold!

PAUL: It's got to be forty below out there!

CAL: [*Reaching for* PAUL's *coat.*] Sir?

HANNAH: ...unbearable!

PAUL: And with the wind chill factor, it's more like sixty below.

HANNAH: ...and only *November*!

CAL: They say the worst is yet to come.

HANNAH: [*Hands over her ears.*] Don't....

PAUL: [*To* CAL.] Yes, I heard that too. Arctic storms are due down from Canada sometime in mid-January....

CAL: [*To* PAUL.] In February we're supposed to have the worst blizzard this country has ever seen! The National Guard's being prepared for this one....

HANNAH: [*Looking around the room.*] Oh, Paul, look! It's charming!

CAL: Please, won't you follow me to your table? We'll warm you up in no time. [*He pulls out the chair for* HANNAH.] Madame?

HANNAH: [*Is enthralled with one of the merry-go-round horses.*] Ooooooh, merry-go-round horses!

PAUL: [*Unwittingly sits down in the chair meant for* HANNAH.]

CAL: *Monsieur*!

HANNAH: I love them!

PAUL: [*To* CAL, *sitting down.*] Thank you.

HANNAH: I WANT THEM!

PAUL: I haven't felt wind like that since...

HANNAH: Aren't they wonderful?

CAL: Could I warm you up with something from the bar?

PAUL: [*Sighs, looking around.*] This is very nice.

CAL: ...a cocktail?

PAUL: Oh, look, Hannah. They have your merry-go-round horses!

HANNAH: They're almost impossible to find these days.

CAL: Some sherry?

PAUL: Those are old!

HANNAH: Aren't they wonderful? I wonder where they got them?

CAL: [*To* HANNAH.] Would you care for something from the bar?

HANNAH: I'll bet you've gotten plenty of offers for those....

PAUL: I don't know about you, but I am starved!

HANNAH: [*To* CAL.] A word of advice: Don't sell them!

CAL: A glass of white wine?...

PAUL: I could eat a horse!

HANNAH: ...no matter what they offer you!

PAUL: I need a drink!

CAL: Yes, Sir?

HANNAH: [*To* CAL.] Every year, they triple in value!

PAUL: Give me a double Scotch, straight up.

CAL: Very good, and you Madame?

HANNAH: [*Comes to the table and sits down.*] *You hang on to them*!

PAUL: I don't know why I should be so hungry, I had a perfectly good lunch!

HANNAH: [*To* PAUL, *under her breath.*] God, I'd love to get my hands on those!

CAL: And for you, Madame?

PAUL: Tartar steak and salad...

HANNAH: Let's see, I guess I'll have a Vodka Gimlet.

CAL: Thank you.

[*He retires to the bar area to mix their drinks.*]

PAUL: I even had a pastry for dessert.

HANNAH: I'm hungry.

PAUL: A plum tart...

HANNAH: I only had a small omelette for lunch.

PAUL: ...with an apricot glaze.

HANNAH: Mushroom...

PAUL: It was...incredible!

HANNAH: ...with a hint of dill.

PAUL: Melts...in...your...mouth.

HANNAH: I behaved myself and skipped dessert.

PAUL: I almost ordered a second.

HANNAH: What did you have for lunch today?

PAUL: *Almost...*

HANNAH: I hardly had anything....

PAUL: You should have seen the plum tart I had for dessert....

HANNAH: Just an omelette.

PAUL: The pastry shell alone...

HANNAH: I thought of having a muffin with it....

PAUL: ...was unbelievable!

HANNAH: Only a half, of course...

PAUL: It could have been served on its own.

HANNAH: But I didn't.

PAUL: I almost broke down and had a second.

HANNAH: Paul!

PAUL: I know, I know!

HANNAH: You shouldn't even *think* of having a second dessert!

PAUL: Well, did I have it? Did I?

HANNAH: I don't know. How would I know?

PAUL: I JUST SAID THAT I DIDN'T. JESUS!

[*A silence.*]

HANNAH: I only had an omelette....

[*A silence.*]

PAUL: I didn't have a second dessert, all right???!

HANNAH: ...a small mushroom omelette...

PAUL: All right????

HANNAH: [*Patting her stomach.*] Uuuuh, it was so filling!

[*A silence.*]

PAUL: [*Depressed, sighs.*]

HANNAH: It's amazing how filling a small mushroom omelette is....But then again mushrooms are very...starchy....

[*A silence.*]

CAL: [*Returns from the bar, puts down* HANNAH's *drink with a flourish.*] A Vodka Gimlet for Madame!

HANNAH: Thank you very much.

CAL: [*Sensing the tension between them, sets down* PAUL's *drink with even more flair.*] And a double Scotch for you, Sir. I hope you enjoy it.

HANNAH: [*Leans back, takes a long sip of her drink, sighs.*]

PAUL: [*Mutters and takes a gulp.*]

CAL: Would you be interested in seeing the menu now, or would you rather wait?

PAUL: Yes, now please.   HANNAH: Oh, let's wait!

CAL: [*More and more flashy in his gestures.*] Very good, I'll bring them right over. [*He fetches them and hands one to* HANNAH.] Madame?

HANNAH: Now, what was it that Ken and Diva said was so good?

CAL: [*Handing one to* PAUL.] Monsieur?

HANNAH: Sole Veronique?

PAUL: [*Under his breath.*] You know I'd never have two desserts for lunch on a day we were going out for dinner!

HANNAH: ... or was it Sole Meunière?

PAUL: I'm not that stupid!

HANNAH: No, wait, I think it was Sole Florentine!

PAUL: ... and in case you've forgotten, I jogged three miles after I got home from the office.

HANNAH: I'VE GOT IT! IT WAS SOLE BONNE FEMME!

PAUL: In fact, it was closer to four and a half.

HANNAH: Ken had Poulet Farci... and Diva had Sole Bonne Femme!

PAUL: I've never been in such good shape!

HANNAH: Or was it the other way around?

PAUL: [*Punching his stomach.*] See that? Hard as a rock!

HANNAH: Ken had the Sole Bonne Femme, and Diva had the Poulet Farci!

PAUL: Go on, hit me in the stomach, I won't even feel it!

HANNAH: No, wait a minute...

PAUL: [*Thrusting out his stomach.*] Come on!

HANNAH: Diva had Poulet Bonne Femme....

PAUL: Hit me!

HANNAH: ... and Ken had Sole Farci!

PAUL: [*Slugs himself.*] See, I didn't feel a thing!

HANNAH: No, that can't be right. There's no such dish as Sole Farci.

PAUL: I'll do it harder. [*He does.*] Nothing!...

HANNAH: Anyway, both of them said it was the most delicious Sole Bonne Femme they'd ever had!

PAUL: [*Really socks himself.*] See that? Didn't even feel it. [*A silence.*] Want me to do it again? [*He repeatedly pommels himself in the stomach. A silence. Then cheerful.*] What was it that Ken and Diva said was so good?

HANNAH: I'm in the mood for veal.

PAUL: Sole Almondine?

HANNAH: You know how on some days you wake up with a craving for something?

CAL: [*Hovering nearby.*] We change our menus every day.

PAUL: Oh?

HANNAH: Friends of ours had your Sole Bonne Femme last week. They said it was out of this world!

CAL: Yes, my wife is a remarkable cook.

HANNAH: Oh, it's your wife who's the chef. I didn't know that.

PAUL: Remember that Chicken Bonne Femme we had at the Pavillion years ago?

HANNAH: It's very rare to come across a woman who's a paid chef.

PAUL: Remember the sauce? . . .

HANNAH: There are only a handful in this country.

PAUL: . . . with white wine and truffles . . .

CAL: Julia Child . . .

HANNAH: Dionne Lucas.

CAL: She's been dead for several years.

HANNAH: She died? I didn't know that!

PAUL: . . . salt pork and meat glaze . . .

CAL: There aren't many.

PAUL: . . . and remember the baby potatoes served with it?

HANNAH: [*To* CAL.] Do you cook too?

CAL: No, I'm afraid I just eat.

HANNAH: We both cook.

CAL: How nice!

HANNAH: [*Nodding towards* PAUL.] He's very good.

PAUL: [*Fingering his menu.*] Well, shall we begin?

CAL: I'm sure.

HANNAH: He does much better soups than me.

CAL: Soups are tricky.

PAUL: [*Holding up his menu.*] Are you ready?

HANNAH: You should taste his gazpacho!

CAL: I love gazpacho!

HANNAH: Well you should taste his!... [*She purrs, remembering the taste.*]

PAUL: [*Holding out her menu for her.*] Hannah!

HANNAH: ...out...of...this...world!

PAUL: Are you ready?

HANNAH: [*Sighs again.*]

PAUL: I'm opening mine....
   [*He looks at her and waits.*]

CAL: If I can assist you in any way, just...

PAUL: Hannah, I'm hungry!

CAL: [*Goes to the rear of the room and flicks on a tape of the Adagio from J. S. Bach's Sonata No. 3 in E Major for violin and harpsichord. The opening measures sound before the* GALTS *begin.*]

PAUL: [*Flicks open his menu with a meaningful look.*]

HANNAH: [*Follows suit.*]

PAUL: [*Glances down the length of it, a tremulous sigh.*]

HANNAH: [*Also glances but in tense silence.*]

PAUL: [*Inhales, takes a deep breath.*]

HANNAH: [*Pushes a strand of hair up off her forehead.*]

PAUL: [*Exhales.*]

HANNAH: [*Tosses her head in bewilderment.*]

PAUL: [*Another sigh, louder.*]
   [*Silence.*]

HANNAH: [*Overcome, shuts her menu and puts it face down on the table.*]

PAUL: [*Gently picks it up and hands it back to her, smiling.*]

HANNAH: [*Scans it again. There's such a feast of choices, she can't decide. She moans.*]

PAUL: [*Pushes back in his chair, eyeing the menu.*]

HANNAH: Oh, Paul!

PAUL: [*Covers her hand with his.*]

HANNAH: It's...

PAUL: Sssssssh!

HANNAH: [*Makes a helpless little sound.*]

PAUL: I know. I know.

HANNAH: Help me.

PAUL: Sweetheart!

HANNAH: Oh, Paul!

PAUL: Take your time....

HANNAH: I...

PAUL: There's no rush....

HANNAH: I'm so...

PAUL: Relax.

HANNAH: [*With a sob.*] I can't!

PAUL: Of course you can!

HANNAH: [*Her head in her hands.*] I'm scared.

PAUL: [*Lifting her head up, cupping it in his hands.*] Trust me.

CAL: [*Turns up the volume of the music.*]

PAUL: [*Under his breath, to* CAL.] Not so loud.

CAL: Sorry! [*Lowers the volume.*]

PAUL: [*Leans close to* HANNAH *and points to something on her menu.*] To start...

HANNAH: [*Melting.*] Oh, Paul!...

PAUL: [*Points to something else.*]

HANNAH: [*A low sexy giggle.*]

PAUL: [*Points again.*] And maybe...

HANNAH: [*Kisses him lightly and coos.*]

PAUL: [*Pointing to something else.*] Or, how about?...

HANNAH: [*Goes off into a shower of giggles.*]

PAUL: [*Pointing.*] With a side order of...

HANNAH: [*Horrified, closes her menu on his hand.*] Paul!

PAUL: [*Reaches over and kisses her.*] Forgive me!
[*A silence.*]

HANNAH: [*Suddenly aggressive, leans over him until she's almost in his lap. She points.*] OK...how about?...

PAUL: [*Shocked.*] Hannah!

HANNAH: [*Pointing elsewhere.*] Plus some...
[*They both go off into gales.*]

CAL: [*Watches them with amusement and laughs to himself.*]

PAUL: [*Out of breath.*] Stop it!

HANNAH: [*Points again.*] And...

PAUL: [*Reaches over and kisses her.*] Darling! You're being obscene and you know it!

HANNAH: [*Laughing, points again.*] And...for dessert!

PAUL: [*Noticing that* CAL *is watching them.*] People are staring....

CAL: [*Quickly looks the other way as...*]

HANNAH: [*Shoots him a dirty look.*]
　　[*The doorbell rings.*]

CAL: [*Saved, heads for the door.*]
　　[*The lights fade on the* GALTS. *The music stops.*]

Scene 3

CAL: [*Opens the door.*] Yes?

ELIZABETH BARROW COLT: [*Is blown in. She's a writer in her thirties who is exceedingly shy and nearsighted. Every move is a stagger and when she speaks she's virtually inaudible.*]

CAL: Good evening, you're with the uh...which party?

ELIZABETH BARROW COLT: [*Inaudible.*] I'm meeting David Osslow.

CAL: Pardon me?

ELIZABETH BARROW COLT: [*Inaudible.*] Mr. Osslow.

CAL: [*Straining to hear.*] I'm sorry....

ELIZABETH BARROW COLT: [*In a terrified whisper, looks around the room.*] David Osslow.

CAL: [*Looking at his reservations list.*] Ah yes, David Osslow!

ELIZABETH BARROW COLT: [*Cringes.*]

CAL: He hasn't come yet. May I take your coat and show you to your table?

ELIZABETH BARROW COLT: [*Panic-stricken.*] I'm early?

CAL: I beg your pardon?

ELIZABETH BARROW COLT: Oh dear.

CAL: Let me take your coat and I'll show you to your table.

ELIZABETH BARROW COLT: [*Clutches her coat around her and stands rooted to the spot.*]

CAL: Wouldn't you like me to show you to your table? I'm sure Mr. Osslow will be here any minute.

ELIZABETH BARROW COLT: [*Looking around the room furtively, opens her pocketbook, and head lowered, takes out a comb and starts combing her hair. As she does, several things fall out of her pocketbook. She dives for them, bumping into* CAL *as he tries to help her retrieve them.*]

CAL: I'm sorry. Excuse me, I was just trying to...I'm sorry...wanted to help you get that...here's your toothbrush.

ELIZABETH BARROW COLT: Oh dear, I dropped my...I'm sorry, I didn't mean to...my lipstick and diary....Oh dear!

CAL: [*Hands her a few things.*] Here, I hope I didn't...

ELIZABETH BARROW COLT: [*Very softly.*] I'm not wearing my glasses.

CAL: [*Jovial.*] It sure is cold out there!

ELIZABETH BARROW COLT: [*Dumping everything back into her pocketbook.*] I can't see very well....

CAL: [*Gently.*] May I take your coat?

ELIZABETH BARROW COLT: [*With a sudden wild giggle.*] I CAN'T SEE ANYTHING AT ALL! [*She sneaks her glasses out of her pocketbook and quickly holds them up to her eyes to get her bearings.*] Oh, look at those merry-go-round horses! Gracious!
[*She bumps into the serving cart which careens towards* HANNAH *who screams.*]

CAL: [*To the* GALTS.] I'm terribly sorry, I'll have her seated in just one moment....

ELIZABETH BARROW COLT: [*Opens her pocketbook again and head lowered, sneaks on a smear of bright lipstick.*]

CAL: I heard it's thirty below with the wind chill factor.

ELIZABETH BARROW COLT: [*Drops the lipstick back in her bag, reaches for her comb and combs her hair again.*] I look a mess.

CAL: And next year, if you can believe it, we're supposed to get hit even harder!

ELIZABETH BARROW COLT: [*Takes out her glasses again, puts them on for a second, lowers her head, and makes several strange muffled sobs.*]

CAL: [*Touching her arm.*] Could I take your coat for you?

ELIZABETH BARROW COLT: [*Her wild giggle again.*] OH...MY COAT!!! [*She fumbles with the buttons.*]

CAL: It's all right, take your time. [*Pause.*] We're supposed to get some relief over the weekend.

ELIZABETH BARROW COLT: [*As she struggles with her coat buttons, drops her bag again and everything spills out.*] Oh dear.

CAL: Here, I'll get it.... [*He dives for the floor and scoops it all back into her bag which he finally hands to her.*] Here you go.

ELIZABETH BARROW COLT: [*Barely audible.*] I can't see very well.

CAL: I beg your pardon?

ELIZABETH BARROW COLT: I can't see very well.

CAL: [*Helping her off with her coat which becomes a great muddle as she can't get her arms out of the sleeves properly.*] Here, let me help you.

ELIZABETH BARROW COLT: [*Struggling between* CAL *and the coat.*] I'M AS BLIND AS A BAT!

CAL: [*Gets the coat off, sighs.*] Please...follow me. [*And he leads her to her table, pulling her chair way way out to give her plenty of leeway.*]

ELIZABETH BARROW COLT: [*Rigid with panic, muddles the timing of when to sit down, plops awkwardly. Sneaks out her glasses for another look, drops them back in her bag.*]

CAL: [*Pushing her the long distance to her table.*] Could I get you something to drink while you wait?

ELIZABETH BARROW COLT: [*Her sob again.*]

CAL: Something from the bar?

ELIZABETH BARROW COLT: [*Inaudible.*] What time is it?

CAL: I beg your pardon?

ELIZABETH BARROW COLT: [*Very shrill.*] TIME?

CAL: [*Startled, jumps, looks at his watch.*] 7:15.

ELIZABETH BARROW COLT: [*Faintly.*] I don't know what he looks like.

CAL: [*Leaning down close to her.*] I'm sorry....

ELIZABETH BARROW COLT: I've only talked to him on the phone.

CAL: [*Mystified.*] Could I get you something from the bar?

ELIZABETH BARROW COLT: How will I know him? [*Her sob.*]

CAL: Are you all right?

ELIZABETH BARROW COLT: [*Fishes in her pocketbook, hauls out a paperback edition of Thomas Mann's* The Magic Mountain, *opens it in the middle and starts reading, holding the book very close to her face.*] I brought my book....

CAL: How about a little appetizer or something while you wait?

ELIZABETH BARROW COLT: [*Keeps reading, making her little sob every now and then. She twists a strand of her hair.*]

CAL: He should be here any minute now.... It's this awful weather...slows everyone down...cars won't start...batteries frozen up...he should be here any time now...worst winter we've had since I can remember....

PAUL: Waiter? Waiter, we're ready to order.

CAL: Would you excuse me, Mademoiselle?

[*He heads towards the* GALTS' *table.*]

[*The light slowly fades on* ELIZABETH BARROW COLT...]

Scene 4

And rise on ELLEN *who is holding up a beautiful fresh bass.*

ELLEN: Just look at you, you sad beauty, you prehistoric fluke...where do you come from, anyway? All silver and slippery, with such a mournful face... [*She holds*

its face up to hers and imitates its pout.] You don't
even know you're a fish, do you? Aaaaaahhh, but *we*
do... and we know how good you taste.... Oh, yes... we
know all about that....
[*She starts sharpening her knife. The light fades on
her busy hands...*]

Scene 5

And rise on CAL *hovering over the* GALTS.

PAUL: Hannah?
HANNAH: Oh, Paul, I'm not ready!
PAUL: Take your time.
HANNAH: I keep changing my mind.
PAUL: There's no rush.
HANNAH: I'm so... tense.
PAUL: We have all the time in the world.
HANNAH: [*Motioning to* CAL.] The Belgian Oxtail Soup
is...
CAL: A hearty beef broth with winter vegetables, smoked
ham, and Madeira.
HANNAH: Madeira...
CAL: Madeira...
HANNAH: And the Billi Bi is...
CAL: Is a cream of mussel soup seasoned with fresh herbs,
shallots, white wine, and a thread of saffron.
HANNAH: [*Impressed.*] ...a thread of saffron...
CAL: Saffron...
HANNAH: And the Veal Prince Orloff is...
CAL: Roast veal stuffed with onions and wild mush-
rooms, served with Sauce Mornay...
HANNAH: [*Rolling it on her tongue.*] Sauce Mornay...
CAL: Sauce Velouté with Gruyère cheese added...
HANNAH: Sauce Velouté...
PAUL: Mornay!
HANNAH: And the Roast Duckling in Wine with Green
Grapes is...

CAL: Fresh.

HANNAH: Fresh!

HANNAH: And the Striped Bass with Shrimp Mousse...is...

CAL: In season!

HANNAH: In season!

PAUL: [*Grunts with anticipation.*]

HANNAH: Your vegetable of the day?

CAL: Braised celery.

PAUL: [*Kissing his fingers.*] My favorite!
[*A silence.*]

HANNAH: Oh, Paul!

PAUL: [*Reaching for her hand.*] Sssssshhhhh...

HANNAH: I'm just so...

PAUL: I know, I know...

HANNAH: I love roast duck!

CAL: The duck is...

PAUL: I'm having the bass!

HANNAH: But I woke up with a craving for veal.

PAUL: I don't care for duck....

CAL: The veal is...

HANNAH: You know how I love veal!

PAUL: I had veal last week....

HANNAH: But I haven't had fresh roast duckling in...

CAL: You might like the bass....

PAUL: My rule of thumb: always order fish that's in season.

HANNAH: I only had an omelette for lunch.

CAL: The duckling is...

PAUL: I don't know about you, but I am starving!

HANNAH: I've been good all week.

PAUL: I can almost taste that mussel soup!
[*Faster and faster.*]

HANNAH: I've got to decide!

PAUL: I can't wait much longer....

HANNAH: I always have veal....

PAUL: I don't care for duck....

HANNAH: I could have the bass....

PAUL: I just want to start....

HANNAH: I need some more time....

97

PAUL: I can't wait much more....

HANNAH: I think I can go....

PAUL: I just want to...

HANNAH: I know I can....

PAUL: I...

HANNAH: I...

PAUL: [*In a burst.*] I'll have the Belgian Oxtail Soup to start, the bass with shrimp, and Floating Island for dessert! [*He pants slightly.*]

CAL: [*Writing it down.*] Very good, sir...and you, Madame?

HANNAH: [*Takes a deep breath, shuts her eyes, clenches her hands, pauses, then very fast.*] Billi Bi, Duckling in Wine with Green Grapes, and Pears in Cointreau with Frozen Cream.

PAUL: [*Applauds her.*] Nice going, Hannah! Very nice! Good work!

[*He leans over the table and kisses her.*]

CAL: [*Writing it down.*] Yes, you did very well. [*He shakes her hand.*] Congratulations.

HANNAH: [*Eyes still shut, murmurs.*] Oh, thank you, thank you, thank you so much....

CAL: [*Puts the last flourish on his pad and pushes through the swinging door into the kitchen.*]

[*The light fades on the rhapsodic* GALTS.]

Scene 6

ELLEN: [*Is more frantic than ever. She has several bass out and is dressing them.*]

CAL: [*Bursting in.*] One oxtail...one Billi, one bass, one duck, one Floating Island, and one pears!

ELLEN: [*Eyes closed, reciting.*] One oxtail, one Billi, one bass, one duck, one Floating Island, and one pears...

CAL: One oxtail, one Billi, one bass, one duck, one Floating Island, and one pears!...

ELLEN: You do the shrimp and I'll do the eggs!
   [*She starts whipping egg whites with an automatic mixer as...*]

CAL: [*Removes the shrimp from the refrigerator and dumps them into the Cuisinart. He turns it on. They both make a fearful clatter.*]

ELLEN: [*Over the din.*] Heavy cream!

CAL: How much?

ELLEN: Half a cup.

CAL: [*Starts pouring it into the Cuisinart.*] Watch...

ELLEN: That's enough. [*They finish their chores simultaneously.*] You slice the mushrooms and I'll finish the mousse!
   [*She pours the mousse out of the Cuisinart and carefully folds in the egg whites she's just whipped as...*]

CAL: [*Slices the mushrooms with lightning speed and precision.*]

ELLEN: You cut the grapes and I'll do the soups....
   [*She returns to her soups on the stove.*]

CAL: I'll cut the grapes....

ELLEN: While I do the soups...

CAL: Where are the grapes?

ELLEN: [*Muttering as she works on the soup.*] One oxtail...one Billi, one bass, and one duck...

CAL: Where are the grapes?

ELLEN: Second shelf of the refrigerator.

CAL: Of course.
   [*Starts rooting around in the refrigerator.*]

ELLEN: One oxtail...one Billi, one bass, and one duck...

CAL: Second shelf.

ELLEN: That's right....[*Tastes the soup.*]

CAL: It's not there.

ELLEN: Then look in the bin....

CAL: [*Thumping around.*] Nope.

ELLEN: Try in the door.

CAL: [*Making more and more noise.*] Nothing.

ELLEN: Check the top shelf.

CAL: I already did.

ELLEN: They're not with the pears?

CAL: Not with the pears.

ELLEN: Not in the bin?

CAL: Not in the bin.

ELLEN: Start taking things out.

CAL: [*Does.*] I am!

ELLEN: They're not in the back?

CAL: Not...in...the back!

ELLEN: Under the bass?

CAL: Nowhere in sight!

ELLEN: Try by the cream.

CAL: I already have.

[*He's now spread a great arc of food around the refrigerator.*]

ELLEN: They've got to be there.

CAL: Ellen, I'm looking!

ELLEN: Next to the stock.

CAL: Nowhere in sight!

ELLEN: Oh, honey, I need them!

CAL: Yes, I know....

ELLEN: Should I come and help?

CAL: Son of a bitch!

ELLEN: I can't do the duck.... [*Reaches for the salt and notices the bowl of empty grape stems.*] OH, NO!

CAL: [*Picking over the mess strewn on the floor.*] They've got to be here!

ELLEN: *I don't believe this!*

[*She lifts up the bowl to show* CAL.]

CAL: [*His back to her.*] I remember seeing them....

ELLEN: CAL, YOU ATE THEM!

CAL: [*His back to her, finds something tempting, starts eating it.*] Mmmmmmmm...

ELLEN: [*Holding up an empty branch.*] There's nothing left but the stems!

CAL: What *is* this?

ELLEN: LOOK!

CAL: [*Facing her.*] What?

ELLEN: You ate all the grapes.

CAL: No, I didn't. I didn't eat those.

ELLEN: [*Waving the branch.*] CAL!

CAL: I didn't eat any grapes.

ELLEN: I saw you!

CAL: Why would I eat those grapes?

ELLEN: I don't know, but I saw you!

CAL: I don't even like grapes.

ELLEN: I asked you to stop, don't you remember?

CAL: I'd never eat grapes.

ELLEN: CAL, YOU ATE THOSE GRAPES, I SAW YOU!

CAL: [*In a whisper.*] Not so loud, they'll hear you out front.

ELLEN: [*Whispering.*] How are we going to serve Duckling in Wine with Green Grapes?

CAL: I didn't do it.

ELLEN: You've ruined the dish.

CAL: You've made a mistake.

ELLEN: I can't go on like this....

CAL: Serve it with something else.

ELLEN: What's scary is, you don't even know you're doing it.

CAL: Peaches or cherries.

ELLEN: It's like a disease....

CAL: Roast duck with Bing Cherries is a classic!

ELLEN: YOU ATE THE BING CHERRIES THIS MORNING! [*She starts to cry.*]

CAL: Well, we have peaches, don't we? Substitute peaches!

ELLEN: Cal, I can cook. I can *really* cook!

CAL: It's even better with peaches!

ELLEN: I could win us three stars, maybe even four!

CAL: [*Starts opening cupboard doors.*] Now where are those peaches?

ELLEN: I've trained with the best...

CAL: [*Thumping in one of the cupboards.*] I know they're in here somewhere....

ELLEN: ...cooked with the best!

CAL: [*Finds a can of peaches.*] You see!

ELLEN: But I can't do this alone. I need you to help.

CAL: [*Starts opening the can.*] You golden babies...

ELLEN: You always had such good taste....

CAL: [*The lid off, he inhales the fragrance, then reaches down for one, lifts it up, and pops it in his mouth.*]

ELLEN: ...a razor sharp instinct. I need it, Cal!

CAL: There's nothing wrong with canned peaches, they're just as good as fresh. [*He then takes a swig of the juice.*] I don't know when I've tasted such a delicious peach....

ELLEN: Do you still have it? [*She rushes to a cupboard and sweeps down an armful of spice tins.*] SHOW ME IT'S THERE, SHOW ME YOUR TALENT! [*Concealing its identity, she pours out a heaping teaspoon of mustard and offers it to him.*] Taste this!

CAL: [*Offering her a large syrupy peach, still garbled.*] I really wish you'd try this, it's...

ELLEN: [*Fierce, forces the teaspoon of mustard into his mouth.*] Taste!

CAL: [*Spitting.*] What you are doing?

ELLEN: [*Shoveling in another batch.*] I SAID, TASTE IT!

CAL: [*Sputtering.*] Jesus, what is this?

ELLEN: You tell me. Cal!

CAL: [*Gagging.*] It's poison.

ELLEN: Try again!

CAL: [*Is certainly strong enough to overpower her, but it is food and he can't resist anything that's put into his mouth. Coughs.*]

ELLEN: What is it?

CAL: How am I supposed to tell, my mouth is on fire?!

ELLEN: Well, you'd better be able to tell if you want to stay in business, my dear!
[*Forces in another spoonful.*]

CAL: [*Weakly.*] It's...curry powder!

ELLEN: Wrong!

CAL: Paprika...

ELLEN: Wrong!

CAL: Clove...

ELLEN: Wrong!

CAL: [*In pain.*] ...Horseradish.

ELLEN: Think, Cal. Think!

CAL: Soy sauce?

ELLEN: Wrong!

CAL: Saffron?

ELLEN: Wrong!

CAL: Ginger?

ELLEN: Wrong!

CAL: [*With a sob.*] I don't know!

ELLEN: IT'S MUSTARD, CAL. SIMPLE MUSTARD! [*She pours out another teaspoon of spice and puts it in his mouth.*] . . . And this?

CAL: [*Spits it out.*] Uuugh! You've gone crazy.

ELLEN: You don't know, do you!

CAL: Dill . . .

ELLEN: You're so glutted, you can't even tell! . . .

CAL: Cinnamon.

ELLEN: You can't even tell bitter from sweet.

CAL: Coffee?

ELLEN: It could be dirt for all you know! [*Shoves in another taste.*]

CAL: Nutmeg?

ELLEN: Unbelievable!

CAL: Anise? . . . Brown sugar? . . . Oregano? . . . Coriander? . . . Tarragon? . . .

ELLEN: It's salt, Cal. [*The doorbell rings.*]

CAL: No!

ELLEN: What are we going to do?

CAL: It didn't taste anything like . . .

ELLEN: *Salt!*

CAL: [*Pouring some in his hand.*] Salt . . .

ELLEN: You drank all the Floating Island. . . .

CAL: It didn't taste anything like salt!

ELLEN: You ate all the grapes. . . .

CAL: [*Tastes the bit in his palm.*] Son of a bitch . . .

ELLEN: And now, canned peaches . . . *canned*!

CAL: You know, that is amazing. I never would have guessed it was . . . salt. . . .

ELLEN: It makes no difference to you anymore. You'd eat *anything* and like it. [*The doorbell rings again.*]

ELLEN: [*Goes back to stirring her oxtail soup, tastes it, pours the remaining beaten egg yolk into the Billi Bi, tastes that, adding spices. She starts to cry.*] There's someone at the door, you'd better get it....

CAL: I'm sorry, El....I'll watch it from now on....I didn't realize....

ELLEN: [*Crying softly as she stirs the soup.*] I can't do it all by myself, I just can't....It's too hard...so much to do....I get lost sometimes, afraid I've done something wrong....I need you to help me....Reassure me, Cal....Tell me it's good....Tell me it's fine....Give me that strength....Tell me it's fine....

CAL: [*Wraps his arms around her, rocks her.*] Ssssshhhh, come on El....It will be all right....We can still do it....We'll work it out....I'll watch the eating....They love you out there.... They're breaking the doors down....Listen to them...baby ...baby... please...

[*The doorbell rings again and again as...*]

THE CURTAIN SLOWLY FALLS

ACT II

Scene 1

One hour later. A general view of the restaurant. HAN-
NAH *and* PAUL GALT *are lingering over their desserts.*
DAVID OSSLOW *has finally arrived and is eating his soup
as* ELIZABETH BARROW COLT *stares at hers. The lights
settle on the latest arrivals, a trio of lively women in
their thirties:* HERRICK SIMMONS, *a hearty eater,* NESSA
VOX, *a guilty eater, and* TONY STASSIO, *a sneaky eater
who's on a perpetual diet. A Telemann trio sonata plays
softly, then fades.*

HERRICK SIMMONS: [*Is looking at the wine list, trying to
  make up her mind.*] Puligny-Montrachet!
  [*Hands the list to* NESSA.]
NESSA VOX: [*Scanning it, considering.*] Puligny-Mon-
  trachet?...
TONY STASSIO: [*Takes the list from* NESSA *and points.*]
  Pinot Chardonnay!
HERRICK SIMMONS: Pinot Chardonnay?
NESSA VOX: [*Takes the list from* TONY *and announces.*]
  Chateau de Lascombes!
HERRICK SIMMONS: Spare me!
  [*A pause.*]
CAL: [*Sensing trouble, comes to their table.*] Could I be
  of any assistance?
TONY STASSIO: [*Taking the list back from* NESSA, *makes
  another choice. She knows nothing about wine.*] Côtes-
  du-Rhône!
CAL: Would you like a red wine or white?

TONY STASSIO: [*Pointing to another selection, mispronouncing it.*] Châteauneuf-du-Pape!

CAL: A Burgundy or Beaujolais?

NESSA VOX: I'd like a chateau-bottled red Bordeaux!

CAL: [*Making suggestions for her.*] Château Belgrave ...Château La Lagune...

HERRICK SIMMONS: I think a white Burgundy would serve us much better.

CAL: [*Now to* HERRICK.] Pouilly-Fuissé...Puligny-Montrachet...

TONY STASSIO: [*Stubborn.*] Nuits St. Georges!

CAL: [*Suggesting more Burgundies to* HERRICK.] Corton-Charlemagne...

TONY STASSIO: Pinot Chardonnay!

HERRICK SIMMONS: [*A tremendous sigh.*] Corton-Charlemagne, that's more like it!

TONY STASSIO: [*Has made up her mind, with stunning authority.*] PULIGNY-FUISSÉ!

CAL: [*Bewildered, as no such brand exists.*] Puligny-Fuissé?

HERRICK SIMMONS: [*Trying to correct* TONY.] Puligny-*Montrachet*!

NESSA VOX: [*Likewise.*] Pouilly-Fuissé!

TONY STASSIO: [*More and more stubborn.*] Montrachet-Fuissé!

CAL: Montrachet-*Puligny*!

NESSA VOX: Puligny...Pouilly!

HERRICK SIMMONS: Pouilly-Fuissé!

CAL: Pouilly-Montrachet!

HERRICK SIMMONS: Pouilly-Montrachet?

NESSA VOX: Montrachet-Puligné [*Pronounced "Pulignay."*]

CAL: [*Repeating after her.*] Montrachet-Puligné!

HERRICK SIMMONS: [*Correcting his pronunciation.*] Nee!

CAL: [*Quickly, embarrassed.*] Nee!

TONY STASSIO: Montrachet-Romanee!

CAL: [*Correcting her pronunciation.*] Montrachet-Romanée, *nay*!

TONY STASSIO: [*Triumphant in her ignorance.*] MONTRACHET-PULIGNAY!

CAL, HERRICK AND NESSA: Nee, Nee!
  [*A pause.*]
HERRICK SIMMONS: [*Turns to* CAL *and gives him their
  order.*] Montrachet-Puligny!
CAL: [*Dutifully repeats after her.*] Montrachet-Puligny!
TONY STASSIO: [*Realizes they've reversed the order.*] Pu-
  ligny-*Montrachet*!
CAL, HERRICK AND TONY: [*All realize she's right and start
  laughing, repeating after her.*] Puligny-Montrachet!
  [*And the lights fade...*]

Scene 2

And rise on ELIZABETH BARROW COLT *and* DAVID OSSLOW.
ELIZABETH *is staring at her soup, motionless.* DAVID OS-
SLOW, *the successful head of his own publishing company, a man with a glowing appetite and glowing literary
taste, is happily eating his. He's in his fifties, is dapper,
at ease, and ready for anything.*

DAVID OSSLOW: I like your work very much.
ELIZABETH BARROW COLT: [*Drops her head and mur-
  murs.*]
DAVID OSSLOW: We all like it....
ELIZABETH BARROW COLT: [*Shuts her eyes, murmurs
  again.*]
DAVID OSSLOW: I beg your pardon?
ELIZABETH BARROW COLT: [*Flinches.*]
DAVID OSSLOW: Are you all right?
ELIZABETH BARROW COLT: [*Nodding, eyes closed.*] Fine,
  fine, fine, fine, fine...
  [*A silence.*]
DAVID OSSLOW: For some reason I imagined you very
  differently. [*A silence.*] I thought you'd have a very
  large head.
ELIZABETH BARROW COLT: [*Starts laughing, wishing she
  could stop.*]
DAVID OSSLOW: No, really I did. I thought you'd have
  this...[*Indicating the size with his hands.*] huge head!

ELIZABETH BARROW COLT: [*Finds this hysterical, and trying not to laugh, makes peculiar squeaking sounds.*]

DAVID OSSLOW: You know how you form an image of someone you haven't met?

ELIZABETH BARROW COLT: [*Keeps laughing.*]

DAVID OSSLOW: I also pictured you as having very bushy eyebrows. You know, the kind that almost meet over the bridge of the nose....

ELIZABETH BARROW COLT: [*Helpless with laughter and embarrassment, tries to hide her face in her napkin and accidentally knocks over her bowl of soup, spilling the entire contents into her lap. She leaps to her feet, flapping like a wet puppy.*] Oh dear!

DAVID OSSLOW: [*Bolts out of his seat to help her.*] Are you all right?

ELIZABETH BARROW COLT: [*Frantically wiping at her dress with her napkin.*] I spilled...

DAVID OSSLOW: [*Lifting his napkin to help.*] Did you burn yourself?

ELIZABETH BARROW COLT: [*Shrinking from him.*] I spilled all my soup....

DAVID OSSLOW: [*Starts wiping at her dress with his napkin.*] Here, let me help....

ELIZABETH BARROW COLT: [*Turning her back to him.*] No, no, I can...

DAVID OSSLOW: Are you sure you're...

ELIZABETH BARROW COLT: I'm sorry....

DAVID OSSLOW: Let me get the waiter. Waiter!

ELIZABETH BARROW COLT: [*Her back turned, hunches over her spilled dress as if the most secret part of her body had suddenly sprung a leak.*] I can...

CAL: [*Striding over.*] Yes?

DAVID OSSLOW: I'm afraid we've had a slight spill. Could you please bring us some water and extra napkins?

ELIZABETH BARROW COLT: It's fine....It's coming right out....It's nothing...really nothing.... [*Showing her dress.*] See, I got it all out....

CAL: Yes, right away, I'll get you some fresh napkins and we'll clean it up in no time! [*He produces several napkins from his pocket and joins* DAVID OSSLOW *in wiping* ELIZABETH *off.*]

ELIZABETH BARROW COLT: [*Dying of embarrassment since the spill hit her squarely in her crotch.*] No, really I can... let me....

CAL: It shouldn't stain. A good dry cleaner should be able to get this right out....[*Feeling the material.*] What is the material, anyway? Cotton?

ELIZABETH BARROW COLT: It isn't my dress....[*She keeps fussing over it.*]

CAL: [*To* DAVID OSSLOW, *feeling the fabric.*] Wouldn't you say this was cotton?

DAVID OSSLOW: [*Feels it.*] No, that isn't cotton, it feels more like...rayon to me....

CAL: [*Feeling another section of it.*] Rayon? It's too light-weight to be rayon....

DAVID OSSLOW: It could be a wool challis....

CAL: I say it's either cotton or a cotton blend.

ELIZABETH BARROW COLT: I don't have a proper dress....

DAVID OSSLOW: As long as it's not a synthetic, she should have no problems....

CAL: [*Feeling it again.*] You know, it might just be...silk!

DAVID OSSLOW: [*Feels.*] Silk?

CAL: That's right: silk!

DAVID OSSLOW: [*Still feeling.*] It certainly has the weight of silk....

CAL: It's silk! That's what it is!

ELIZABETH BARROW COLT: She'll kill me.

CAL: Don't worry, this will come right out. Silk sheds stains like water!
[*Pushes into the kitchen with the soiled napkins.*]

DAVID OSSLOW: It's a nice dress.

ELIZABETH BARROW COLT: [*Trying to hide the immense stain with her napkin, heads back towards her chair.*] I'm sorry....

DAVID OSSLOW: [*Pulls out her chair for her.*] These kinds of things happen all the...

ELIZABETH BARROW COLT: [*Collapses in the chair before he's pulled it out all the way, making a loud plop.*] Oh dear, I...

DAVID OSSLOW: [*Strains to push the chair, with her in it, closer to the table.*] There we go....[*He returns to his seat, looks at her, reaches across the table and picks up her hand, squeezes it and then lets it go.*] Are you all right?

ELIZABETH BARROW COLT: [*Head down.*] Fine, fine, fine, fine fine...

[*A silence.*]

CAL: [*Returns with a brand new bowl of steaming soup which he sets down before* ELIZABETH.] There we go! [*And he turns on his heel.*]

ELIZABETH BARROW COLT: [*Her shoulders giving way, looks at it.*] Oh dear.

[*A slight pause.*]

DAVID OSSLOW: Elizabeth, I'd like to publish your short stories.

ELIZABETH BARROW COLT: [*Looking into the soup, stunned.*] Oh my.

DAVID OSSLOW: They're wonderful.

ELIZABETH BARROW COLT: Mercy!

DAVID OSSLOW: What did you say?

ELIZABETH BARROW COLT: [*Softly.*] I don't know what to say....

DAVID OSSLOW: ...Really wonderful!

ELIZABETH BARROW COLT: I never imagined...[*Starts fishing around in her pocketbook.*]

DAVID OSSLOW: You're incredibly gifted....

ELIZABETH BARROW COLT: Oh, no, I'm...[*Pulls out her lipstick, lowers her head and sneaks on a smear, hands shaking. Suddenly she drops the lipstick. It falls into her soup with a splash.*] Oh, no!

DAVID OSSLOW: What was that?

ELIZABETH BARROW COLT: [*Dives for it.*] Oh, nothing, I just dropped my lipstick....

[*She repeatedly tries to retrieve it with her spoon, but it keeps splashing back down into her soup. She fi-*

nally gives up, fishes it out with her hands, and drops it into her purse.]

DAVID OSSLOW: Don't you like the soup?

ELIZABETH BARROW COLT: [*Hunched over her pocketbook.*] Oh, yes, it's...

DAVID OSSLOW: It looks delicious.

ELIZABETH BARROW COLT: [*Staring at it.*] Yes, it's very nice.

DAVID OSSLOW: I've always loved French Provincial....I'm sorry....I...

ELIZABETH BARROW COLT: Would you like it?

[*A pause.*]

ELIZABETH BARROW COLT: OH, YOU HAVE IT!

DAVID OSSLOW: No, really, I...

ELIZABETH BARROW COLT: [*Picks up the bowl with trembling hands and starts lifting it across the table to him, her spoon still in it.*] I want you to have it!

DAVID OSSLOW: *Careful!*

ELIZABETH BARROW COLT: [*Giddy, the soup sloshing wildly.*] I never have soup!

DAVID OSSLOW: *Look out!*

ELIZABETH BARROW COLT: In fact, I hardly ever have dinner, either!

DAVID OSSLOW: Really, I...

ELIZABETH BARROW COLT: [*Sets it down in front of him, spilling some.*] THERE!

DAVID OSSLOW: [*Looks at it. Weakly.*] Well, thank you.

ELIZABETH BARROW COLT: [*Incredibly relieved, looks at him and sighs.*]

DAVID OSSLOW: [*Picks up her spoon and dips it into the soup.*]

ELIZABETH BARROW COLT: This is nice.

DAVID OSSLOW: [*Starts eating it.*]

ELIZABETH BARROW COLT: How is it?

DAVID OSSLOW: Very good. Would you like a taste?

ELIZABETH BARROW COLT: Oh, no, thank you!

[*A silence.*]

DAVID OSSLOW: Do you cook at all?

ELIZABETH BARROW COLT: Oh, no.

DAVID OSSLOW: [*Reaches a spoonful of soup across the table to her.*] Come on, try some.

ELIZABETH BARROW COLT: [*She tastes it.*] My mother didn't cook, either.

DAVID OSSLOW: Now isn't that good?
[*Gives her another taste.*]

ELIZABETH BARROW COLT: Mmmmmmmm ... [*Quickly wipes her mouth with her napkin.*]

DAVID OSSLOW: [*Takes a taste himself.*] My mother was a great cook.

ELIZABETH BARROW COLT: She didn't know how. She grew up with servants.

DAVID OSSLOW: Her Thanksgiving dinners! ...

ELIZABETH BARROW COLT: We had a cook. Lacey. She was awful and she smelled.

DAVID OSSLOW: I cook every once in a while.

ELIZABETH BARROW COLT: We all hated her. Especially my mother.

DAVID OSSLOW: My wife is a great cook! Some night you'll have to come over for dinner!
[*He settles into his soup, eating with less and less relish as her story progresses.*]

ELIZABETH BARROW COLT: In fact, when I was young I never even saw my mother in the kitchen. The food just appeared at mealtime as if by magic, all steaming and ready to eat. Lacey would carry it in on these big white serving platters that had a rim of raised china acorns. Our plates had the same rim. Twenty-two acorns per plate, each one about the size of a lump of chewed gum. When I was very young I used to try and pry them off with my knife.... We ate every night at eight o'clock sharp because my parents didn't start their cocktail hour until seven, but since dinner time was meant for exchanging news of the day, the emphasis was always on talking ... and not on eating. My father bolted his food, and my mother played with hers: sculpting it up into hills and then mashing it back down through her fork. To make things worse, before we sat down at the table she'd always put on a fresh smear of lipstick. I still remember the shade. It was called "Fire and Ice"...a dark throbbing red that rubbed off on her fork in waxy clumps that stained her food pink, so that by the end of the first course she'd have rended everything into a kind of...rosy puree. As my father wolfed down his meat and vegetables, I'd watch my mother thread this puree through the raised acorns on her plate, fanning it out into long runny pink ribbons....I could never eat a thing...."WAKE UP, AMERICA!" she'd trumpet to me. "You're not being excused from this table until you clean up that plate!" So, I'd take several mouthfuls and then, when no one was looking, would spit them out into my napkin. Each night I systematically transferred everything on my plate into that lifesaving napkin....

DAVID OSSLOW: Jesus Christ.

ELIZABETH BARROW COLT: It's amazing they never caught on.

DAVID OSSLOW: [*Lights a cigarette and takes a deep drag.*]

ELIZABETH BARROW COLT: I mean, you'd think Lacey would have noticed the huge bundles of half-chewed food I left in my chair....

DAVID OSSLOW: I have never had trouble eating!

ELIZABETH BARROW COLT: We used cloth napkins, after all. They were collected after each meal.

DAVID OSSLOW: I can always eat, no matter where I am!

ELIZABETH BARROW COLT: We had a fresh one each evening.

DAVID OSSLOW: Believe me, I could use a little of your problem....

ELIZABETH BARROW COLT: Lacey washed and ironed them.

DAVID OSSLOW: That is, if you call not eating a problem.

ELIZABETH BARROW COLT: To launder them, she had to dump the food out.

DAVID OSSLOW: [*Patting his stomach.*] I should have such problems!

ELIZABETH BARROW COLT: She must have noticed. I left so much, at least a pound....

DAVID OSSLOW: I'm so bad, I start thinking about my

113

next meal before I've even finished the one I'm eating!

ELIZABETH BARROW COLT: I wonder what she thought? If she was hurt that I could never get it down...

DAVID OSSLOW: Now *that's* serious!...

ELIZABETH BARROW COLT: I lived in constant fear that she'd tell my parents. You see I was terribly underweight....

DAVID OSSLOW: I love to eat!

ELIZABETH BARROW COLT: Or worse, that she'd sneak into my room some night, lugging all those bulging napkins...and spill everything out...from one end of my bed to the other...and *force* me to eat it...

DAVID OSSLOW: I've always loved to eat....It will be the death of me....Every time I see my doctor, he says the same thing. He says, "David, you've got to lose some of that weight!"
[*A silence.*]

ELIZABETH BARROW COLT: I used to bite my nails. I think it was because I was so hungry all the time.

DAVID OSSLOW: [*Hands her back her empty soup bowl.*] Thank you, it was delicious.

ELIZABETH BARROW COLT: [*Hiding her hands.*] I still bite them sometimes. [*A silence. She looks around the room, a sigh.*] This is wonderful.
[*Another silence.*]

DAVID OSSLOW: Oh! I forgot to return your spoon!
[*He hands it to her, covering her hand with both of his.*]

ELIZABETH BARROW COLT: [*Grasps it, turns it gently in her hands, sneaks it up against her cheek for a moment...and then drops it into her pocketbook.*] I can't believe this is happening.
[*The lights fade...*]

Scene 3

And rise on the entire restaurant and kitchen.

CAL: [*Is pouring the wine for* HERRICK.] Puligny-Montrachet.

ELLEN: [*Is fussing over her entrees.*] Ooooooooohhhhhhh!

HERRICK SIMMONS: [*Tasting the wine*] Mmmmmmmmmmm...

ELLEN: [*Inhaling the fragrance.*] Aaaaaaaahhhhhhh!

HERRICK SIMMONS: [*Crooning over her wine in a different register.*] Uuuuuuuuhhhhhh!

NESSA VOX: [*Eagerly, to* HERRICK.] How is it?

HANNAH: Oh, Paul, that was...

ELLEN: Arrange the peach slices on the duck....

HERRICK SIMMONS: Symphonic!

HANNAH: ...divine!

DAVID OSSLOW: [*To* ELIZABETH.] That...was an outstanding soup!

ELLEN: [*Gazing at the veal.*]...beautiful!

PAUL: Better than the Pavillion, better than the Tour d'Argent...

CAL: [*Pouring wine for* NESSA.] Mademoiselle...

TONY STASSIO: I can hardly wait.

ELIZABETH BARROW COLT: I wasn't sure how to get here....

ELLEN: ...Ladle the Mornay on the veal....

NESSA VOX: [*Tastes her wine and makes little mewing sounds.*]

HANNAH: ...better than *any* meal I've had anywhere...

ELLEN: [*Handling the duck.*]...inspired!

PAUL: Here, here...

TONY STASSIO: [*Grabs* NESSA's *hand.*] I'm going to have a heart attack!

ELLEN: [*Fussing over the bass.*] Yes, my little bass...

PAUL: The best!...

TONY STASSIO: [*Her hand on her heart.*] No, really, I am!

HANNAH: Well, Ken and Diva did rave, remember?

NESSA VOX: [*To* TONY.] Just don't keel over until the food comes!

DAVID OSSLOW: In fact, *both* soups were outstanding!

ELLEN: [*Inhaling the bass.*] Devastating...

ELIZABETH BARROW COLT: [*To* DAVID.] I almost got on the wrong bus.

HERRICK SIMMONS: [*Raises her glass to her friends.*] To the meal!

NESSA VOX: To the meal!

TONY STASSIO: To the meal!

CAL: [*Dives back into the kitchen, to* ELLEN.] They can hardly wait!

ELLEN: [*Has put the final touches on her entrees.*] All set...

CAL: [*Hoists the tray over his head.*] So far...so good.... [*And plunges back into the dining room.*]

ELLEN: [*As he disappears.*] So far...so good.

CAL: [*Glides towards the women's table with his tray.*]

HERRICK SIMMONS: [*Catching sight of the food.*] Ooooooooohhhhhh!

NESSA VOX: Aaaaaaaahhhhhhhhhhh!

TONY STASSIO: Mmmmmmmmmmmmmmmmmmmm!

CAL: [*Sets his tray down on a folding waiter's table. Picks up the duckling and sets it down before* HERRICK.] Duckling in Wine with...Sliced Peaches!

TONY STASSIO: Ohhhh, look!

NESSA VOX: It's a masterpiece! Look at the color of those peaches...pure Cezanne!

TONY STASSIO: Sir, I think you made a mistake, *I* was the one who ordered...
[*She starts to reach for the duck but is stopped as...*]

CAL: [*Sets down the veal at her place. Each dish he presents is more spectacular than the last one.*]...and for Mademoiselle, Veal Prince Orloff!

TONY STASSIO: [*Stops her hand's flight towards the duck and gasps.*] Yesssss!

NESSA VOX: [*Staring at it.*] My God!

HERRICK SIMMONS: [*Weakly.*] Do you see that...stuffing?

NESSA VOX: It's...overwhelming! Absolutely...

TONY STASSIO: [*Looking down at it, very pleased.*] Perfect!

HERRICK SIMMONS: Do you smell that sauce? That's Sauce Velouté!...Phillip's favorite!

NESSA VOX: I think I'm going to die!

HERRICK SIMMONS: I'd know it anywhere!

NESSA VOX: [*To* TONY.] I thought you wanted the duck.

HERRICK SIMMONS: No, she ordered the bass. He made a mistake, the veal is mine!

TONY STASSIO: I didn't order bass!

NESSA VOX: [*To* CAL.] Excuse me, Sir, but I believe that veal belongs to *me*!

HERRICK SIMMONS: [*Holding out her plate of duck.*] Who ordered this duck?

TONY STASSIO: I'd never order bass with shrimp, I'm on a diet!

HERRICK SIMMONS: That veal is mine!

TONY STASSIO: [*To* HERRICK.] The *duck* is yours!

NESSA VOX: [*To* TONY.] I thought the duck was *yours*!

HERRICK SIMMONS: No, it's *hers*! [*Indicating* NESSA.] The veal is mine.

NESSA VOX: Then who ordered the bass?

HERRICK SIMMONS: [*To* TONY.] You did!

TONY STASSIO: [*Indicating* NESSA.] She did!

CAL: [*Sets the bass down before* NESSA. *It's the triumph of the three dishes. They all want it.* CAL *exits.*]

NESSA VOX: [*Gasps.*] My God!

TONY STASSIO: [*Reaches for the bass.*] No, no, *that's* mine! *I* ordered the bass!

HERRICK SIMMONS: [*Snatches the bass out from under* NESSA *and gives* NESSA *her duck in exchange. To* TONY.] Oh, no you didn't!

NESSA VOX: [*Looking at the duck.*] Hey, where's my bass?

TONY STASSIO: [*Grabs the bass away from* HERRICK *and gives her the veal in exchange.*] Now, wait just one minute!

NESSA VOX: I didn't order duck!

HERRICK SIMMONS: . . . and I didn't order veal!

TONY STASSIO: [*Starts to eat the bass.*] Mmmmmmm-mmmm . . .

NESSA VOX: [*Pulls the bass away from* TONY *and gives her the duck.*] HEY, YOU CAN'T EAT THAT BASS. IT'S MINE!

HERRICK SIMMONS: [*To* TONY.] You ordered the duck, don't you remember?

TONY STASSIO: [*Handing* NESSA HERRICK'S *veal.*] She ordered the veal . . . [*Handing* HERRICK NESSA'S *duck.*]

You ordered the duck...and [*Taking* NESSA's *bass.*]
I ordered the bass!

NESSA VOX: I would never order veal!

HERRICK SIMMONS: You think I'd order...*duck?*

TONY STASSIO: Of course you'd order duck!

[*This entree snatching speeds up into a whirlwind.*]

HERRICK SIMMONS: [*Taking the bass from* TONY *and giving her the duck in exchange.*] That is, if *you* hadn't
ordered it first!

NESSA VOX: [*Totally confused, to* HERRICK.] I thought
you wanted the veal.

TONY STASSIO: [*Takes* NESSA's *veal and gives it to* HER-
RICK...*then takes* HERRICK's *bass and gives* NESSA
the duck.] Yes! [*To* HERRICK.] You did!

HERRICK SIMMONS: [*Grabs the bass back from* TONY *and
gives her the veal in exchange.*] I did!

NESSA VOX: Oh, no you didn't...this bass is *mine!*
[*She takes the bass from* HERRICK *and gives her the
duck.*]

TONY STASSIO: NO, THE VEAL IS YOURS! [*She gives*
NESSA *the veal and snatches the bass.*] IT'S MY
BIRTHDAY, SO THE BASS IS MINE!
[*She starts eating the bass.*]
[*Silence.*]

HERRICK SIMMONS: [*To* NESSA.] She's eating all my bass!

NESSA VOX: Well, you're eating all her duck! [*Raises her
glass to* TONY.] Happy Birthday!

HERRICK SIMMONS: [*Likewise.*] Happy Birthday!

DAVID OSSLOW: Waiter, the wine list please.
[*The three women start eating with gusto, save* TONY,
who takes tiny bites. As CAL *passes, he croons with
delight.*]

TONY STASSIO: [*To* NESSA.] How's the veal, it looks delicious.
[*They continue to eat.*]

TONY STASSIO: [*Suddenly pushes her bass away.*] I don't
know about you two, but I am stuffed!

NESSA VOX: But we've hardly started....

TONY STASSIO: Can't...eat...another...bite!

HERRICK SIMMONS: You ought to taste this duck, it's heaven!

TONY STASSIO: I think I'm going to burst.

NESSA VOX: Tony, you haven't eaten anything!

HERRICK SIMMONS: [*Offering* TONY *a forkful of duck.*] Come on, try it....

TONY STASSIO: [*Shaking her head.*] Really, I'm...

NESSA VOX: [*Lays down her fork.*] I don't believe this!

HERRICK SIMMONS: [*Plows into her duck with renewed vigor.*] Well, you're missing something fabulous!

NESSA VOX: [*To* HERRICK.] She says she's finished....

HERRICK SIMMONS: Mmmmmmmm!

NESSA VOX: Look at her plate!

TONY STASSIO: Don't let me spoil your dinner just because I'm dieting....

HERRICK SIMMONS: Aaaaaaahhhhhh!

NESSA VOX: She hasn't touched it.

HERRICK SIMMONS: Nessa, you've got to try some of this duck.
[*Offers her a forkful.*]

TONY STASSIO: You two just go right ahead....

NESSA VOX: Well if she's not going to eat, then neither am I!

HERRICK SIMMONS: [*Offering* NESSA *the duck more forcefully.*] Come on, it's sensational!

NESSA VOX: [*Tastes it.*] Mmmmmmmmmmm!

HERRICK SIMMONS: Isn't that something?

TONY STASSIO: [*Lifting up her plate.*] Would anyone like my bass?

HERRICK SIMMONS: [*Giving* NESSA *another bite.*] And now taste it with some of the peaches....

NESSA VOX: [*Does.*] MY GOD!

HERRICK SIMMONS: Hmm?

NESSA VOX: [*Flutters.*]

TONY STASSIO: I've already lost four pounds this week!

NESSA VOX: TONY, YOU'VE GOT TO TRY THIS DUCK, YOU'LL DIE!

HERRICK SIMMONS: [*Reaching a forkful over to* TONY.] It's unbelievable....

NESSA VOX: It's the best duck I've ever...

HERRICK SIMMONS: Here, let me get you more sauce. [*She offers* TONY *a heaping spoonful.*]

NESSA VOX: You won't know what hit you!

TONY STASSIO: [*Shielding her mouth with her hand.*] No really, I couldn't....

NESSA VOX: [*To* HERRICK.] Wouldn't you say that was the best duck you ever...

TONY STASSIO: [*Trying to ward them off.*] Please...

HERRICK SIMMONS: [*More threatening with her fork.*] Just a little taste!...

NESSA VOX: Come on, it won't kill you!

HERRICK SIMMONS: Open!

NESSA VOX: [*Scoops some up with her fork and also menaces* TONY *with it.*] We insist!

HERRICK SIMMONS: It really is...

NESSA VOX: Quite...

TONY STASSIO: Please!

NESSA VOX: Wonderful.

TONY STASSIO: Don't...

HERRICK SIMMONS: You should...

TONY STASSIO: ...force me!

HERRICK SIMMONS: ...try it!

NESSA VOX: Come on, Tony! You promised....

HERRICK SIMMONS: Eat the duck!

NESSA VOX: You've hardly eaten anything.

TONY STASSIO: I've got to lose ten more pounds!

NESSA VOX: [*Dumps the duck off her fork and threatens* TONY *with some of her veal.*] At least try the veal!

TONY STASSIO: [*Shielding her face with both hands.*] Only ten pounds! [*She starts to cry.*]

NESSA VOX: [*Slams down her fork.*] FUCK IT THEN. JUST FUCK IT!

[*Silence.*]

HERRICK SIMMONS: [*Resumes eating her duck.*] Ignore her.

NESSA VOX: HOW CAN I IGNORE HER WHEN WE'RE SITTING AT THE SAME TABLE AND SHE REFUSES TO EAT?

HERRICK SIMMONS: It's her problem. [*Offering* NESSA *an-*

other forkful of duck.] Come on, help me with this duck.

TONY STASSIO: I'm fat.

NESSA VOX: She says she's fat!

HERRICK SIMMONS: [*Reaching across for a taste of NES-SA's veal.*] How's your veal?

TONY STASSIO: [*Lifts up her arm, pulls the underpart of it.*] Look at that!

NESSA VOX: That isn't fat! That's your arm!

HERRICK SIMMONS: [*Eating NESSA's veal.*] Mmmmmmm! Very nice!

TONY STASSIO: It's fat.

NESSA VOX: [*Lifts up her plate of veal and gives it to HERRICK.*] Here, have it all, I don't want any.

HERRICK SMITH: Don't give it all to me!

TONY STASSIO: [*Gives HERRICK her bass.*] You can have my bass too.

NESSA VOX: She ruined the whole meal.

HERRICK SIMMONS: I can't eat all of this! [*As she starts to do just that.*]

TONY STASSIO: [*Smiling, to NESSA.*] How was the veal?

NESSA VOX: You'd think I'd learn....

HERRICK SIMMONS: What's going on here?

TONY STASSIO: [*To NESSA, referring to the veal.*] It looks good.

NESSA VOX: She does it every time!

TONY STASSIO: [*To HERRICK.*] And your bass looks really...

NESSA VOX: IT'S NOT AS IF SHE EVER STICKS TO ANY OF HER DIETS! AS SOON AS SHE GETS HOME, SHE'LL OPEN UP THE REFRIGERATOR AND HAVE HERSELF ONE WHOLLOPING ORGY!...

HERRICK SIMMONS: Take it easy....

NESSA VOX: SHE DENIES HERSELF IN FRONT OF US, BUT OH, WHEN SHE GETS INTO THE PRIVACY OF HER OWN REFRIGERATOR...

TONY STASSIO: [*Hands over her ears.*] I don't know what she's talking about....

HERRICK SIMMONS: [*To NESSA.*] Come on....

NESSA VOX: DOES SHE EVER GO AT IT! I know her. [*To* HERRICK.] Would you like to hear?

HERRICK SIMMONS: Nessa, don't...

NESSA VOX: First...just to warm up, she wolfs down a twin-pack of Golden Ridges potato chips followed by a fistful of Nabisco Nilla Wafers. Then, it's on to the freezer for the real stuff: Hungry Man TV dinners flash frozen by Swansons, Howard Johnson's, Stouffers, Mortons, Mrs. Paul, Ronzoni, and Chun King!...But...can she wait for them to heat up? ...God knows, it's a long wait for a Hungry Man TV dinner when you're languishing for it...the piquant steak in onion gravy, the hashed brown potato nuggets, the peas and carrots in seasoned sauce, and the delectable little serving of apple cake cobbler, pristine and golden in its tidy aluminum compartment. ...So, while it's warming at four hundred degrees, she'll help herself to some Pepperidge Farm corn muffins, fully baked and ready to serve. Still frozen, mind you...still frosted with a thin sheen of ice, but there's nothing wrong with eating frozen corn muffins...especially if you turn out the lights and eat them in the dark...lift them up to your mouth...in the dark...roll your tongue over them...in the...

HERRICK SIMMONS: NESSA, THAT'S ENOUGH!

[*A silence.*]

TONY STASSIO: [*Trying to recover, in a quavering voice.*] Well, I wonder if it's warmed up at all outside....

[*She wets her finger and rubs it around the rim of her glass making eerie music.*]

[*Another silence.*]

HERRICK SIMMONS: [*Pushing her bass away.*] Well, I guess I'm done. Anyone want the rest of this food?

TONY STASSIO: It's actually dangerous to go out on a night like this....

[*A silence.*]

NESSA VOX: Well, if you two are finished, then so am I....

[*Pushes her veal towards the center of the table.*]

HERRICK SIMMONS: ...can't eat another bite!

TONY STASSIO: I don't know when I've been so full!

NESSA VOX: If I have one more taste, I'm going to explode!

HERRICK SIMMONS: You're going to explode! What about me? I won't be able to fit behind the wheel of the car to drive us home!

[*This gets slower and slower.*]

TONY STASSIO: I can't go on....

NESSA VOX: I've had it....

HERRICK SIMMONS: I am stuffed!

TONY STASSIO: I can't move....

NESSA VOX: I'm in pain!

HERRICK SIMMONS: I feel sick....

TONY STASSIO: I'm...dying....

[*The lights fade around them...*]

Scene 4

And rise on PAUL *and* HANNAH GALT. *They have just been presented with snifters of after-dinner brandy.*

PAUL: [*Picks his up and sloshes it around, inhaling the fragrance.*]

HANNAH: [*Does the same, then holds out her glass to* PAUL.] A toast!

PAUL: [*Offering her his glass.*] Oh good, I love toasts!

HANNAH: [*Clinking his glass.*] To...us! [*She drinks.*]

PAUL: [*Drinks.*] That's very sweet, Hannah.

HANNAH: [*Reaches out her glass and clinks his again.*] You and me all the way. [*She drinks.*]

PAUL: [*Drinks again.*] Here, here!

[*A silence.*]

HANNAH: [*Lifts up her glass again.*] I want to make another toast!

PAUL: You're on!

HANNAH: [*Clinking his glass.*] To our wonderful children...Brian and Michelle! [*She drinks.*]

PAUL: Brian and Michelle...super kids! [*He drinks.*]

HANNAH: Gee, I'm having a good time.
[*She kicks off her shoes.*]
[*A silence.*]

PAUL: [*Leans back in his chair, swirling his brandy.*] This is very pleasant... very pleasant indeed.

HANNAH: [*Leaning forward.*] Another toast!

PAUL: Not again!

HANNAH: [*Clinking his glass.*] Oh, come on, Paul... toast!

PAUL: [*Clinks with her.*] Toast.

HANNAH: Guess.

PAUL: What do you mean, "guess"?

HANNAH: Guess what I'm going to toast.

PAUL: Hannah, I couldn't possibly *guess*....

HANNAH: Of course you can, just try....

PAUL: [*Raising his glass.*] To... oh, Hannah, we could sit here all night, there's no way I could *guess* what you're...

HANNAH: All right, all right! I thought you could guess, but if you can't... you can't! [*A pause, she lifts her glass, clinks it to his.*] To your long and curly eyelashes!

PAUL: [*Pulls back his glass.*] To my... long and curly *eyelashes*???!

HANNAH: Yes, they're gorgeous! [*She drinks again.*]

PAUL: [*In a whisper.*] Hannah, I can't drink to my... *eyelashes*!

HANNAH: Well, I can... and I'm going to because they're gorgeous!

PAUL: They are?

HANNAH: Very long... and very curly!

PAUL: You never told me that before.

HANNAH: Well, I'm telling you now....

PAUL: [*Studies his reflection in his brandy glass.*] Son of a bitch!

HANNAH: [*Getting tipsy, clinking his glass again.*] Toast... toast!

PAUL: Not so loud.

HANNAH: [*Clanks softer.*] Sorry....

PAUL: [*Still peering at his reflection in his glass.*] They're really long and curly?

HANNAH: [*Touching his glass.*] Toast, toast!...To your kneecaps! You have fabulous kneecaps! [*She drinks.*]

PAUL: [*Looks around the room, embarrassed.*] Hannah!

HANNAH: Come on, drink! [*She drinks again.*]

PAUL: [*In a whisper.*] Not to my *kneecaps*, for Christsakes!

HANNAH: [*Raps his glass again.*] TO ONE...STUNNING PAIR OF KNEECAPS! [*She drinks.*]

PAUL: [*Embarrassed, laughs.*] Hannah, stop it!

HANNAH: Really...*stunning*!
[*A few of the diners look over at them.*]

PAUL: OK...if that's the way you want to play...[*He holds out his glass to her.*] I would like to propose a toast!

HANNAH: [*Sitting back in her chair.*] Oh goody! [*She offers her glass.*]

PAUL: To your snowy white thighs! [*He clinks and drinks.*]

HANNAH: [*Snatches her glass away, embarrassed.*] Paul!

PAUL: [*Clinking her glass again.*] May they continue to bewitch and excite....[*He drinks.*]

HANNAH: [*In a hiss.*] Paul, stop it, it's not funny!...People are looking!
[HERRICK, NESSA, *and* TONY *stare openly and try not to laugh.*]

PAUL: [*Directly to them.*] Well, it's true, she's got one terrific pair of snowy white thighs!

HANNAH: [*Dying of embarrassment.*] I don't believe this....

PAUL: Would I lie?

HANNAH: [*In a dry whisper.*] Paul, stop it! Just...stop it!

PAUL: [*Stands and toasts everyone in the room.*] Well, bon appetit to one and all. [*He drinks, then sits back down.*]

HANNAH: I've never been so embarrassed....

PAUL: Oh, come on, Hannah, we're just fooling around....

HANNAH: Maybe *you're* fooling around, but *I'm* not!...

PAUL: So, all of a sudden *I'm* fooling around, is that it?...

HANNAH: You brought it up, not me!

PAUL: You think I'm fooling around, is that what you're saying?

HANNAH: I never said you were fooling around...*you* said *we* were fooling around.

PAUL: Are you fooling around?

HANNAH: What do you mean, am *I* fooling around? What kind of a question is that?

PAUL: *Are* you fooling around?

HANNAH: [*After a pause.*] Well, I'm not telling.

PAUL: You mean, you are fooling around?

HANNAH: What do you think?

PAUL: Frankly, I don't know what to think!

HANNAH: Well, neither do I...I mean, what a thing to ask me after a nice dinner and everything.

PAUL: [*Putting his hand over hers.*] I'm sorry.

HANNAH: [*Sulking.*] So am I....

PAUL: [*After a pause.*] Forgive me?

HANNAH: I have to think about it.

[*A silence as they both sip their brandies.*]

PAUL: Have you thought about it yet?

HANNAH: Maybe.

PAUL: Would you care to tell me what you decided?

HANNAH: That depends...

PAUL: Yes?

HANNAH: Do you promise never to embarrass me in public again?

PAUL: I promise.

HANNAH: Cross your heart?

PAUL: [*Crosses his heart.*] Cross my heart! [*Then lifts his glass to hers.*] I'll never embarrass you in public again! [*He drinks.*]

HANNAH: [*She drinks, mournful.*] I'm not fooling around. [*A silence.*]

PAUL: [*Eager, reaches his glass forward.*] A toast, another toast!

HANNAH: [*Offering her glass.*] Yes?

PAUL: To our next meal!

[*He clinks.*]

HANNAH: Oh, I like that!

PAUL: [*Drinks.*]

HANNAH: That's more like it. [*She drinks.*] To our next
meal!
　[*And leans over and kisses him.*]
　[*The lights fade...*]

Scene 5

And rise on ELLEN *and* CAL *in the kitchen. The food that*
ELLEN *was working with in the first act has multiplied*
tenfold. It's tumbling off the counters and overflowing
on the stove. ELLEN *and* CAL *race in the midst of it like*
figures in a speeded up old-time movie.

ELLEN: [*Is adding raw
mushrooms and spices
to a salad. She then
tosses it, all the while
talking on the
telephone which she
has tucked under her
chin.*] COULD YOU
SPEAK INTO THE
PHONE A LITTLE
LOUDER, PLEASE?
I'M HAVING
TROUBLE HEARING
YOU. YES
...THAT'S MUCH
BETTER. Now, you
were saying, you'd
like reservations for
how many? Three for
Thursday the
ninth...I'm sorry,
we're completely filled

CAL: [*Prepares a tray of
coffee, cups, sugar,
cream, and silverware
for the* GALTS, *while
talking on the other
telephone which he has
tucked under his chin.*]
No, nothing pleases us
more than hearing
from satisfied
customers, you're not
bothering us in the
least.... You've never
tasted such inspired
Chicken Kiev in your
life? ELLEN,
THEY'VE NEVER
TASTED SUCH
INSPIRED CHICKEN
KIEV IN THEIR
LIVES! And you'd like
to come back for

the ninth. Could I suggest Tuesday the fourteenth?... I SAID, TUESDAY THE FOURTEENTH! Yes, that's right, you could choose any time you like. I BEG YOUR PARDON? SOFT-SHELLED CRABS? Yes, I agree with you, they are delicious. ... Yes.... yes... NO, I WOULDN'T DREAM OF DEEP FRYING THEM, I NEVER DEEP FRY ANYTHING.... Yes, yes... you'd like to call me back after you've talked it over with your husband? Fine... I SAID, THAT WOULD BE FINE. THANK YOU FOR CALLING. Goodbye. [*She hangs up.*]

more? We change our menu every day, you realize, so I couldn't guarantee you that same Chicken Kiev again.... Now, which evening were you thinking of coming back? Thursday the ninth at 7:30? Yes, that would be fine.... Your name please? Kipner?... OH, YES, OF COURSE, I REMEMBER YOU FROM LAST WEEK. YOU WERE THE PARTY OF FOUR WHO ORDERED EXTRA SALADS. Well, thank you for calling. We'll see you on the ninth. Good-bye. [*He hangs up.*]

ELLEN: That was three for the fourteenth... maybe.

CAL: Six for the ninth...?

ELLEN: Six for the ninth? We're filled on the ninth!

CAL: You said, fourteen on the third?

ELLEN: You should have made it for the eighteenth. The salads are ready to go. [CAL *exits to the dining room with the salads.*] We have plenty of room on the eighteenth. He could have made it for the twenty-first which is a holiday....[*Turning towards her sauce and picking up three eggs.*] And now for my Hollandaise, my thick and rich Hollandaise for the bass! [*She separates the eggs for the Hollandaise Sauce.*]

CAL: [*Careening back into the kitchen.*] Fourteen on the

third is fantastic. That's what I like to hear: *big numbers.* Fourteen on the third...nineteen on the tenth...twenty-five on the sixteenth!

ELLEN: [*Beating the yolks.*] Slow down. It's not fourteen on the third. It's three on the fourteenth, but we're talking about the ninth, and we're filled on the ninth.

CAL: [*Fussing with his coffee tray.*] We can divide them up into two tables of seven....

ELLEN: We have plenty of room on the eighteenth! Vinegar...[*She adds a drop.*]

CAL: ...or three tables of five minus one...

ELLEN: I could handle four on the eighteenth....

CAL: How about one table of six and two tables of four?

ELLEN: Or even five on the nineteenth...salt...[*She adds a pinch.*]

CAL: Or...four tables of three...

ELLEN: ...but six on the ninth?...Impossible!

CAL: [*As he swings out the door with his tray of coffees.*] No problem!

ELLEN: Pepper! MY BASS! [*She rushes to the oven and pulls out her bass, takes the lid off.*] Oh, just look how lovely you are! And how delicious you smell...a garden full of herbs...perfect!

[*She puts the bass on a counter top.*]

CAL: [*And back into the kitchen.*] Baby, we are going to expand!

ELLEN: OH NO WE'RE NOT! Fish juices. [*She pours off the fish juices into her Hollandaise.*]

CAL: We are going to build onto the side of the house....

ELLEN: Over my dead body! Heavy cream. [*She beats in the heavy cream.*]

CAL: Enclose the back yard...

ELLEN: Just try it...twelve tablespoons of melted butter. Smooth and easy. Come on, baby....

CAL: [*Refilling the water pitcher for the bar.*] Break through the bedroom...

ELLEN: [*Beats and grunts.*]

CAL: Knock out those back walls.

ELLEN: Cal, you're losing your mind! Raving like a madman.

CAL: Add a good two hundred feet.

ELLEN: NO!

CAL: If we use our heads, Ellen, we can fit fifty more tables in there!

[*He rushes back to the dining room to pour the ladies their wine and deposit his water pitcher.*]

ELLEN: The next time he comes through that door, he'll announce we're opening a franchise! [*She returns to her sauce with a joyous fury.*] Oh, yes... you little yellow sweetheart... you thick and creamy love of mine... you luscious baby... thicken!... Break through the bedroom?... Thaaaaat's the way... you're doing fine.... Oh, yes... just fine... you tangy heart-breaker, you zesty tease... fifty more tables? ...NEVER!

[*She dances around the pot, grunting and whipping her sauce.*]

CAL: [*Comes careening back into the kitchen.*] With a little planning, we could be feeding two hundred people a night!

ELLEN: Not in this house! Not in *my* restaurant! [*She gives the sauce one more stroke and sets it aside on the counter.*] EVERYTHING'S GOING TO BE FINE! Lemon juice... [*She adds a final drop of lemon juice.*]

CAL: That's over five thousand dollars! [*He eyes the Hollandaise she's just made.*]

ELLEN: Just... fine!

CAL: [*Reaches for a spoon and unconsciously scoops out a taste of the Hollandaise.*] Five thousand dollars a night, comes to thirty thousand dollars a week!

ELLEN: [*Turns to the wild rice simmering on another burner, stirs it, adjusting the seasoning.*] They'll love it!

CAL: At that rate we could pay back our loan within six months!

ELLEN: They'll die over it!

CAL: We'd be in the clear.... [*He takes another taste of the sauce.* (ELLEN *has planted a decoy pan of lemon yogurt for* CAL *to drink so the actor won't die of heartburn, she simply switches pans at the last minute.*)]

ELLEN: Oh, Cal, I want them to die over it!

CAL: If we could just pay off that loan.... [*He picks up the saucepan of Hollandaise and starts drinking it.*]

ELLEN: [*Her back to him as she dishes out the rice.*] I am a cook who takes chances!

CAL: [*Gulping it down.*] Ellen, I gave up my law practice for this!

ELLEN: [*Transferring the bass to a serving platter.*] ...a cook...who delivers!

CAL: Eight years of a successful business!

ELLEN: [*Smells the bass, tastes the drippings.*] ...and I keep getting better!

CAL: [*Starts to spill the sauce down his front.*] A lot of people told me I was crazy....*You* even told me I was crazy....Give up an assured annual income of forty thousand and go seventy-five thousand into debt...for what?

ELLEN: [*One more taste.*] It's...perfect!

CAL: To open a restaurant in our living room!

ELLEN: [*Croons over the bass.*]

CAL: Insanity!

ELLEN: [*Reaches for her sauce.*] And now for the crowning glory...my sauce...my Hollandaise...

CAL: A wonderful little restaurant that would serve out-of-this-world food...an old dream of ours...

ELLEN: [*Her back to him, scans the counter top.*] Now where did I put it? I just had it....

CAL: You could cook to your heart's content....

ELLEN: Damn!

CAL: I could run the place, show off my entrepreneurial skills....

ELLEN: Where's my sauce?

CAL: *But we'd have to be serious about it and make some money!* I'm having trouble sleeping at night!

ELLEN: [*Finally sees him with the pan.*] Oh, Cal! You...can't...you...didn't!
[*She staggers to the stove.*]

CAL: [*Stops drinking, unaware of his action.*]

ELLEN: [*Blindly rushes to him and tries to wrest the pan from his hands.*] HOW...COULD...YOU...*DRINK*

131

...HOLLANDAISE SAUCE???... THE *TASTE*, CAL...

CAL: [*Trying to ward her off.*] Hey, take it easy....

ELLEN: How could you just take it off the burner...pick up the whole pan...and drink out of it?
[*She starts swatting him with a towel.*]

CAL: Watch it!

ELLEN: You're like some animal...an animal drinking out of its trough....

CAL: [*As the sauce sloshes wildly.*] Look out!

ELLEN: [*She finally wrenches it from him...holds the pan aloft and with deadly calm, pours it on the floor.*] Go on, Cal, drop down to the floor and lap it up! Lower your muzzle into it...*and drink*!
[*She pushes him from behind.*]

CAL: [*Loses his balance and sprawls on his hands and knees in front of the sauce...he backs away from it, horrified.*]

ELLEN: [*In a towering rage.*] THAT DOES IT, I'M SORRY, BUT...*THAT DOES IT*!!! [*She starts hurling pots and dishes into the sink. She picks up whatever is big and makes noise and throws it across the room. She then pulls out all the cords to her appliances, turns off the burners on the stove and switches off the overhead lights. The whole room goes black except for the sliver of light coming from underneath the door to the restaurant.*] No more cooking. I'm through!

CAL: [*Still on his knees, starts cleaning up the sauce with some towels.*] Ellen, what are you doing? There are people out there waiting for their food.

ELLEN: [*In a whisper.*] Too bad.

CAL: Half of them still haven't had their main course.

ELLEN: Go on, finish up the sauce on the floor. No one can see you.

CAL: Table One is still waiting for its entrees.

ELLEN: It's kind of nice like this....

CAL: Table Three may order second desserts....

ELLEN: ...cozy...

CAL: Table Two can't make up its mind....

ELLEN: ...comforting...

CAL: The next sitting will be here soon....

ELLEN: It's so quiet.

    [*She sits on one of the counters and hugs her legs to her chest.*]

CAL: A party of five is coming at nine.

ELLEN: Look at the stove, Cal, it's moving.

CAL: We've got to keep ahead of them.

ELLEN: It's like some wonderful dark ocean liner....

CAL: ELLEN, LISTEN TO ME! All hell is going to break loose out there!

ELLEN: Cut free from its anchor...

CAL: I'm the one on the spot.

ELLEN: ...pushing through the night...

CAL: What am I going to do?

ELLEN: No one can stop it.

CAL: [*In a panicky whisper.*] What am I going to do?

ELLEN: It's broken free and is heading out to places unknown.

    [*And the lights fade totally.*]

Scene 6

They rise on DAVID OSSLOW *and* ELIZABETH BARROW COLT *who are waiting for their entrees.*

DAVID OSSLOW: Most publishing houses shy away from short story collections.

ELIZABETH BARROW COLT: [*Murmurs.*] Oh well, I didn't really...

DAVID OSSLOW: They just don't sell....

ELIZABETH BARROW COLT: [*Murmurs.*] Yes, I suppose when the chips are down...

DAVID OSSLOW: But yours are so remarkable. I'm sure people have told you that before.

ELIZABETH BARROW COLT: Actually, I don't see that many...

DAVID OSSLOW: I really appreciate you meeting me like this on such a cold...

133

ELIZABETH BARROW COLT: [*Giddy.*] I HAD NO IDEA WHAT YOU LOOKED LIKE. I COULDN'T IMAGINE HOW WE'D EVER...

CAL: [*Upset and rushed, plunges into the restaurant and up to their table with the bass. Under his breath.*] Please God, don't let them notice there's no Hollandaise Sauce on the bass...Bar au Mousse de Crevettes.

[*He places it on the table with a flourish.*]

DAVID OSSLOW: Aaahhh, here comes our entree!

ELIZABETH BARROW COLT: Oh.

CAL: [*With very elaborate gestures.*] And would you like me to divide it for you?

DAVID OSSLOW: Please.

CAL: [*Does a spectacular job preparing the fish.*]

DAVID OSSLOW: [*In a whisper.*] Look at that bass! It's a masterpiece!

[ELIZABETH BARROW COLT *peers at* CAL *nearsightedly, then sneaks on her glasses to see better.*]

DAVID OSSLOW: I didn't know you wore glasses.

ELIZABETH BARROW COLT: [*Quicky takes them off.*] Oh, I don't! These are someone else's.

DAVID OSSLOW: You wear someone else's glasses?

ELIZABETH BARROW COLT: Sylvia Tussman, she works downtown at Hyde and Johnsons....

DAVID OSSLOW: You could ruin your eyes wearing someone else's glasses....

ELIZABETH BARROW COLT: ...in the typing pool, she's also good at steno.

DAVID OSSLOW: You should get your own prescription.

ELIZABETH BARROW COLT: She has several different pairs of glasses, so she said...

DAVID OSSLOW: [*Looking at her closely.*] You know, you have very beautiful eyes.

ELIZABETH BARROW COLT: Oh, no...

DAVID OSSLOW: You do. They're so pale, transparent almost....

ELIZABETH BARROW COLT: [*Blazing with embarrassment, drops her head, murmurs.*]

DAVID OSSLOW: [*Cups her face in his hands.*] Let me see them again....

ELIZABETH BARROW COLT: It's nothing, they're just... eyes...

DAVID OSSLOW: [*Drawing her head closer.*] No, really, they're...extraordinary.

ELIZABETH BARROW COLT: I don't know, I...

DAVID OSSLOW: I bet they glow in the dark.... They do, don't they?

ELIZABETH BARROW COLT: [*Has fallen in love with* DAVID OSSLOW.] Not really, I...
[CAL, *finished with his handiwork, tries to set* ELIZABETH's *plate down, but she's all over the place. Just as he's about to put it down, she moves, blocking him. They play a dreadful kind of hesitation dance.*]

CAL: Sorry, I was just	ELIZABETH BARROW COLT:
trying to...excuse me,	I'm sorry, I'm sorry,
I just wanted...*I'm*	I'm sorry, I'm sorry,
sorry!...Hold it right	I'm sorry, I'm sorry....
there....*If you could*	
just hold her...	

DAVID OSSLOW: [*Holds her still with both hands.*]

CAL: [*Finally sets it down.*] There we are!

ELIZABETH BARROW COLT: [*Looks down at it.*] Gosh.

CAL: [*Sets down* DAVID's *plate with ease.*] And for Monsieur...

ELIZABETH BARROW COLT: [*Looking at her bass, unable to face* DAVID OSSLOW.] Gosh.

DAVID OSSLOW: [*Lifts his fork to her.*] Bon appetit! [*And dives in.*]

ELIZABETH BARROW COLT: [*Is paralyzed by shyness and can't move.*] Gosh...beautiful eyes!

DAVID OSSLOW: Are you all right?

ELIZABETH BARROW COLT: Oh dear.

DAVID OSSLOW: What's wrong?

ELIZABETH BARROW COLT: [*Starts to laugh breathlessly.*]

DAVID OSSLOW: Don't you like the bass?

ELIZABETH BARROW COLT: [*Trying to stop laughing.*] Oh dear, oh dear, oh dear.

DAVID OSSLOW: [*Laughs tentatively with her.*]

ELIZABETH BARROW COLT: [*Puts her napkin over her face in an effort to stop. Snorts and gasps under it.*] No one ever said I had beautiful...

DAVID OSSLOW: [*Watches her with amusement and then returns to his bass.*]

ELIZABETH BARROW COLT: [*Suddenly rises, pushes her chair back almost knocking it over, and with the napkin partially over her head, lurches towards the rear of the room.*]

DAVID OSSLOW: [*Stands.*] Are you all right?

CAL: The Ladies' Room is upstairs to the left.

ELIZABETH BARROW COLT: [*Great peals of laughter erupting from her, lurches into the kitchen.*]

CAL: She went into the kitchen....

DAVID OSSLOW: She's been wearing someone else's glasses.

CAL: Oh.

[ELIZABETH BARROW COLT *wanders nearsightedly through the dark kitchen, amazed at the confusion of food and pots.*]

DAVID OSSLOW: She's been wearing someone else's glasses. May we have our wine now, please? [*He keeps eating.*]

CAL: Certainly, Sir.

DAVID OSSLOW: She's a writer.

CAL: Yes?

DAVID OSSLOW: And a very good one.

CAL: She looks like a writer.

DAVID OSSLOW: Mmmmm...

CAL: Strange eyes...

DAVID OSSLOW: I don't think she's been out to restaurants very often.

ELIZABETH BARROW COLT: [*Bursts back into the room, laughing.*] I was in the...kitchen....[*She whirls around, confused, still looking for the Ladies' Room...and following another route, ends up in the kitchen again.*]

DAVID OSSLOW: [*Eating.*] This bass is delicious!

CAL: I'm so glad you like it! [*He puts down the bottle of wine.*] Puligny-Montrachet.

DAVID OSSLOW: [*Nods that* CAL *should pour it, as he continues to eat.*]

CAL: [*Uncorks the bottle and begins the ritual of pouring it. He gives* DAVID *the cork to smell, pours him a tiny taste, waits for his approval, fills* ELIZABETH's *glass, and then returns to* DAVID's *as...*]

ELIZABETH BARROW COLT: [*Continues to wander through the dark kitchen. She eventually comes upon* ELLEN *who's sitting on the counter. She peers nearsightedly at her, but is unable to make any sense of what's happening. More embarrassed than ever, she lunges back out into the restaurant.*] I was in the kitchen...again.... [*And helplessly tries to get her moorings.*]

CAL: *Upstairs*...the Ladies' Room is *upstairs*...to the left....

ELIZABETH BARROW COLT: [*Almost on all fours, creeps up the stairs.*]

CAL: [*As he watches her.*] Maybe she needs her glasses, she was wearing them earlier.

DAVID OSSLOW: No, I don't think so.

CAL: She seems lost....

DAVID OSSLOW: [*Drinking his wine.*] She'll be all right. [*A silence.*]

ELIZABETH BARROW COLT: [*Has been calmed by her flight upstairs and gingerly reenters the room. She waves to* DAVID *from afar.*] Oh dear...

DAVID OSSLOW: [*Rises, waves back.*] Hi.

ELIZABETH BARROW COLT: [*Softly.*] Hi.

DAVID OSSLOW: Are you feeling better? [*He pulls out her chair.*]

ELIZABETH BARROW COLT: [*She collapses into it.*] I'm sorry....

DAVID OSSLOW: Don't be sorry.... [*He starts pushing her back to the table.*]

ELIZABETH BARROW COLT: I'm so embarrassed....

DAVID OSSLOW: Your bass is getting cold.

ELIZABETH BARROW COLT: [*She starts to cry.*] I'm sorry....

CAL: Can I get you anything else?

DAVID OSSLOW: No, we're fine, thank you.

CAL: Then I'll be getting back to the kitchen. [*As he plunges through the door, to* ELLEN, *angry.*] ELLEN, PLEASE!

ELIZABETH BARROW COLT: Oh dear.

DAVID OSSLOW: [*Moving closer to her.*] Calm down.

ELIZABETH BARROW COLT: [*Can't stop crying.*] Oh dear, oh dear, oh dear...

DAVID OSSLOW: Elizabeth, it happens all the time.

ELIZABETH BARROW COLT: No.

DAVID OSSLOW: Yes. All the time. Now dry your eyes and eat your bass.

ELIZABETH BARROW COLT: [*Doesn't move.*] Yes.

DAVID OSSLOW: I've seen writers fall to the floor in a dead faint.

ELIZABETH BARROW COLT: Oh.

DAVID OSSLOW: I've seen it all, believe me!

ELIZABETH BARROW COLT: [*Looks at her bass.*] Oh my...

DAVID OSSLOW: Now try some of that bass.

ELIZABETH BARROW COLT: Yes.

DAVID OSSLOW: It's superb. You'll love it.

ELIZABETH BARROW COLT: [*Looks at her bass again, helpless. Sighs. A silence, then very loud and intense.*] ONE AFTERNOON WHEN I CAME HOME FROM SCHOOL, MOTHER WAS IN TEARS BECAUSE LACEY HAD QUIT, WALKED OUT IN A TORRENT OF INSULTS. "NEVER AGAIN!" MOTHER SOBBED. "FROM NOW ON, I'LL DO THE COOKING MYSELF!"...IT WAS A BIG MISTAKE. SHE DIDN'T KNOW HOW AND SHE WAS IN THE MIDST OF MENOPAUSE. SHE KEPT BREAKING DISHES AND CUTTING HER FINGERS WITH THE CARVING KNIFE. ONE NIGHT SHE SLICED OFF THE TIP OF HER THUMB AND GROUND IT UP IN THE GARBAGE DISPOSAL!

[HANNAH GALT *lurches towards the Ladies' Room upstairs. The lights rise a little to reveal the other diners. They're startled by* ELIZABETH's *sudden outburst and*

*stare, then turn away feigning indifference, while
hanging on every word.*]

ELIZABETH BARROW COLT: Mealtime was much the same
as it had always been....Father still talked a blue
streak, Mother still mashed her food into a pink
soup...and I still spit everything out into my napkin. But they were paper napkins now, and since I
cleared the table, there was no chance of discovery.
I breathed easier. What changed then, was the vio-
lence that went into the cooking beforehand....I never
saw such bloodletting over meals! If she didn't knick
herself while cutting the tomatoes, she'd deliberately
slice a finger while waiting for the rice to boil. "Why
bother cooking?" she'd cry, holding her bleeding
hands under the faucet. "We'll all be dead soon
enough!"...It was around this time that Mother was
starting to get...suicidal....[*She starts to laugh.*]
Oh dear, I shouldn't laugh....It was just so...comical!
You see, Mother was very comical. She wore hats all
the time, great turban-type creations piled high with
artificial flowers and papier-mâché fruits. She wore
them outside and she wore them in the house. She
wore them when she cooked and when she ate...great
teetering crowns that bobbed and jingled with every
move...poor Mother....I don't know what it was
that made her so unhappy...her menopause, her
cocktails before dinner, some private anguish...but
during this period, she used to threaten to kill herself. After another bloodstained dinner, she'd throw
herself facedown on our driveway and beg my father
to put the car in reverse and drive over her. "Don't
be ridiculous, dear," he'd say. But she meant it and
would lie there sobbing, "PLEASE...DO IT!" It was
a ritual we went through every night....

DAVID OSSLOW: [*Does his best to eat his dinner, stopping
only when he's too shaken to swallow.*] And did she
ever?...I mean...succeed?

ELIZABETH BARROW COLT: [*Sighs.*] Oh dear.

DAVID OSSLOW: She did....

ELIZABETH BARROW COLT: Poor Mother.

TINA HOWE

DAVID OSSLOW: How...awful....
ELIZABETH BARROW COLT: [*Sighs.*]
DAVID OSSLOW: Your father finally gave in and ran over her....
ELIZABETH BARROW COLT: Not that.
DAVID OSSLOW: Sleeping pills...
ELIZABETH BARROW COLT: If only it had been....
DAVID OSSLOW: Poor thing...
ELIZABETH BARROW COLT: Yes...
DAVID OSSLOW: She shot herself?...
ELIZABETH BARROW COLT: Can't you guess?
DAVID OSSLOW: How could I guess...with someone like...*that*?
ELIZABETH BARROW COLT: Think! It's so in character!
DAVID OSSLOW: She slit her throat with a carving knife?
ELIZABETH BARROW COLT: [*A bit bloodthirsty.*] Better...
DAVID OSSLOW: [*After a pause.*] Of course...I know....

DAVID OSSLOW: She turned on the gas....	ELIZABETH BARROW COLT: She turned on the gas....

ELIZABETH BARROW COLT: She turned on the gas and opened that big mouth of an oven door and stuck her head in...with her hat firmly in place....
DAVID OSSLOW: Yes, of course...the hat!
ELIZABETH BARROW COLT: [*Starts laughing.*] It must have been quite a sight...Mother down on all fours, trying to fit her head in without knocking her hat off....
DAVID OSSLOW: And?...
ELIZABETH BARROW COLT: Oh dear, I shouldn't laugh....
DAVID OSSLOW: No, go on....
ELIZABETH BARROW COLT: Well, after she'd been in there for ten minutes or so, getting groggier and groggier, something went wrong. The papier-mâché trinkets on her hat began to sizzle and explode like little firecrackers. Within moments the entire hat was in flames. She came to like a shot and raced to the sink....her head actually...*cooking*! She turned on the water full blast....Her hat and all of her hair was consumed...but she survived. [*Pause.*] She joked about it afterwards...after the hospital stay and

140

plastic surgery...about almost having barbecued herself like some amazing delicacy...some exotic...roast! "I BET I WOULD HAVE TASTED DAMNED GOOD!" she used to say, smacking her lips. [*Long pause.*] My mother is very beautiful, you know....She's so beautiful...people turn around.

HANNAH: [*Reenters the room and sits down.*]
[*A silence.*]

DAVID OSSLOW: You haven't eaten any of your bass.

ELIZABETH BARROW COLT: [*Looking at it.*] Oh, yes, my bass...

DAVID OSSLOW: [*With great tenderness.*] You haven't touched it.

ELIZABETH BARROW COLT: I'm sorry, I...

DAVID OSSLOW: [*Touching her cheek.*] It's getting cold....

ELIZABETH BARROW COLT: Yes, I guess it is....

DAVID OSSLOW: [*Dips her fork into her bass and holds it out to her like a father feeding his child.*] Come...just try it...one taste....

[ELIZABETH BARROW COLT *looks at him helplessly, unable to take it. Neither of them move, and the lights fade around them.*]

Scene 7

The kitchen. Everything is still in a blackout.

CAL: [*Softly.*] Ellen, I beg of you. Don't do this to me...to us!

Scene 8

The lights rise on HERRICK SIMMONS, NESSA VOX *and* TONY STASSIO.

HERRICK SIMMONS: [*In a whisper.*] The things you overhear in restaurants....

NESSA VOX: [*Whistles her disbelief.*]

TONY STASSIO: I don't know....

HERRICK SIMMONS: Very strange...
NESSA VOX: [*Whistles again.*]
HERRICK SIMMONS: Poor thing...
NESSA VOX: She has such...beautiful eyes.
   [*Silence.*]
HERRICK SIMMONS: Guess what happened to me today?
TONY STASSIO: What?
HERRICK SIMMONS: [*Starts to laugh.*] You'll die!
NESSA VOX: Tell us!
HERRICK SIMMONS: I was...flashed.
TONY STASSIO: So?...
HERRICK SIMMONS: By a...woman!
TONY STASSIO: Gee!
NESSA VOX: What did she flash?
HERRICK SIMMONS: A breast!
NESSA VOX: How wonderful!
TONY STASSIO: How sick!
HERRICK SIMMONS: It wasn't sick at all, it was really
   quite beautiful. I mean, it was so unexpected. I'd just
   had lunch with Phillip and was looking in Tiffany's
   windows. I turned to cross Fifty-seventh Street, and
   this very pretty blond woman was crossing towards
   me. As we passed each other, she smiled at me, low-
   ered one side of her blouse, and flashed a gleaming
   breast....
TONY STASSIO: Sick...
NESSA VOX: I love it!
TONY STASSIO: What did you do?
HERRICK SIMMONS: Nothing. I just looked at it.
TONY STASSIO: [*Starts sneaking tastes of her bass.*] God!
   Did she say anything?
HERRICK SIMMONS: Not a word.
NESSA VOX: [*Also lighting into her veal.*] I love it! Women
   finally getting up enough nerve to be flashers!
HERRICK SIMMONS: [*Starts gobbling her duck.*]
   [*This sneaking of food begins as innocent picking,
   but gets uglier and uglier as their real hunger sur-
   faces.*]
TONY STASSIO: But imagine...doing that...showing your
   breast to a stranger....

NESSA VOX: What was it like?

TONY STASSIO: It's really kind of...

HERRICK SIMMONS: What was *what* like?

NESSA VOX: Her breast...

HERRICK SIMMONS: It was nice.

NESSA VOX: Was it round...or pendulous?

TONY STASSIO: [*Sneaks more bass.*]

HERRICK SIMMONS: Round.

NESSA VOX: [*Sneaks more veal.*] I think I'd die if I had pendulous breasts.

[*At times only one of them sneaks her food, at other times they sneak in concert.*]

HERRICK SMITH: *Why?*

NESSA VOX: They're so...*ugly!*

TONY STASSIO: [*In a small voice.*] Mine are pendulous.

NESSA VOX: They are not!

TONY STASSIO: They are so!

HERRICK SIMMONS: [*To* TONY.] You have lovely breasts!

TONY STASSIO: [*Softly.*] I have shitty breasts.

HERRICK SIMMONS: NO WOMAN HAS SHITTY BREASTS!

NESSA VOX: Listen, mine are dappled.

HERRICK SIMMONS: I'M SORRY, BUT BREASTS ARE LIFE-GIVING!

TONY STASSIO: Dappled?

NESSA VOX: [*Her head lowered.*] Spotted. You know how sometimes they get all...

HERRICK SIMMONS: I've never heard of spotted breasts!

NESSA VOX: Whenever I'm upset, they get...mottled.

HERRICK SIMMONS: Listen, a lot of women...

TONY STASSIO: [*In a low voice.*] When I gain weight, mine get *really* pendulous! "Old bananas," my brother used to call me!

HERRICK SIMMONS: A lot of women are ashamed of their breasts, it's ridiculous!

NESSA VOX: There's some imbalance in my hormones.

TONY STASSIO: ...In front of his friends.

HERRICK SIMMONS: They should be proud of them!

NESSA VOX: [*To* TONY.] At least you're not...spotted.

HERRICK SIMMONS: [*To* TONY.] One of mine is bigger than

143

the other, but they're still terrific!

TONY STASSIO: I have trouble finding clothes that fit.

NESSA VOX: And don't think it isn't painful!

HERRICK SIMMONS: What the hell...

TONY STASSIO: It's a real problem.

NESSA VOX: It's not fair.

TONY STASSIO: Of course when I diet, they do deflate somewhat....

NESSA VOX: [*To* HERRICK.] How would you like a blotchy bosom?

HERRICK SIMMONS: I MEAN, WHAT CAN WE DO ABOUT IT? WHAT CAN WE POSSIBLY DO? [*The lights fade on their ravenous and unhappy faces as they openly plunge into their food...*]

Scene 9

But they don't rise in the kitchen because ELLEN *is still sitting in the dark.* CAL *paces nervously. All is stillness for several moments.*

CAL: [*Turns on the speaker connected with the tape that plays in the restaurant. The Adagio from J. S. Bach's Sonata No. 5 in F Minor for violin and harpischord goes on.*] Ellen...

ELLEN: Oh, that's nice....

CAL: I can't even see you.

ELLEN: Nice to stop and rest...

CAL: Could I light a candle at least?

ELLEN: [*A long sigh.*]

CAL: [*Gets a candle and sets it into a head of lettuce or some other unlikely object and then lights it.*]

ELLEN: How pretty...

CAL: That's better.... [*Silence.*] Remember when you used to make us dinner by candlelight when we were first married? How I loved it! Watching you cook in the dark...it was so romantic. I could hear your heart race as you tended your filets, stirred your sauces.... I could never quite see what you were adding, rending, sautéing....

ELLEN: You'd never get too close, but would watch from a distance, give me my room...and all the time in the world. So much time and so much love...

CAL: Yes, I could feel it thickening all around us. I'd sneak glances at you in the darkness and reel at your grace.... We were so happy! My God! That new-lywed cooking, those honeymoon suppers that lasted and lasted...

ELLEN: And here we are again except now you've eaten everything before I could get started.... *Why, Cal?*

CAL: Because it's so good.

ELLEN: But it's *not* good! You're eating everything before it's done!

CAL: You're such a good cook....

ELLEN: You're eating it raw!

CAL: You have such a gift....

ELLEN: ...gobbling it up...

CAL: ...an incredible gift!

ELLEN: ...swallowing it whole!

CAL: It's wonderful.

ELLEN: I can't go on like this.

CAL: Really...wonderful.

ELLEN: You've got to give me a chance.... LET ME DO MY WORK! PLEASE!...
   [*A silence.*]

CAL: [*Starts eating a roll.*] It's this damned not sleeping. I lie awake half the night worrying.

ELLEN: Just let me cook!

CAL: Will we pay off the loan?

ELLEN: I'll go sour without it, you know, soft at the edges!

CAL: ...bring in some cash?

ELLEN: I don't care about cash!

CAL: Worry makes me hungry, you know. Not sleeping makes me hungry.

ELLEN: I can't stop cooking, I've been at it too long.
   [*She turns on the overhead light.*]

CAL: It all adds up.

ELLEN: You can still make a choice.

CAL: I know it's a problem.

ELLEN: And you must...or we're done for. Totally done for.

[*A silence.*]

CAL: I'll try and watch it.

ELLEN: You have to watch it.

CAL: And if for some terrible reason I can't?

ELLEN: But it's over.

CAL: The restaurant will close?

ELLEN: No, everything's over. Finished.

[*A silence.*]

CAL: Even me?

ELLEN: [*Looks at him, takes her time.*] Even you...

CAL: Ellen, don't say that.

ELLEN: It's true.

CAL: I said *don't*!

ELLEN: [*Starts working on a dessert.*]

CAL: You don't help matters, you know.... "Taste this...try that...is it good? Oh, Cal, will they like it?...I want them to die over it!"...There's no escaping you and your outstretched spoons, did you ever think about that?

ELLEN: I was just asking you to taste!

CAL: Well, you're playing with fire!

ELLEN: You're right, you're right....From now on, I'll cook on my own and taste on...my...own! [*She grates orange peel into a sizzling pan.*]

CAL: [*Advances towards her.*] What are you doing?

ELLEN: [*Brandishing her spoon.*] Stay where you are!

CAL: What have you got there?

ELLEN: Don't make a move!

CAL: [*Inches closer.*] That smell...

ELLEN: Cal...I'm warning you!

CAL: [*Backs off.*] I won't...I won't...see, I'm not moving!

ELLEN: [*Taking a taste.*] I'll taste *on my own*!...

CAL: This isn't going to be easy.

ELLEN: [*Tasting her handiwork.*] Good...good...yes, it's getting there....

CAL: I'll try to change....I'll really try....

ELLEN: [*Turns toward him.*] OK, set everything up for us...come on...do your stuff!

[*She drapes his waiter's napkin over his arm with gentleness and respect.*]

CAL: [*Moved.*] The specialty of the house?

ELLEN: [*Smiling.*] The specialty of the house!

CAL: [*Gets the dessert dishes from the pantry and extra silverware, pauses by the door for a minute.*] I don't want to lose you.

ELLEN: Neither do I.

CAL: [*As he pushes through to the dining room.*] You're tough! You know....

ELLEN: [*With a smile.*] So are you!

Scene 10

The lights rise on the diners who are in considerable agitation.

DAVID OSSLOW: Waiter, could we see the dessert menu, please?

HANNAH: *There* he is!

NESSA VOX: [*Hailing him.*] Sir?

PAUL: Well, finally! I thought he'd died in there!

NESSA VOX: *Sir*??

CAL: [*Makes the necessary preparations for serving the specialty of the house. He hears his customers but is intent on his own work.*]

HANNAH: [*To* PAUL.] Ask him if they take Master Charge?

DAVID OSSLOW: Waiter?

NESSA VOX: Excuse me, Sir. Could you possibly turn up the heat a little more? It's freezing in here!

TONY STASSIO: [*Rising to get her coat.*] I'm getting my coat. It must be ninety below out there.

NESSA VOX: [*Also rises, stands by the window.*] Get mine too....

PAUL: Waiter, the check please!

DAVID OSSLOW: Anytime you're ready with the dessert menu...

HANNAH: [*To* CAL.] Excuse me, but do you take Master Charge?

DAVID OSSLOW: We'd also like a look at the pastry tray.

PAUL: Waiter? It's been half an hour!

ELLEN: [*Has made the final preparations on her dessert. She puts on a clean white apron and perhaps a chef's hat. She stands by the door bearing it aloft.*]

CAL: [*Opens the door for her.*]

ELLEN: [*Steps into the restaurant and puts the dessert down on a chafing dish.*]

TONY STASSIO: What's happening?

HANNAH: What's this?

NESSA VOX: Who's that?

PAUL: What's going on?

TONY STASSIO: Who's she?

DAVID OSSLOW: It must be their dessert....

HERRICK SIMMONS: [*Returning from the Ladies' Room.*] It must be my Zabaglione....

HANNAH: But we've already...

PAUL: Sssssshhhhhh!

HANNAH: Oh, Paul, smell!

HERRICK SIMMONS: I love it!

ELLEN: [*To* CAL.] The matches please.

CAL: [*Lights a match to her dessert. Orange and blue flames leap up.*]

HANNAH: [*Gasps.*]

PAUL: Hannah, hold still!

NESSA VOX: It looks like...

DAVID OSSLOW: It must be...

HANNAH: Oh, what's that called?...

NESSA VOX: I've got it!

[*A pause.*]

NESSA, DAVID AND HANNAH: It's Crepes Suzettes!

HANNAH: Crepes Suzettes!

HERRICK SIMMONS: Crepes Suzettes!

PAUL: I knew it!

CAL: [*Stands back and announces.*] CREPES CARROU-SELS!

EVERYONE: [*Bursts into applause and sighs, murmuring "Crepes Carrousels!"*]

ELLEN: ... on the house!

EVERYONE: [*Even louder cheers and echoes of "on the house!"*]

ELLEN: [*Starts transferring the crepes into a large serving platter.*]

TONY STASSIO: I don't believe this!

HERRICK SIMMONS: [*Sidles over to the platter and looks in.*]

ELLEN: [*Motions her to help herself.*]

HERRICK SIMMONS: [*She does and sits back down at her place, smiling.*]

DAVID OSSLOW: [*Advances to take his piece.*] I've been to *many* restaurants in my day, but this is the first time I've ever seen anything like this!

NESSA VOX: Wait for me!
[*She rushes to the platter and takes her share.*]

TONY STASSIO: I'm right behind you!

HANNAH: [*Helping herself.*] This is extraordinary.

ELIZABETH BARROW COLT: No, not really.

EVERYONE: [*Looks at her, suddenly hushed.*]

ELIZABETH BARROW COLT: It's the beginning of time ...

NESSA VOX AND TONY STASSIO: [*Start to laugh.*]

DAVID OSSLOW: Ssssshhhhh!

HERRICK SIMMONS: Be quiet!

ELIZABETH BARROW COLT: [*With great simplicity.*] ... long, long ago when men ate by a fire ... crouched close to its warmth ... entwined their great arms ... gave thanks for the kill ... opened their mouths ... and shared in the feast!
[*She rises and joins the other diners at the flaming platter. She helps herself to some crepe and for the first time all evening, she eats. She looks at ELLEN, who smiles at her.*]

[*The diners become more jovial around ELLEN and eat with increasing gusto, wiping their greasy faces, grunting with pleasure. ELLEN throws CAL a backward glance, but he shakes his head indicating he's had enough for the evening.* EVERYONE's *movements slow down to simple gestures, their language becomes less familiar. The fury of the November wind increases outside and the light from* ELLEN's *bonfire burns brighter and brighter as the diners gather close to its warmth.* ELLEN *stands above them, churning up the flames, her face glowing with a fierce radiance. Purified of their collective civilization and private grief, they feast as . . .*]

THE CURTAIN SLOWLY FALLS

PAINTING CHURCHES

PAINTING CHURCHES was initially produced by The
Second Stage at the South Street Theatre in 1983; artistic directors, Robyn Goodman and Carole Rothman.

DIRECTOR: Carole Rothman
SETTING: Heidi Landesman
LIGHTING: Frances Aronson
COSTUMES: Nan Cibula
SOUND: Gary Harris

CAST

(in order of appearance)

FANNY CHURCH ....Marian Seldes
GARDNER CHURCH......................Donald Moffat
MARGARET CHURCH (MAGS) ....Frances Conroy

Lamb's Theatre production, 1984; producers, Elizabeth
I. McCann, Nelle Nugent, Ray Larsen, Lee Guber, Shelly
Gross.

DIRECTOR: Carole Rothman
SETTING: Heidi Landesman
LIGHTING: Frances Aronson
COSTUMES: Linda Fisher
SOUND: Gary Harris

CAST

(in order of appearance)

FANNY CHURCH .... Marian Seldes
GARDNER CHURCH.................... George N. Martin
MARGARET CHURCH (MAGS) ...... Elizabeth McGovern

CHARACTERS

FANNY SEDGWICK CHURCH, *a Bostonian from a fine old
family, in her sixties*
GARDNER CHURCH, *her husband, an eminent New En-
gland poet from a finer family, in his seventies*
MARGARET CHURCH (MAGS), *their daughter, a painter,
in her early thirties*

During the scene changes, the opening measures of the following Chopin waltzes are played:

As the house lights dim, the Waltz in A Minor, opus posthumous

Setting up Act I, Scene 2, the Waltz in E Minor, opus posthumous

Setting up Act I, Scene 3, the Waltz in E Major, opus posthumous

To close Act I, the final notes of the Waltz in B Minor, opus 69, no. 2. As the house lights dim for Act II, the Waltz in A flat Major, opus 64, no. 3

Setting up Act II, Scene 2, repeat the Waltz in A Minor, opus posthumous

To accompany the final moments of GARDNER's and FAN-NY's dance, the Waltz in D flat Major, Opus 70, no. 3

ACT I

Scene 1

TIME: *Several years ago.*
PLACE: *The living room of the Church's townhouse on Beacon Hill one week before everything will be moved to Cape Cod. Empty packing cartons line the room and all the furniture has been tagged with brightly colored markers. At first glance it looks like any discreet Boston interior, but on closer scrutiny one notices a certain flamboyance. Oddities from secondhand stores are mixed in with the fine old furniture, and exotic handmade curios vie with tasteful family objets d'art. What makes the room remarkable, though, is the play of light that pours through three soaring arched windows. At one hour it's hard edged and brilliant; the next, it's dappled and yielding. It transforms whatever it touches, giving the room a distinct feeling of unreality. It's several years ago, a bright spring morning.*

FANNY *is sitting on the sofa, wrapping a valuable old silver coffee service. She's wearing a worn bathrobe and fashionable hat. As she works, she makes a list of everything on a yellow legal pad.* GARDNER *can be heard typing in his study down the hall.*

FANNY: [*She picks up a coffee pot.*] God, this is good-looking! I'd forgotten how handsome Mama's old silver was! It's probably worth a fortune. It certainly weighs enough! [*Calling out.*] GARRRRR-RRRRRRRRRRRRRDNERRRRRRRRRRRR?

157

...Well, it should bring us a pretty penny, that's for sure. [*Wraps it, places it in a carton, and then picks up the tray that goes with it. She holds it up like a mirror and adjusts her hat. Louder in another register.*] OH, GARRRRRRRRRRRRRRRDNER-RRRR?...

[*He continues typing.*]

FANNY: [*She then reaches for a small box and opens it with reverence.*] Grandma's Paul Revere teaspoons!...[*She takes out several and fondles them.*] I don't care how desperate things get, these will never go! One has to maintain some standards! [*She writes on her list.*] "Grandma's Paul Revere teaspoons, Cotuit!"...WASN'T IT THE AMERICAN WING OF THE METROPOLITAN MUSEUM OF ART THAT WANTED GRANDMA'S PAUL REVERE TEA-SPOONS SO BADLY?...[*She looks at her reflection in the tray again.*] This is a very good-looking hat, if I do say so. I was awfully smart to grab it up. [*Silence.*]
DON'T YOU REMEMBER A DISTINGUISHED-LOOKING MAN COMING TO THE HOUSE AND OFFERING US FIFTY THOUSAND DOLLARS FOR GRANDMA'S PAUL REVERE TEASPOONS?... HE HAD ON THESE MARVELOUS SHOES! THEY WERE SO POINTED AT THE ENDS WE COULDN'T IMAGINE HOW HE EVER GOT THEM ON AND THEY WERE SHINED TO WITH-IN AN INCH OF THEIR LIVES AND I REMEM-BER HIM SAYING HE CAME FROM THE... AMERICAN WING OF THE METROPOLITAN MUSEUM OF ART!...HELLO?...GARDNER?... ARE YOU THERE!

[*The typing stops.*]

FANNY: YOO-HOOOOOOO...[*Like a fog horn.*] GARRRRRRRRRRRDNERRRRRRR?...

GARDNER: [*Offstage; from his study.*] YES, DEAR...IS THAT YOU?...

FANNY: OF COURSE IT'S ME! WHO ELSE COULD IT

POSSIBLY BE?...DARLING, PLEASE COME
HERE FOR A MINUTE.
[*The typing resumes.*]

FANNY: FOR GOD'S SAKE, WILL YOU STOP THAT
DREADFUL TYPING BEFORE YOU SEND ME
STRAIGHT TO THE NUT HOUSE?... [*In a new
register.*] GARRRRRRRRRRRRRDNERRRRRR?...
[*He stops.*]

GARDNER: [*Offstage.*]
WHAT'S THAT?
MAGS IS BACK
FROM THE NUT
HOUSE?...

FANNY: I SAID...Lord, I
hate this yelling....
PLEASE...COME....
HERE!

[*Brief silence.*]

GARDNER: [*Offstage.*] I'LL
BE WITH YOU IN A
MOMENT, I DIDN'T
HEAR HER RING.
[*Starts singing.*]
"Nothing Could be
Finer Than to be in
Carolina."

FANNY: It's a wonder I'm
not in a strait jacket
already. Actually, it
might be rather nice
for a
change...peaceful.
DARLING...I WANT
TO SHOW YOU MY
NEW HAT!

[*Silence.* GARDNER *enters, still singing. He's wearing
mismatched tweeds and is holding a stack of papers
which keep drifting to the floor.*]

GARDNER: Oh, don't you look nice! Very attractive, very
attractive!

FANNY: But I'm still in my bathrobe.

GARDNER: [*Looking around the room, leaking more papers.*] Well, where's Mags?

FANNY: Darling, you're dropping your papers all over
the floor.

GARDNER: [*Spies the silver tray.*] I remember this! Aunt
Alice gave it to us, didn't she? [*He picks it up.*] Good
Lord, it's heavy. What's it made of? Lead?!

FANNY: No, Aunt Alice did *not* give it to us. It was Mama's.

GARDNER: Oh, yes...

[*He starts to exit with it.*]

FANNY: Could I have it back, please?

GARDNER: [*Hands it to her, dropping more papers.*] Oh, sure thing.... Where's Mags? I thought you said she was here.

FANNY: I didn't say Mags was here, I asked *you* to come here.

GARDNER: [*Papers spilling.*] Damned papers keep falling....

FANNY: I wanted to show you my new hat. I bought it in honor of Mags' visit. Isn't it marvelous?

GARDNER: [*Picking up the papers as more drop.*] Yes, yes, very nice...

FANNY: Gardner, you're not even looking at it!

GARDNER: Very becoming...

FANNY: You don't think it's too bright, do you? I don't want to look like a traffic light. Guess how much it cost?

GARDNER: [*A whole sheaf of papers slides to the floor; he dives for them.*] OH, SHIT!

FANNY: [*Gets to them first.*] It's all right, I've got them, I've got them. [*She hands them to him.*]

GARDNER: You'd think they had wings on them....

FANNY: Here you go...   GARDNER: ...damned
things won't hold still!

FANNY: Gar?...

GARDNER: [*Has become engrossed in one of the pages.*] Mmmmm?

FANNY: HELLO?

GARDNER: [*Startled.*] What's that?

FANNY: [*In a whisper.*] My hat. Guess how much it cost.

GARDNER: Oh, yes. Let's see...ten dollars?

FANNY: Ten dollars...IS THAT ALL?...

GARDNER: Twenty?

FANNY: GARDNER, THIS HAPPENS TO BE A DESIGNER HAT! DESIGNER HATS START AT FIFTY DOLLARS...SEVENTY-FIVE!

GARDNER: [*Jumps.*] Was that the door bell?

FANNY: No, it wasn't the door bell. Though it's high time Mags were here. She was probably in a train wreck!

GARDNER: [*Looking through his papers.*] I'm beginning to get fond of Wallace Stevens again.

FANNY: This damned move is going to kill me! Send me straight to my grave!

GARDNER: [*Reading from a page.*]
"The mules that angels ride come slowly down
The blazing passes, from beyond the sun.
Descensions of their tinkling bells arrive.
These muleteers are dainty of their way..."
[*Pause.*] Don't you love that! "These muleteers are *dainty* of their way"!?...

FANNY: Gar, the hat. How much?
[GARDNER *sighs.*]

FANNY: Darling?...

GARDNER: Oh, yes. Let's see...fifty dollars? Seventy-five?

FANNY: It's French.

GARDNER: Three hundred!

FANNY: [*Triumphant.*] No, eighty-five cents.

GARDNER: Eighty-five cents!...I thought you said...

FANNY: That's right...eighty...five...*cents!*

GARDNER: Well, you sure had me fooled!

FANNY: I found it at the thrift shop.

GARDNER: I thought it cost at least fifty dollars or seventy-five. You know, designer hats are very expensive!

FANNY: It was on the mark-down table. [*She takes it off and shows him the label.*] See that? Lily Daché! When I saw that label, I nearly keeled over right into the fur coats!

GARDNER: [*Handling it.*] Well, what do you know, that's the same label that's in my bathrobe.

FANNY: Darling, Lily Daché designed hats, not men's bathrobes!

GARDNER: Yup...Lily Daché...same name...

FANNY: If you look again, I'm sure you'll see...

GARDNER: ...same script, same color, same size. I'll show you.
[*He exits.*]

FANNY: Poor lamb can't keep anything straight anymore. [*Looks at herself in the tray again.*] God, this is a good-looking hat!

GARDNER: [*Returns with a nondescript plaid bathrobe. He points to the label.*] See that?...What does it say?

FANNY: [*Refusing to look at it.*] Lily Daché was a *hat* designer! She designed ladies' *hats*!

GARDNER: What...does...it...say?

FANNY: Gardner, you're being ridiculous.

GARDNER: [*Forcing it on her.*] Read...the label!

FANNY: Lily Daché did *not* design this bathrobe, I don't care what the label says!

GARDNER: READ! [FANNY *reads it.*] ALL RIGHT, NOW WHAT DOES IT SAY?...

FANNY: [*Chagrined.*] Lily Daché.

GARDNER: I told you!

FANNY: Wait a minute, let me look at that again. [*She does; then throws the robe at him in disgust.*] Gar, Lily Daché never designed a bathrobe in her life! Someone obviously ripped the label off one of her hats and then sewed it into the robe.

GARDNER: [*Puts it on over his jacket.*] It's damned good-looking. I've always loved this robe. I think you gave it to me....Well, I've got to get back to work. [*He abruptly exits.*]

FANNY: Where did you get that robe anyway?...I didn't give it to you, did I?...

[*Silence.* GARDNER *resumes typing.*]

FANNY: [*Holding the tray up again and admiring herself.*] You know, I think I *did* give it to him. I remember how excited I was when I found it at the thrift shop...fifty cents and never worn! *I* couldn't have sewn that label in to impress him, could I?...I can't be that far gone!...The poor lamb wouldn't even notice its label, let alone understand its cachet....Uuuuuuh, this damned tray is even heavier than the coffee pot. They must have been amazons in the old days! [*Writes on her pad.*] "Empire tray, Parke-Bernet Galleries," and good riddance! [*She wraps it and drops it into the carton with the coffee pot.*] Where *is* that wretched Mags? It would be just like her to get into a train wreck! She was supposed to be here hours ago. Well, if she doesn't show up soon, I'm going to drop dead of exhaustion. God, wouldn't that be wonderful?...Then they could just cart me off into storage with all the old chandeliers and china...

[*The doorbell rings.*]

FANNY: IT'S MAGS, IT'S MAGS! [*A pause. Dashing out of the room, colliding into* GARDNER.] GOOD GOD, LOOK AT ME! I'M STILL IN MY BATHROBE!

GARDNER: [*Offstage.*] COMING, COMING...I'VE GOT IT...COMING! [*Dashing into the room, colliding into* FANNY.] I'VE GOT IT...HOLD ON... COMING... COMING....

FANNY: [*Offstage.*] MAGS IS HERE! IT'S MAGS....SHE'S FINALLY HERE!

[GARDNER *exits to open the front door.* MAGS *comes staggering in carrying a suitcase and an enormous duffle bag. She wears wonderfully distinctive clothes and has very much her own look. She's extremely out of breath and too wrought up to drop her heavy bags.*]

MAGS: I'm sorry....I'm sorry I'm so late....Everything went wrong! A passenger had a heart attack outside of New London and we had to stop....It was terrifying! All these medics and policemen came swarming onto the train and the conductor kept running up and down the aisles telling everyone not to leave their seats under any circumstances....Then the New London fire department came screeching down to the tracks, sirens blaring, lights whirling, and all these men in black rubber suits started pouring through the doors....*That* took two hours....

FANNY: DARLING...DARLING...WHERE ARE YOU?...

MAGS: *Then,* I couldn't get a cab at the station. There

just weren't any! I must have circled the block fifteen times. Finally I just stepped out into the traffic with my thumb out, but no one would pick me up...so I walked....

FANNY: [*Offstage.*] Damned zipper's stuck....

GARDNER: You walked all the way from the South Station?

MAGS: Well actually, I ran....

GARDNER: You had poor Mum scared to death.

MAGS: [*Finally puts the bags down with a deep sigh.*] I'm sorry....I'm really sorry. It was a nightmare.

FANNY: [*Reenters the room, her dress over her head. The zipper's stuck; she staggers around blindly.*] Damned zipper! Gar, will you please help me with this?

MAGS: I sprinted all the way up Beacon Hill.

GARDNER: [*Opening his arms wide.*] Well, come here and let's get a look at you. [*He hugs her.*] Mags!...

MAGS: [*Squeezing him tight.*] Oh, Daddy...Daddy!

GARDNER: My Mags!

MAGS: I never thought I'd get here!...Oh, you look wonderful!

GARDNER: Well, you don't look so bad yourself!

MAGS: I love your hair. It's gotten so...white!

FANNY: [*Still lost in her dress, struggling with the zipper.*] This is *so* typical...just as Mags arrives, my zipper has to break! [FANNY *grunts and struggles.*]

MAGS: [*Waves at her.*] Hi, Mum....

FANNY: Just a minute, dear, my zipper's...

GARDNER: [*Picks up* MAG'S *bags*] Well, sit down and take a load off your feet....

MAGS: I was so afraid I'd never make it....

GARDNER: [*Staggering under the weight of her bags.*] What have you got in here? Lead weights?

MAGS: I can't believe you're finally letting me do you.

FANNY: [*Flings her arms around* MAGS, *practically knocking her over.*] OH, DARLING...MY   GARDNER: [*Lurching*

164

PRECIOUS MAGS, YOU'RE HERE AT LAST. *around in circles.*] Now let's see ... where should I put these? ...

FANNY: I was sure your train had derailed and you were lying dead in some ditch!

MAGS: [*Pulls away from* FANNY *to come to* GARDNER'S *rescue.*] Daddy, please, let me ... these are much too heavy.

FANNY: [*Finally noticing* MAGS.] GOOD LORD, WHAT HAVE YOU DONE TO YOUR HAIR?!

MAGS: [*Struggling to take the bags from* GARDNER.] Come on, give them to me ... please? [*She sets them down by the sofa.*]

FANNY: [*As her dress starts to slide off one shoulder.*] Oh, not again! ... Gar, would you give me a hand and see what's wrong with this zipper. One minute it's stuck, the next it's falling to pieces.

[GARDNER *goes to her and starts fussing with it.*]

MAGS: [*Pacing.*] I don't know, it's been crazy all week. Monday, I forgot to keep an appointment I'd made with a new model.... Tuesday, I overslept and stood up my advanced painting students.... Wednesday, the day of my meeting with Max Zoll, I forgot to put on my underpants....

FANNY: GOD DAMNIT, GAR, CAN'T YOU DO ANY-THING ABOUT THIS ZIPPER?!

MAGS: I mean, there I was, racing down Broome Street in this gauzy Tibetan skirt when I tripped and fell right at his feet ... SPLATTT! My skirt goes flying over my head and there I am ... everything staring him in the face ...

FANNY: COME ON, GAR, USE A LITTLE MUSCLE!

MAGS: [*Laughing.*] Oh, well, all that matters is that I finally got here.... I mean ... there you are....

GARDNER: [*Struggling with the zipper.*] I can't see it, it's too small!

FANNY: [*Whirls away from* GARDNER, *pulling her dress off altogether.*] OH, FORGET IT! JUST FORGET

165

IT!...The trolley's probably missing half its teeth, just like someone else I know. [*To* MAGS.] I grind my teeth in my sleep now, I've worn them all down to stubs. Look at that! [*She flings open her mouth and points.*] Nothing left but the gums!

GARDNER: I never hear you grind your teeth....

FANNY: That's because I'm snoring so loud. How could you hear anything through all that racket? It even wakes me up. It's no wonder poor Daddy has to sleep downstairs.

MAGS: [*Looking around.*] Jeez, look at the place! So, you're finally doing it...selling the house and moving to Cotuit year round. I don't believe it. I just don't believe it!

GARDNER: Well, how about a drink to celebrate Mags' arrival?

MAGS: You've been here so long. Why move now?

FANNY: Gardner, what are you wearing that bathrobe for?...

MAGS: You can't move. I won't let you!

FANNY: [*Softly to* GARDNER.] Really, darling, you ought to pay more attention to your appearance.

MAGS: You love this house. *I* love this house...this room...the light.

GARDNER: So, Mags, how about a little... [*He drinks from an imaginary glass.*] to wet your whistle?

FANNY: We can't start drinking now, it isn't even noon yet!

MAGS: I'm starving. I've got to get something to eat before I collapse!

[*She exits towards the kitchen.*]

FANNY: What *have* you done to your hair, dear? The color's so queer and all your nice curl is gone.

GARDNER: It looks to me as if she dyed it.

FANNY: Yes, that's it. You're absolutely right! It's a completely different color. She dyed it bright red!

[MAGS *can be heard thumping and thudding through the icebox.*]

FANNY: NOW, MAGS, I DON'T WANT YOU FILLING UP ON SNACKS....I'VE MADE A PERFECTLY

BEAUTIFUL LEG OF LAMB FOR LUNCH!
...HELLO?...DO YOU HEAR ME?... [*To* GARD-
NER.] No one in our family has *ever* had red hair, it's
so common looking.

GARDNER: I like it. It brings out her eyes.

FANNY: WHY ON EARTH DID YOU DYE YOUR HAIR
RED, OF ALL COLORS?!...

MAGS: [*Returns, eating Saltines out of the box.*] I didn't
dye my hair, I just added some highlight.

FANNY: I suppose that's what your arty friends in New
York do...dye their hair all the colors of the rainbow!

GARDNER: Well, it's damned attractive if you ask
me...damned attractive!
[MAGS *unzips her duffle bag and rummages around
in it while eating the Saltines.*]

FANNY: Darling, I told you not to bring a lot of stuff
with you. We're trying to get rid of things.

MAGS: [*Pulls out a folding easel and starts setting it up.*]
AAAAAHHHHHH, here it is. Isn't it a beauty? I
bought it just for you!

FANNY: Please don't get crumbs all over the floor. Crys-
tal was just here yesterday. It was her last time
before we move.

MAGS: [*At her easel.*] God, I can hardly wait! I can't
believe you're finally letting me do you.

FANNY: "*Do*" us?...What *are* you talking about?

GARDNER: [*Reaching for the Saltines.*] Hey, Mags, could
I have a couple of those?

MAGS: [*Tosses him the box.*] Sure! [*To* FANNY.] Your portrait.

GARDNER: Thanks. [*He starts munching on a handful.*]

FANNY: You're planning to paint our portrait now? While
we're trying to move?

GARDNER: [*Sputtering Saltines.*] Mmmmm, I'd forgotten
just how delicious Saltines are!

MAGS: It's a perfect opportunity. There'll be no distrac-
tions; you'll be completely at my mercy. Also, you
promised.

FANNY: I did?

167

MAGS: Yes, you did.

FANNY: Well, I must have been off my rocker.

MAGS: No, you said, "You can paint us, you can dip us in concrete, you can do anything you want with us, just so long as you help us get out of here!"

GARDNER: [*Offering the box of Saltines to* FANNY.] You really ought to try some of these, Fan, they're absolutely delicious!

FANNY: [*Taking a few.*] Why, thank you.

MAGS: I figure we'll pack in the morning and you'll pose in the afternoons. It'll be a nice diversion.

FANNY: These *are* good!

GARDNER: Here, dig in...take some more.

MAGS: I have some wonderful news...amazing news! I wanted to wait 'til I got here to tell you.

[*They eat their Saltines, passing the box back and forth as* MAGS *speaks.*]

MAGS: You'll die! Just fall over into the packing cartons and die! Are you ready?...BRACE YOUR-SELVES....OK, HERE GOES....I'm being given a one woman show at one of the most important galleries in New York this fall. Me, Margaret Church, exhibited at Castelli's, 420 West Broadway.... Can you believe it?!...MY PORTRAITS HANGING IN THE SAME ROOMS THAT HAVE SHOWN RAUSCHENBERG, JOHNS, WARHOL, KELLY, LICHTENSTEIN, STELLA, SERRA, ALL THE HEAVIES....It's incredible, beyond belief...I mean, at my age....Do you know how good you have to be to get in there? It's a miracle...an honest-to-God, star-spangled miracle!

[*Pause.*]

FANNY: [*Mouth full.*] Oh, darling, that's wonderful. We're so happy for you!

GARDNER: [*His mouth full*] No one deserves it more, no one deserves it more!

MAGS: Through some fluke, some of Castelli's people showed up at our last faculty show at Pratt and were knocked out....

FANNY: [*Reaching for the box of Saltines.*] More, more...

MAGS: They said they hadn't seen anyone handle light like me since the French Impressionists. They said I was this weird blend of Pierre Bonnard, Mary Cassat and David Hockney....

GARDNER: [*Swallowing his own mouthful.*] I told you they were good.

MAGS: Also, no one's doing portraits these days. They're considered passé. I'm so out of it, I'm in.

GARDNER: Well, you're loaded with talent and always have been.

FANNY: She gets it all from Mama, you know. Her miniature of Henry James is still one of the main attractions at the Atheneum. Of course no woman of breeding could be a professional artist in her day. It simply wasn't done. But talk about talent...that woman had talent to burn!

MAGS: I want to do one of you for the show.

FANNY: Oh, do Daddy, he's the famous one.

MAGS: No, I want to do you both. I've always wanted to do you and now I've finally got a good excuse.

FANNY: It's high time somebody painted Daddy again! I'm sick to death of that dreadful portrait of him in the National Gallery they keep reproducing. He looks like an undertaker!

GARDNER: Well, I think you should just do Mum. She's never looked handsomer.

FANNY: Oh, come on, I'm a perfect fright and you know it.

MAGS: I want to do you both. Side by side. In this room. Something really classy. You look so great. Mum with her crazy hats and everything and you with that face. If I could just get you to hold still long enough and actually pose.

GARDNER: [*Walking around, distracted*] Where are those papers I just had? God damnit, Fanny....

MAGS: I have the feeling it's either now or never.

GARDNER: I can't hold on to anything around here. [*He exits to his study.*]

MAGS: I've always wanted to do you. It would be such a challenge.

FANNY: [*Pulling* MAGS *next to her onto the sofa.*] I'm so glad you're finally here, Mags. I'm very worried about Daddy.

MAGS: Mummy, please. I just got here.

FANNY: He's getting quite gaga.

MAGS: Mummy!...

FANNY: You haven't seen him in almost a year. Two weeks ago he walked through the front door of the Codman's house, kissed Emily on the cheek and settled down in the maid's room, thinking he was home!

MAGS: Oh, come on, you're exaggerating.

FANNY: He's as mad as a hatter and getting worse every day! It's this damned new book of his. He works on it around the clock. I've read some of it, and it doesn't make one word of sense, it's all at sixes and sevens....

GARDNER: [*Poking his head back in the room, spies some of his papers on a table and grabs them.*] Ahhh, here they are.

[*He exits.*]

FANNY: [*Voice lowered.*] Ever since this dry spell with his poetry, he's been frantic, absolutely...frantic!

MAGS: I hate it when you do this.

FANNY: I'm just trying to get you to face the facts around here.

MAGS: There's nothing wrong with him! He's just as sane as the next man. Even saner, if you ask me.

FANNY: You know what he's doing now? You couldn't guess in a million years!...He's writing criticism! Daddy! [*She laughs.*] Can you believe it? The man doesn't have one analytic bone in his body. His mind is a complete jumble and always has been!

[*There's a loud crash from* GARDNER's *study.*]

GARDNER: [*Offstage.*] SHIT!

MAGS: He's abstracted....That's the way he is.

FANNY: He doesn't spend any time with me anymore. He just holes up in that filthy study with Toots. God, I hate that bird! Though actually they're quite cunning together. Daddy's teaching him Grey's Elegy. You ought to see them in there, Toots perched on top of Daddy's head, spouting out verse after verse...Daddy, tap-tap-tapping away on his typewriter. They're quite a pair.

GARDNER: [*Pokes his head back in.*] Have you seen that Stevens' poem I was reading before?

FANNY: [*Long suffering.*] NO, I HAVEN'T SEEN THAT STEVENS' POEM YOU WERE READING BEFORE!.... Things are getting very tight around here, in case you haven't noticed. Daddy's last Pulitzer didn't even cover our real estate tax, and now that he's too doddery to give readings anymore, that income is gone.... [*Suddenly handing* MAGS *the sugar bowl she'd been wrapping.*] Mags, *do* take this sugar bowl. You can use it to serve tea to your students at that wretched art school of yours....

MAGS: It's called Pratt! The Pratt Institute.

FANNY: Pratt, Splatt, whatever...

MAGS: And I don't serve tea to my students, I teach them how to paint.

FANNY: Well, I'm sure none of them has ever seen a sugar bowl as handsome as this before.

GARDNER: [*Reappearing again.*] You're sure you haven't seen it?...

FANNY: [*Loud and angry.*] YES, I'M SURE I HAVEN'T SEEN IT! I JUST TOLD YOU I HAVEN'T SEEN IT!

GARDNER: [*Retreating.*] Right you are, right you are. [*He exits.*]

FANNY: God!
[*Silence.*]

MAGS: What do you have to yell at him like that for?

FANNY: Because the poor thing's as deaf as an adder! [MAGS *sighs deeply; silence.*]

FANNY: [*Suddenly exuberant, leads her over to a lamp.*] Come, I want to show you something.

MAGS: [*Looking at it.*] What is it?

FANNY: Something I made. [MAGS *is about to turn it on.*]WAIT, DON'T TURN IT ON YET! It's got to be dark to get the full effect. [*She rushes to the windows and pulls down the shades.*]

MAGS: What *are* you doing?...

FANNY: Hold your horses a minute. You'll see.... [*As the room gets darker and darker.*] Poor me, you wouldn't believe the lengths I go to to amuse myself these days....

MAGS: [*Touching the lamp shade.*] What is this? It looks like a scene of some sort.

FANNY: It's an invention I made...a kind of magic lantern.

MAGS: Gee...it's amazing....

FANNY: What I did was buy an old engraving of the Grand Canal....

MAGS: You *made* this?

FANNY: ...and then color it in with crayons. Next, I got out my sewing scissors and cut out all the street lamps and windows...anything that light would shine through. Then I pasted it over a plain lampshade, put the shade on this old horror of a lamp, turned on the switch and... [*She turns it on.*] VOILÀ ...VENICE TWINKLING AT DUSK! It's quite effective, don't you think?...

MAGS: [*Walking around it.*] Jeeez...

FANNY: And see, I poked out all the little lights on the gondolas with a straight pin.

MAGS: Where on earth did you get the idea?

FANNY: Well you know, idle minds...

[*FANNY spins the shade, making the lights whirl.*]

MAGS: It's really amazing. I mean, you could sell this in a store!

GARDNER: [*Enters.*] HERE IT IS. IT WAS RIGHT ON TOP OF MY DESK THE WHOLE TIME. [*He crashes into a table.*] OOOOOWWWWW!

FANNY: LOOK OUT, LOOK OUT!

MAGS: [*Rushes over to him.*] Oh, Daddy, are you all right?

FANNY: WATCH WHERE YOU'RE GOING, WATCH WHERE YOU'RE GOING!

GARDNER: [*Hopping up and down on one leg.*] GOD
DAMNIT!...I HIT MY SHIN.

FANNY: I was just showing Mags my lamp....

GARDNER: [*Limping over to it.*] Oh, yes, isn't that something? Mum is awfully clever with that kind of
thing....It was all her idea. Buying the engraving,
coloring it in, cutting out all those little dots.

FANNY: Not "dots"...lights and windows, lights and
windows!

GARDNER: Right, right...lights and windows.

FANNY: Well, we'd better get some light back in here
before someone breaks their neck. [*She zaps the
shades back up.*]

GARDNER: [*Puts his arm around* MAGS.] Gee, it's good to
have you back.

MAGS: It's good to be back.

GARDNER: And I like that new red hair of yours. It's
very becoming.

MAGS: But I told you, I hardly touched it....

GARDNER: Well, something's different. You've got a glow.
So...how do you want us to pose for this grand portrait of yours?...[*He poses self-consciously.*]

MAGS: Oh, Daddy, setting up a portrait takes a lot of
time and thought. You've got to figure out the background, the lighting, what to wear, the sort of mood
you want to...

FANNY: OOOOH, LET'S DRESS UP, LET'S DRESS UP!
[*She grabs a packing blanket, drapes it around herself and links arms with* GARDNER, *striking an elegant
pose.*] This *is* going to be fun. She was absolutely
right! Come on, Gar, look distinguished!

MAGS: Mummy, please, it's not a game!

FANNY: [*More and more excited.*] You still have your
tuxedo, don't you? And I'll wear my marvelous long
black dress that makes me look like that fascinating
woman in the Sargent painting! [*She strikes the famous profile pose.*]

MAGS: MUMMY?!...

FANNY: I'm sorry, we'll behave, just tell us what to do.

[*They settle down next to each other.*]

GARDNER: That's right, you're the boss.

FANNY: Yes, you're the boss.

MAGS: But I'm not ready yet; I haven't set anything up.

FANNY: Relax, darling, we just want to get the hang of it....

[*They stare straight ahead, trying to look like suitable subjects, but they can't hold still. They keep making faces, lifting an eyebrow, wriggling a nose, twitching a lip. Nothing big and grotesque, just flickering changes; a half-smile here, a self-important frown there. They steal glances at each other every so often.*]

GARDNER: How am I doing, Fan?

FANNY: Brilliantly, absolutely brilliantly!

MAGS: But you're making faces.

FANNY: *I'm* not making faces. [*Turning to* GARDNER *and making a face.*] Are *you* making faces, Gar?

GARDNER: [*Instantly making one.*] Certainly not! I'm the picture of restraint!

[*Without meaning to, they get sillier and sillier. They start giggling, then laughing.*]

MAGS: [*Can't help but join in.*] You two are impossible...completely impossible! I was crazy to think I could ever pull this off! [*Laughing away.*] Look at you...just...look at you!

BLACKOUT

Scene 2

Two days later, around five in the afternoon. Half of the Church household has been dragged into the living room for packing. Overflowing cartons are everywhere. They're filled with pots and pans, dishes and glasses, and the entire contents of two linen closets. MAGS *has placed a stepladder under one of the windows. A pile of tablecloths and curtains is flung beneath it. Two side chairs are in readiness for the eventual pose.*

MAGS: [*Has just pulled a large crimson tablecloth out of a carton. She unfurls it with one shimmering toss.*] PERFECT...PERFECT!...

FANNY: [*Seated on the sofa, clutches an old pair of galoshes to her chest.*] Look at these old horrors; half the rubber is rotted away and the fasteners are falling to pieces....GARDNER?...OH, GARRRRRRRRRRDNERRRRR?...

MAGS: [*Rippling out the tablecloth with shorter snapping motions.*] Have you ever seen such a color?....

FANNY: I'VE FOUND YOUR OLD SLEDDING GALOSHES IN WITH THE POTS AND PANS. DO YOU STILL WANT THEM?

MAGS: It's like something out of a Rubens!... [*She slings it over a chair and then sits on a footstool to finish the Sara Lee banana cake she started. As she eats, she looks at the tablecloth making happy grunting sounds.*]

FANNY: [*Lovingly puts the galoshes on over her shoes and wiggles her feet.*] God, these bring back memories! There were real snow storms in the old days. Not these pathetic little two inch droppings we have now. After a particularly heavy one, Daddy and I used to go sledding on the Common. This was way before you were born....God, it was a hundred years ago!...Daddy would stop writing early, put on these galoshes and come looking for me, jingling the fasteners like castanets. It was a kind of mating call, almost.... [*She jingles them.*] The Common was always deserted after a storm; we had the whole place to ourselves. It was so romantic....We'd haul the sled up Beacon Street, stop under the State House, and aim it straight down to the Park Street Church, which was much further away in those days. ...Then Daddy would lie down on the sled, I'd lower myself on top of him, we'd rock back and forth a few times to gain momentum and then... WHOOOOOOOOOSSSSSSSHHHHH...down we'd plunge like a pair of eagles locked in a spasm of lovemaking. God, it was wonderful!...The city whizzing past us at ninety miles an hour...the cold...the darkness...Daddy's hair in my mouth...GAR...REMEMBER HOW WE USED TO GO SLEDDING IN THE OLD DAYS?...Sometimes he'd lie on top of me. That was fun. I liked that even more. [*In her foghorn voice.*] GARRRRRRRRRD-NERRRRR?...

MAGS: Didn't he say he was going out this afternoon?

FANNY: Why, so he did! I completely forgot. [*She takes off the galoshes.*] I'm getting just as bad as him. [*She drops them into a different carton—wistful.*] Gar's galoshes, Cotuit.

[*A pause.*]

MAGS: [*Picks up the tablecloth again; holds it high over her head.*] Isn't this fabulous?... [*She then wraps FANNY in it.*] It's the perfect backdrop. Look what it does to your skin.

FANNY: Mags, what *are* you doing?

MAGS: It makes you glow like a pomegranate.... [*She whips it off her.*] Now all I need is a hammer and nails.... [*She finds them.*] YES! [*She climbs up the stepladder and starts hammering a corner of the cloth into the moulding of one of the windows.*] This is going to look so great!...I've never seen such color!

FANNY: Darling, what is going on?...

MAGS: Rembrandt, eat your heart out! You seventeenth-century Dutch has-been, you. [*She hammers more furiously.*]

FANNY: MARGARET, THIS IS NOT A CONSTRUC-TION SITE....PLEASE...STOP IT....YOOHOOO-OO...DO YOU HEAR ME?...

[GARDNER *suddenly appears, dressed in a raincoat.*]

GARDNER: YES, DEAR,	FANNY: [*To* MAGS.]
HERE I AM. I JUST	YOU'RE GOING TO
STEPPED OUT FOR	RUIN THE WALLS
A WALK DOWN	TO SAY NOTHING
CHESTNUT STREET.	OF MAMA'S BEST
BEAUTIFUL	TABLECLOTH....
AFTERNOON,	MAGS, DO YOU
ABSOLUTELY	HEAR ME?...YOO-

BEAUTIFUL!

GARDNER: WHY, THAT LOOKS VERY NICE, MAGS, very nice indeed....

HOO!...

FANNY: DARLING, I MUST INSIST you stop that dreadful...

MAGS: [*Steps down; stands back and looks at it.*] That's it. That's IT!

FANNY: [*To* GARDNER, worried.] Where have *you* been? [MAGS *kisses her fingers at the backdrop and settles back into her banana cake.*]

GARDNER: [*To* FANNY.] You'll never guess who I ran into on Chestnut Street...Pate Baldwin! [*He takes his coat off and drops it on the floor. He then sits in one of the posing chairs.*]

MAGS: [*Mouth full of cake.*] Oh, Daddy, I'm nowhere near ready for you yet.

FANNY: [*Picks up his coat and hands it to him.*] Darling, coats do *not* go on the floor.

GARDNER: [*Rises, but forgets where he's supposed to go.*] He was in terrible shape. I hardly recognized him. Well, it's the Parkinson's disease....

FANNY: You mean, Hodgkin's disease....

GARDNER: Hodgkin's disease?...

MAGS: [*Leaves her cake and returns to the tablecloth.*] Now to figure out exactly how to use this gorgeous light....

FANNY: Yes, Pate has Hodgkin's disease, not Parkinson's disease. Sammy Bishop has Parkinson's disease. In the closet...your coat goes...in the closet!

GARDNER: You're absolutely right! Pate has Hodgkin's disease. [*He stands motionless, the coat over his arm.*]

FANNY: ...and Goat Davis has Addison's disease.

GARDNER: I always get them confused.

FANNY: [*Pointing towards the closet.*] That way.... [GARDNER *exits to the closet;* FANNY *calls after him.*] Grace Phelps has it too, I think. Or, it might be Hodgkin's, like Pate. I can't remember.

GARDNER: [*Returns with a hanger.*] Doesn't the Goat have Parkinson's disease?

FANNY: No, that's Sammy Bishop.

TINA HOWE

GARDNER: God, I haven't seen the Goat in ages! [*The coat still over his arm, he hands* FANNY *the hanger.*]

FANNY: He hasn't been well.

GARDNER: Didn't Heppy...*die*?!

FANNY: What are you giving me this for?...Oh, Heppy's been dead for years. She died on the same day as Luster Bright, don't you remember?

GARDNER: I always liked her.

FANNY: [*Gives him back the hanger.*] Here, I don't want this.

GARDNER: She was awfully attractive.

FANNY: Who?

GARDNER: Heppy!

FANNY: Oh, yes, Heppy had real charm.

MAGS: [*Keeps adjusting the tablecloth.*] Better ...better...

GARDNER: ...which is something the Goat is short on, if you ask me. He has Hodgkin's disease, doesn't he? [*Puts his raincoat back on and sits down.*]

FANNY: Darling, what *are* you doing? I thought you wanted to hang up your coat!

GARDNER: [*After a pause.*] OH, YES, THAT'S RIGHT! [*He goes back to the closet; a pause.*]

FANNY: Where were we?

GARDNER: [*Returns with yet another hanger.*] Let's see....

FANNY: [*Takes both hangers from him.*] FOR GOD'S SAKE, GAR, PAY ATTENTION!

GARDNER: It was something about the Goat....

FANNY: [*Takes the coat from* GARDNER.] HERE, LET ME DO IT!... [*Under her breath to* MAGS.] See what I mean about him? You don't know the half of it! [She hangs it up in the closet.] ...Not the half.

MAGS: [*Still tinkering with the backdrop.*] Almost...almost...

GARDNER: [*Sitting back down in one of the posing chairs.*] Oh, Fan, did I tell you, I ran into Pate Baldwin just now. I'm afraid he's not long for this world.

FANNY: [*Returning.*] Well, it's that Hodgkin's disease.... [*She sits on the posing chair next to him.*]

GARDNER: God, I'd hate to see him go. He's one of the

178

great editors of our times. I couldn't have done it without him. He gave me everything, everything!

MAGS: [*Makes a final adjustment.*] Yes, that's it! [*She stands back and gazes at them.*] You look wonderful!...

FANNY: Isn't it getting to be... [*She taps at an imaginary watch on her wrist and drains an imaginary glass.*] *cocktail time*?!

GARDNER: [*Looks at his watch.*] On the button, on the button! [*He rises.*]

FANNY: I'll have the usual, please. Do join us, Mags! Daddy bought some Dubonnet especially for you!

MAGS: Hey. I was just getting some ideas.

GARDNER: [*To* MAGS, *as he exits for the bar.*] How about a little...*Dubonnet* to wet your whistle?

FANNY: Oh, Mags, it's like old times having you back with us like this!

GARDNER: [*Offstage.*] THE USUAL FOR YOU, FAN?

FANNY: I wish we saw more of you....PLEASE! ...Isn't he darling? Have you ever known anyone more darling than Daddy?...

GARDNER: [*Offstage. Hums Jolson's "You Made Me Love You."*] MAGS, HOW ABOUT YOU?...A LITTLE ...DUBONNET?...

FANNY: Oh, *do* join us!   MAGS: [*To* GARDNER.] No, nothing, thanks

FANNY: Well, what do you think of your aged parents picking up and moving to Cotuit year round? Pretty crazy, eh what?...Nothing but the gulls, oysters and us!

GARDNER: [*Returns with* FANNY's *drink.*] Here you go....

FANNY: Why thank you, Gar. [*To* MAGS.] You sure you won't join us?

GARDNER: [*Lifts his glass towards* FANNY *and* MAGS.] Cheers!

[GARDNER *and* FANNY *take that first life-saving gulp.*]

FANNY: Aaaaahhhhh!   GARDNER: Hits the spot, hits the spot!

MAGS: Well, I certainly can't do you like that!

FANNY: Why not? I think we look very...*comme il faut!*

[*She slouches into a rummy pose;* GARDNER *joins her.*]
WAIT... I'VE GOT IT! I'VE GOT IT!
[*She whispers excitedly to* GARDNER.]

MAGS: Come on, let's not start this again!

GARDNER: What's that?...Oh, yes...yes, yes...I know the one you mean. Yes, right, right...of course.
[*A pause.*]

FANNY: How's...*this?!*... [FANNY *grabs a large serving fork and they fly into an imitation of Grant Wood's* American Gothic.]

MAGS: ...and I wonder why it's taken me all these years to get you to pose for me. You just don't take me seriously! Poor old Mags and her ridiculous portraits...

FANNY: Oh, darling, your portraits aren't *ridiculous*! They may not be all that one *hopes* for, but they're certainly not...

MAGS: Remember how you behaved at my first group show in Soho?...Oh, come on, you remember. It was a real circus! Think back....It was about six years ago....Daddy had just been awarded some presidential medal of achievement and you insisted he wear it around his neck on a bright red ribbon, and you wore this...*huge* feathered hat to match! I'll never forget it! It was the size of a giant pizza with twenty-inch red turkey feathers shooting straight up into the air....Oh, come on, you remember, don't you?...

FANNY: [*Leaping to her feet.*] HOLD EVERYTHING! THIS IS IT! THIS IS REALLY IT! Forgive me for interrupting, Mags darling, it'll just take a minute.
[*She whispers excitedly to* GARDNER.]

MAGS: I had about eight portraits in the show, mostly of friends of mine, except for this old one I'd done of Mrs. Crowninshield.

GARDNER: All right, all right...let's give it a whirl.
[*A pause; then they mime Michelangelo's* Pietà *with* GARDNER *lying across* FANNY's *lap as the dead Christ.*]

MAGS: [*Depressed.*] The *Pietà*. Terrific!

FANNY: [*Jabbing* GARDNER *in the ribs.*] Hey, we're getting good at this.

GARDNER: Of course it would help if we didn't have all these modern clothes on.

MAGS: AS I WAS SAYING...

FANNY: Sorry, Mags...sorry...

[*Huffing and creaking with the physical exertion of it all, they return to their seats.*]

MAGS: ...As soon as you stepped foot in the gallery you spotted it and cried out, "MY GOD, WHAT'S MILLICENT CROWNINSHIELD DOING HERE?" Everyone looked up what with Daddy's clanking medal and your amazing hat which I was sure would take off and start flying around the room. A crowd gathered....Through some utter fluke, you latched on to *the* most important critic in the city, I mean...Mr. Modern Art himself, and you hauled him over to the painting, trumpeting out for all to hear, "THAT'S MILLICENT CROWNINSHIELD! I GREW UP WITH HER. SHE LIVES RIGHT DOWN THE STREET FROM US IN BOSTON. BUT IT'S A VERY POOR LIKENESS, IF YOU ASK ME! HER NOSE ISN'T NEARLY THAT LARGE AND SHE DOESN'T HAVE SOMETHING QUEER GROWING OUT OF HER CHIN! THE CROWNINSHIELDS ARE REALLY QUITE GOOD-LOOKING, STUFFY, BUT GOOD-LOOKING NONETHELESS!"

GARDNER: [*Suddenly jumps up, ablaze.*] WAIT, WAIT...IF IT'S MICHELANGELO YOU WANT ...I'm sorry, Mags....One more...just one more... please?

MAGS: Sure, why not? Be my guest.

GARDNER: *Fanny, prepare yourself!*
[*More whispering.*]

FANNY: But I think *you* should be God.

GARDNER: Me?...Really?

FANNY: Yes, it's much more appropriate.

GARDNER: Well, if you say so... [FANNY *and* GARDNER *ease down to the floor with some difficulty and lie on their sides,* FANNY *as Adam,* GARDNER *as God, their fingers inching closer and closer in the attitude of*

Michelangelo's The Creation. *Finally they touch.*]

MAGS: [*Cheers, whistles, applauds.*] THREE CHEERS
...VERY GOOD...NICELY DONE, NICELY
DONE! [*They hold the pose a moment more, flushed
with pleasure; then rise, dust themselves off and grope
back to their chairs.*] So, there we were....

FANNY: Yes, *do* go on!...

MAGS: ...huddled around Millicent Crowninshield, when
you whipped into your pocketbook and suddenly an-
nounced, "HOLD EVERYTHING! I'VE GOT A PHO-
TOGRAPH OF HER RIGHT HERE, THEN YOU
CAN SEE WHAT SHE REALLY LOOKS
LIKE!"...You then proceeded to crouch down to the
floor and dump everything out of your bag, and I
mean...*everything*!...leaking packets of sequins and
gummed stars, sea shells, odd pieces of fur, crochet
hooks, a monarch butterfly embedded in plastic, den-
tal floss, antique glass buttons, small jingling bells,
lace...I thought I'd die! Just sink to the floor and
quietly die!...You couldn't find it, you see. I mean,
you spent the rest of the afternoon on your hands
and knees crawling through this ocean of junk, muttering, "It's *got* to be here somewhere; I know I had
it with me!"...Then Daddy pulled me into the thick
of it all and said, "By the way, have you met our
daughter Mags yet? She's the one who did all these
pictures...paintings...portraits...whatever you call
them." [*She drops to her hands and knees and begins
crawling out of the room.*] By this time, Mum had
somehow crawled out of the gallery and was lost on
another floor. She began calling for me..."YOO-HOO,
MAGS...WHERE ARE YOU?...OH, MAGS, DAR-
LING...HELLO?...ARE YOU THERE?..." [*She
reenters and faces them.*] This was at my *first* show.

BLACKOUT

Scene 3

*Twenty-four hours later. The impact of the impending
move has struck with hurricane force.* FANNY *has lugged
all their clothing into the room and dumped it in various
cartons. There are coats, jackets, shoes, skirts, suits, hats,
sweaters, dresses, the works. She and* GARDNER *are seated
on the sofa, going through it all.*

FANNY: [*Wearing a different hat and dress, holds up a
ratty overcoat.*] What about this gruesome old thing?

GARDNER: [*Is wearing several sweaters and vests, a Ha-
waiian holiday shirt, and a variety of scarves and ties
around his neck. He holds up a pair of shoes.*]
God...remember these shoes? Pound gave them to
me when he came back from Italy. I remember it
vividly.

FANNY: *Do* let me give it to the thrift shop! [*She stuffs
the coat into the appropriate carton.*]

GARDNER: He bought them for me in Rome. Said he
couldn't resist; bought himself a pair too since we
both wore the same size. God, I miss him! [*Pause.*]
HEY, WHAT ARE YOU DOING WITH MY OVER-
COAT?!

FANNY: Darling, it's threadbare!

GARDNER: But that's my overcoat! [*He grabs it out of the
carton.*] I've been wearing it every day for the past
thirty-five years!

FANNY: That's just my point: It's had it.

GARDNER: [*Puts it on over everything else.*] There's nothing wrong with this coat!

FANNY: I trust you remember that the cottage is an
eighth the size of this place and you simply won't
have room for half this stuff! [*She holds up a sports
jacket.*] This dreary old jacket, for instance. You've
had it since Hector was a pup!

GARDNER: [*Grabs it and puts it on over his coat.*] Oh, no, you don't....

FANNY: ...and this God-awful hat...

GARDNER: Let me see that.

[*He stands next to her and they fall into a lovely tableau.*]

MAGS: [*Suddenly pops out from beind a wardrobe carton with a flash camera and takes a picture of them.*] PERFECT!

FANNY: [*Hands flying to her face.*] GOOD GOD, WHAT WAS THAT?...

GARDNER: [*Hands flying to his heart.*] JESUS CHRIST, I'VE BEEN SHOT!

MAGS: [*Walks to the center of the room, advancing the film.*] That was terrific. See if you can do it again.

FANNY: What *are* you doing?...

GARDNER: [*Feeling his chest.*] Is there blood?

FANNY: I see lace everywhere....

MAGS: It's all right, I was just taking a picture of you. I often use a Polaroid at this stage.

FANNY: [*Rubbing her eyes.*] Really, Mags, you might have given us some warning!

MAGS: But that's the whole point: to catch you unawares!

GARDNER: [*Rubbing his eyes.*] It's the damndest thing.... I see lace everywhere.

FANNY: Yes, so do I....

GARDNER: It's rather nice, actually. It looks as if you're wearing a veil.

FANNY: I *am* wearing a veil!

[*The camera spits out the photograph.*]

MAGS: OH GOODY, HERE COMES THE PICTURE!

FANNY: [*Grabs the partially developed print out of her hands.*] Let me see, let me see....

GARDNER: Yes, let's have a look.

[*They have another quiet moment together looking at the photograph.*]

MAGS: [*Tiptoes away from them and takes another picture.*] YES!

FANNY: NOT AGAIN!   GARDNER: WHAT WAS
PLEASE, DARLING!   THAT?...WHAT
                                    HAPPENED?...

[*They stagger towards each other.*]

MAGS: I'm sorry, I just couldn't resist. You looked so...

FANNY: WHAT ARE YOU TRYING TO DO... *BLIND*
US?!

GARDNER: Really, Mags, enough is enough....

[GARDNER *and* FANNY *keep stumbling about kid-dingly.*]

FANNY: Are you still there, Gar?

GARDNER: Right as rain, right as rain!

MAGS: I'm sorry; I didn't mean to scare you. It's just a
photograph can show you things you weren't aware
of. Here, have a look.

[*She gives them to* FANNY.] Well, I'm going out to the
kitchen to get something to eat. Anybody want anything?

[*She exits.*]

FANNY: [*Looking at the photos, half-amused, half-hor-
rified.*] Oh, Gardner, have you ever?...

GARDNER: [*Looks at them and laughs.*] Good grief...

MAGS: [*Offstage; from the kitchen.*] IS IT ALL RIGHT
IF I TAKE THE REST OF THIS TAPIOCA FROM
LAST NIGHT?

FANNY: IT'S ALL RIGHT WITH ME. How about you,
Gar?

GARDNER: Sure, go right ahead. I've never been that
crazy about tapioca.

FANNY: What are you talking about, tapioca is one of
your favorites.

MAGS: [*Enters, slurping from a large bowl.*]
Mmmmmmmm...

FANNY: Really, Mags, I've never see anyone eat as much
as you.

MAGS: [*Takes the photos back.*] It's strange. I only do
this when I come home.

FANNY: What's the matter, don't I feed you enough?

GARDNER: Gee, it's hot in here!

[*Starts taking off his coat.*]

FANNY: God knows, you didn't eat anything as a child! I've never seen such a fussy eater. Gar, what *are* you doing?

GARDNER: Taking off some of these clothes. It's hotter than Tofit in here!

[*Shedding clothes to the floor.*]

MAGS: [*Looking at her photos.*] Yes, I like you looking at each other like that....

FANNY: [*To* GARDNER.] Please watch where you're dropping things; I'm trying to keep some order around here.

GARDNER: [*Picks up what he dropped, dropping even more in the process.*] Right, right....

MAGS: Now all I've got to do is figure out what you should wear.

FANNY: Well, I'm going to wear my long black dress, and you'd be a fool not to do Daddy in his tuxedo. He looks so distinguished in it, just like a banker!

MAGS: I haven't really decided yet.

FANNY: Just because you walk around looking like something the cat dragged in, doesn't mean Daddy and I want to, do we, Gar?

[GARDNER *is making a worse and worse tangle of his clothes.*]

FANNY: HELLO?...

GARDNER: [*Looks up at* FANNY.] Oh, yes, awfully attractive, awfully attractive!

FANNY: [*To* MAGS.] If you don't mind me saying so, I've never seen you looking so forlorn. You'll never catch a husband looking that way. Those peculiar clothes, that God-awful hair...really, Mags, it's very distressing!

MAGS: I don't think my hair's so bad, not that it's terrific or anything...

FANNY: Well, I don't see other girls walking around like you. I mean, girls from your background. What would Lyman Wigglesworth think if he saw you in the street?

MAGS: Lyman   Wigglesworth?!...Uuuuuughhhhhh! [*She shudders.*]

FANNY: All right then, that brilliant Cabot boy...what *is* his name?

GARDNER: Sammy.

FANNY: No, not Sammy....

GARDNER: Stephen ... Stanley ... Stuart ... Sheldon ... Sherlock...Sherlock! It's *Sherlock!*

MAGS: Spence!

FANNY: SPENCE, THAT'S IT! HIS NAME IS SPENCE!

GARDNER: THAT'S IT...SPENCE! SPENCE CABOT!

FANNY: Spence Cabot was first in his class at Harvard.

MAGS: Mum, he has no facial hair.

FANNY: He has his own law firm on Arlington Street.

MAGS: Spence Cabot has six fingers on his right hand!

FANNY: So, he isn't the best-looking thing in the world. Looks isn't everything. He can't help it if he has extra fingers. Have a little sympathy!

MAGS: But the extra one has this weird nail on it that looks like a talon....It's long and black and... [*She shudders.*]

FANNY: No one's perfect, darling. He has lovely hand-writing and an absolutely saintly mother. Also, he's as rich as Croesus! He's a lot more promising than some of those creatures you've dragged home. What was the name of that dreadful Frenchman who smelled like sweaty socks?...Jean Duke of Scripto?

MAGS: [*Laughing.*] Jean-Luc Zichot!

FANNY: ...and that peculiar little Oriental fellow with all the teeth! Really, Mags, he could have been put on display at the circus!

MAGS: Oh, yes, Tsu Chin. He was strange, but very sexy....

FANNY: [*Shudders.*] He had such tiny...feet! Really, Mags, you've got to bear down. You're not getting any younger. Before you know it, all the nice young men will be taken and then where will you be?...All by yourself in that grim little apartment of yours with those peculiar clothes and that bright red hair...

MAGS: MY HAIR IS NOT BRIGHT RED!

FANNY: I only want what's best for you, you know that.

You seem to go out of your way to look wanting. I don't understand it.... Gar, what *are* you putting your coat on for?... You look like some derelict out on the street. We don't wear coats in the house. [*She helps him out of it.*] That's the way.... I'll just put this in the carton along with everything else.... [*She drops it into the carton, then pauses.*] Isn't it about time for...*cocktails!*

GARDNER: What's that?

[FANNY *taps her wrist and mimes drinking.*]

GARDNER: [*Looks at his watch.*] Right you are, right you are! [*Exits to the bar.*] THE USUAL?...

FANNY: *Please!*

GARDNER: [*Offstage.*] HOW ABOUT SOMETHING FOR YOU, MAGS?

MAGS: SURE, WHY NOT?...LET 'ER RIP!

GARDNER: [*Offstage.*] WHAT'S THAT?...

FANNY: SHE SAID YES.   MAGS: I'LL HAVE SOME
SHE SAID YES!   DUBONNET!

GARDNER: [*Poking his head back in.*] How about a little Dubonnet?

FANNY: That's just what she said....She'd like some...Dubonnet!

GARDNER: [*Goes back to the bar and hums another Jolson tune.*] GEE, IT'S GREAT HAVING YOU BACK LIKE THIS, MAGS....IT'S JUST GREAT! [*More singing.*]

FANNY: [*Leaning closer to* MAGS.] You have such *potential*, darling! It breaks my heart to see how you've let yourself go. If Lyman Wigglesworth...

MAGS: Amazing as it may seem, I don't *care* about Lyman Wigglesworth!

FANNY: From what I've heard, he's quite a lady killer!

MAGS: But with whom?...Don't think I haven't heard about his fling with...Hopie Stonewall!

FANNY: [*Begins to laugh.*] Oh, God, let's not get started on Hopie Stonewall again...ten feet tall with spots on her neck.... [*To* GARDNER.] OH, DARLING, DO HURRY BACK! WE'RE TALKING ABOUT PATHETIC HOPIE STONEWALL!

MAGS: It's not so much her incredible height and spotted skin; it's those tiny pointed teeth and the size eleven shoes!

FANNY: I love it when you're like this!

[MAGS *starts clomping around the room making tiny pointed teeth nibbling sounds.*]

FANNY: GARDNER...YOU'RE MISSING EVERYTHING! [*Still laughing.*] Why is it Boston girls are always so...tall?

MAGS: Hopie Stonewall isn't a Boston girl; she's a giraffe. [*She prances around the room with an imaginary dwarf-sized Lyman.*] She's perfect for Lyman Wigglesworth!

GARDNER: [*Returns with* FANNY'S *drink, which he hands her.*] Now, where were we?...

FANNY: [*Trying not to laugh.*] HOPIE STONEWALL!...

GARDNER: Oh, yes, she's the very tall one, isn't she? [FANNIE *and* MAGS *burst into gales.*]

MAGS: The only hope for us..."Boston girls" is to get as far away from our kind as possible.

FANNY: She always asks after you, darling. She's very fond of you, you know.

MAGS: Please, I don't want to hear!

FANNY: Your old friends are *always* asking after you.

MAGS: It's not so much how creepy they all are, as how much they remind me of myself!

FANNY: But you're not "creepy," darling...just...shabby!

MAGS: I mean, give me a few more inches and some brown splotches here and there, and Hopie and I could be sisters!

FANNY: [*In a whisper to* GARDNER.] Don't you love it when Mags is like this? I could listen to her forever!

MAGS: I mean...look at me!

FANNY: [*Gasping.*] Don't stop, don't stop!

MAGS: Awkward...plain...I don't know how to dress, I don't know how to talk. When people find out Daddy's my father, they're always amazed...."Gardner Church is YOUR father?! Aw, come on, you're kidding?!"

FANNY: [*In a whisper.*] Isn't she divine?...

MAGS: Sometimes I don't even tell them. I pretend I grew up in the Midwest somewhere...farming people...we work with our hands.

GARDNER: [*To* MAGS.] Well, how about a little refill?...

MAGS: No, no more thanks.

[*Pause.*]

FANNY: What did you have to go and interrupt her for? She was just getting up a head of steam....

MAGS: [*Walking over to her easel.*] The great thing about being a portrait painter, you see, is it's the *other* guy that's exposed; you're safely hidden behind the canvas and easel. [*Standing behind it.*] You can be as plain as a pitchfork, as inarticulate as mud, but it doesn't matter because you're completely concealed: your body, your face, your intentions. Just as you make your most intimate move, throw open your soul...they stretch and yawn, remembering the dog has to be let out at five....To be so invisible while so enthralled...it takes your breath away!

GARDNER: Well put, Mags. Awfully well put!

MAGS: That's why I've always wanted to paint you, to see if I'm up to it. It's quite a risk. Remember what I went through as a child with my great masterpiece?...

FANNY: You painted a masterpiece when you were a child?...

MAGS: Well, it was a masterpiece to me.

FANNY: I had no idea you were precocious as a child. Gardner, do you remember Mags painting a masterpiece as a child?

MAGS: I didn't paint it. It was something I made!

FANNY: Well, this is all news to me! Gar, *do* get me another drink! I haven't had this much fun in years! [*She hands him her glass and reaches for* MAGS'.] Come on, darling, join me....

MAGS: No, no more, thanks. I don't really like the taste.

FANNY: Oh, come on, kick up your heels for once!

MAGS: No, nothing...really.

FANNY: Please? Pretty please?...To keep me company?!

MAGS: [*Hands* GARDNER *her glass.*] Oh, all right, what the hell...

FANNY: That's a good girl!

GARDNER: [*Exiting.*] Coming right up, coming right up!

FANNY: [*Yelling after him.*] DON'T GIVE ME TOO MUCH NOW. THE LAST ONE WAS AWFULLY STRONG...AND HURRY BACK SO YOU DON'T MISS ANYTHING!...Daddy's so cunning, I don't know what I'd do without him. If anything should happen to him, I'd just...

MAGS: Mummy, nothing's going to happen to him!...

FANNY: Well, wait 'til you're our age, it's no garden party. Now...where were we?...

MAGS: My first masterpiece...

FANNY: Oh, yes, but *do* wait 'til Daddy gets back so he can hear it too....YOO-HOO...GARRRRRRD-NERRRRRR?...ARE YOU COMING?...[*Silence.*] Go and check on him, will you?

GARDNER: [*Enters with both drinks. He's very shaken.*] I couldn't find the ice.

FANNY: Well, *finally!*

GARDNER: It just up and disappeared....[*Hands* FANNY *her drink.*] There you go

[FANNY *kisses her fingers and takes a hefty swig.*]

GARDNER: Mags.

[*He hands* MAGS *her drink.*]

MAGS: Thanks, Daddy.

GARDNER: Sorry about the ice.

MAGS: No problem, no problem.

[GARDNER *sits down; silence.*]

FANNY: [*To* MAGS.] Well, drink up, drink up! [MAGS *downs it in one gulp.*] GOOD GIRL!...Now, what's all this about a masterpiece?...

MAGS: I did it during that winter you sent me away from the dinner table. I was about nine years old.

FANNY: We sent you from the dinner table?

MAGS: I was banished for six months.

FANNY: You *were?*...How extraordinary!

MAGS: Yes, it *was* rather extraordinary!

FANNY: But why?

MAGS: Because I played with my food.

FANNY: You did?

MAGS: I used to squirt it out between my front teeth.

FANNY: Oh, I remember that! God, it used to drive me crazy, absolutely...crazy! [*Pause.*] "MARGARET, STOP THAT OOZING RIGHT THIS MINUTE, YOU ARE *NOT* A TUBE OF TOOTHPASTE!"

GARDNER: Oh, yes...

FANNY: It was perfectly disgusting!

GARDNER: I remember. She used to lean over her plate and squirt it out in long runny ribbons....

FANNY: That's enough, dear.

GARDNER: They were quite colorful, actually; decorative almost. She made the most intricate designs. They looked rather like small, moist Oriental rugs....

FANNY: [*To* MAGS.] But why, darling? What on earth possessed you to do it?

MAGS: I couldn't swallow anything. My throat just closed up. I don't know, I must have been afraid of choking or something.

GARDNER: I remember one in particular. We'd had chicken fricassee and spinach....She made the most extraordinary...

FANNY: [*To* GARDNER.] WILL YOU PLEASE SHUT UP?! [*Pause.*] Mags, what *are* you talking about? You never choked in your entire life! This is the most distressing conversation I've ever had. Don't you think it's distressing, Gar?

GARDNER: Well, that's not quite the word I'd use.

FANNY: What word *would* you use, then?

GARDNER: I don't know right off the bat, I'd have to think about it.

FANNY: THEN, THINK ABOUT IT!
   [*Silence.*]

MAGS: I guess I was afraid of making a mess. I don't know; you were awfully strict about table manners. I was always afraid of losing control. What if I started to choke and began spitting up over everything?...

FANNY: All right, dear, that's enough.

MAGS: No, I was really terrified about making a mess;
you always got so mad whenever I spilled. If I just
got rid of everything in neat little curlicues beforehand, you see...

FANNY: I SAID: THAT'S ENOUGH!
[*Silence.*]

MAGS: *I* thought it was quite ingenious, but you didn't
see it that way. You finally sent me from the table
with, "When you're ready to eat like a human being,
you can come back and join us!"...So, it was off to
my room with a tray. But I couldn't seem to eat there
either. I mean, it was so strange settling down to
dinner in my *bedroom*....So I just flushed everything down the toilet and sat on my bed listening to
you: clinkity-clink, clatter clatter, slurp, slurp...but
that got pretty boring after a while, so I looked around
for something to do. It was wintertime, because I
noticed I'd left some crayons on top of my radiator
and they'd melted down into these beautiful shimmering globs, like spilled jello, trembling and puls-
ing.... [overlapping]

GARDNER: [*Eyes closed.*] "This luscious and impeccable
fruit of life

Falls, it appears, of its own weight to earth...."

MAGS: Naturally, I wanted to try it myself, so I grabbed
a red one and pressed it down against the hissing
lid. It oozed and bubbled like raspberry jam!

GARDNER: "When you were Eve, its acrid juice was sweet,
Untasted, in its heavenly, orchard air...."

MAGS: I mean, that radiator was really hot! It took incredible will power not to let go, but I held on, whispering, "Mags, if you let go of this crayon, you'll be
run over by a truck on Newberry Street, so help you
God!"...So I pressed down harder, my fingers steaming and blistering....

FANNY: I had no idea about any of this, did you, Gar?

MAGS: Once I'd melted one, I was hooked! I finished off
my entire supply in one night, mixing color over color
until my head swam!...The heat, the smell, the brilliance that sank and rose...I'd never felt such ex-

hilaration!...Every week I spent my allowance on crayons. I must have cleared out every box of Crayolas in the city!

GARDNER: [*Gazing at* MAGS.] You know, I don't think I've ever seen you looking prettier! You're awfully attractive when you get going!

FANNY: Why, what a lovely thing to say.

MAGS: AFTER THREE MONTHS THAT RADIATOR WAS...SPECTACULAR! I MEAN, IT LOOKED LIKE SOME COLOSSAL FRUIT CAKE, FIVE FEET TALL!...

FANNY: It sounds perfectly hideous.

MAGS: It was a knockout; shimmering with pinks and blues, lavenders and maroons, turquoise and golds, oranges and creams....For every color, I imagined a taste...YELLOW: lemon curls dipped in sugar...RED: glazed cherries laced with rum ...GREEN: tiny peppermint leaves veined with chocolate...PURPLE:...

FANNY: That's quite enough!

MAGS: And then the frosting...ahhhh, the frosting! A satiny mix of white and silver...I kept it hidden under blankets during the day....My huge...[*She starts laughing.*] looming...teetering sweet...

FANNY: I ASKED YOU TO STOP! GARDNER, WILL YOU PLEASE GET HER TO STOP!

GARDNER: See here, Mags, Mum asked you to...

MAGS: I was so...*hungry*...losing weight every week. I looked like a scarecrow what with the bags under my eyes and bits of crayon wrapper leaking out of my clothes. It's a wonder you didn't notice. But finally you came to my rescue...if you could call what happened a rescue. It was more like a rout!

FANNY: Darling... GARDNER: Now, look,
Please! young lady...

MAGS: The winter was almost over....It was very late at night....I must have been having a nightmare because suddenly you and Daddy were at my bed, shaking me....I quickly glanced towards the radiator to see if it was covered....*It wasn't*! It glittered and towered in the moonlight like some...gigantic Viennese pastry! You followed my gaze and saw it. Mummy screamed..."WHAT HAVE YOU GOT IN HERE?...MAGS, WHAT HAVE YOU BEEN DOING?"...She crept forward and touched it, and then jumped back. "IT'S FOOD!" she cried..."IT'S ALL THE FOOD SHE'S BEEN SPITTING OUT! OH, GARDNER, IT'S A MOUNTAIN OF ROTTING GARBAGE!"

FANNY: [*Softly.*] Yes...it's coming back...it's coming back....

MAGS: Daddy exited as usual; left the premises. He fainted, just keeled over onto the floor....

GARDNER: Gosh, I don't remember any of this....

MAGS: My heart stopped! I mean, I knew it was all over. My lovely creation didn't have a chance. Sure enough...out came the blow torch. Well, it couldn't have *really* been a blow torch, I mean, where would you have ever gotten a blow torch?...I just have this very strong memory of you standing over my bed, your hair streaming around your face, aiming this...flame thrower at my confection...my cake... my tart...my strudel...."IT'S GOT TO BE DE-STROYED IMMEDIATELY! THE THING'S ALIVE WITH VERMIN!...JUST LOOK AT IT!...IT'S PRACTICALLY CRAWLING ACROSS THE ROOM!"...Of course in a sense you were right. It *was* a monument of my cast-off dinners, only I hadn't built it with food....I found my own materials. I was languishing with hunger, but oh, dear Mother...I FOUND MY OWN MATERIALS!...

FANNY: Darling...*please*?!

MAGS: I tried to stop you, but you wouldn't lis-ten....OUT SHOT THE FLAME!...I remember these waves of wax rolling across the room and Daddy coming to, wondering what on earth was going on....Well, what did you know about my abili-ties?...You see, I had...I mean, I *have* abilities.... [*Struggling to say it.*] I have abilities. I have...strong abilities. I have...very strong abilities. They are very strong...very, very strong.... [*She rises and runs out of the room overcome as* FANNY *and* GARDNER *watch, speechless.*]

THE CURTAIN FALLS

ACT II

Scene 1

Three days later. Miracles have been accomplished. Almost all of the Churches' furniture has been moved out, and the cartons of dishes and clothing are gone. All that remains are odds and ends. MAGS's *tableau looms, impregnable.* FANNY *and* GARDNER *are dressed in their formal evening clothes, frozen in their pose. They hold absolutely still.* MAGS *stands at her easel, her hands covering her eyes.*

FANNY: All right, you can look now.

MAGS: [*Removes her hands.*] Yes! . . . I told you you could trust me on the pose.

FANNY: Well, thank God you let us dress up. It makes all the difference. Now we really look like something.

MAGS: [*Starts to sketch them.*] I'll say. . . .

[*A silence as she sketches.*]

GARDNER: [*Recites Yeats's "The Song of Wandering Aengus" in a wonderfully resonant voice as they pose.*]
"I went out to the hazel wood,
Because a fire was in my head,
And cut and peeled a hazel wand,
And hooked a berry to a thread,
And when white moths were on the
    wing,
And moth-like stars were flickering
    out,
I dropped the berry in a stream
And caught a little silver trout.

197

TINA HOWE

When I had laid it on the floor
I went to blow the fire aflame,
But something rustled on the floor,
And someone called me by my name:

It had become a glimmering girl
With apple blossoms in her hair
Who called me by my name and ran
And faded through the brightening air.

Though I am old with wandering
Through hollow lands and hilly lands,
I will find out where she has gone,
And kiss her lips and take her hands;
And walk among long dappled grass,
And pluck till time and times are
   done,
The silver apples of the moon,
The golden apples of the sun."

FANNY: That's lovely, dear. Just lovely. Is it one of yours?
GARDNER: No, no, it's Yeats. I'm using it in my book.
FANNY: Well, you recited it beautifully, but then you've
always recited beautifully. That's how you wooed me,
in case you've forgotten.... You must have memo-
rized every love poem in the English language! There
was no stopping you when you got going...your
Shakespeare, Byron, and Shelley...you were
shameless...*shameless*!
GARDNER: [*Eyes closed.*] "I will find out where she has
gone,
And kiss her lips and take her hands..."
FANNY: And then there was your own poetry to do battle
with; your sonnets and quatrains. When you got going
with them, there was nothing left of me! You could
have had your pick of any girl in Boston! Why you
chose me, I'll never understand. I had no looks to
speak of and nothing much in the brains department.... Well, what did you know about women and
the world?...What did any of us know?...[*Silence.*]

GOD, MAGS, HOW LONG ARE WE SUPPOSED
TO SIT LIKE THIS?...IT'S AGONY!

MAGS: [*Working away.*] You're doing fine...just fine....

FANNY: [*Breaking her pose.*] It's so...boring!

MAGS: Come on, don't move. You can have a break soon.

FANNY: I had no idea it would be so boring!

GARDNER: Gee, I'm enjoying it.

FANNY: You would!...

[*A pause.*]

GARDNER: [*Begins reciting more Yeats, almost singing it.*]

"He stood among a crowd at Drumahair;
His heart hung all upon a silken dress,
And he had known at last some tenderness,
Before earth made of him her sleepy care;
But when a man poured fish into a pile,
It seemed they raised their little silver heads..."

FANNY: Gar...PLEASE! [*She lurches out of her seat.*] God, I can't take this anymore!

MAGS: [*Keeps sketching* GARDNER.] I know it's tedious at first, but it gets easier....

FANNY: It's like a Chinese water torture!...[*Crosses to* MAGS *and looks at* GARDNER *posing.*] Oh, darling, you look marvelous, absolutely marvelous! Why don't you just do Daddy!?

MAGS: Because you look marvelous too. I want to do you both!

FANNY: Please!...I have one foot in the grave and you know it! Also, we're way behind in our packing. There's still one room left which everyone seems to have forgotten about!

GARDNER: Which one is that?

FANNY: You know perfectly well which one it is!

GARDNER: I do?...

FANNY: Yes, you do!

GARDNER: Well, it's news to me.

FANNY: I'll give you a hint. It's in...*that* direction. [*She points.*]

GARDNER: The dining room?

FANNY: No.

GARDNER: The bedroom?

FANNY: No.

GARDNER: Mags' room?

FANNY: No.

GARDNER: The kitchen?

FANNY: *Gar*?!...

GARDNER: The guest room?

FANNY: Your God-awful study!

GARDNER: Oh, shit!

FANNY: That's right, "Oh, shit!" It's books and papers up to the ceiling! If you ask me, we should just forget it's there and quietly tiptoe away....

GARDNER: My study!...

FANNY: Let the new owners dispose of everything....

GARDNER: [*Gets out of his posing chair.*] Now, just one minute....

FANNY: You never look at half the stuff in there!

GARDNER: I don't want you touching those books! They're mine!

FANNY: Darling, we're moving to a cottage the size of a handkerchief! Where, pray tell, is there room for all your books?

GARDNER: I don't know. We'll just have to make room!

MAGS: [*Sketching away.*] RATS!

FANNY: I don't know what we're doing fooling around with Mags like this when there's still so much to do....

GARDNER: [*Sits back down, overwhelmed.*] My study!...

FANNY: You can stay with her if you'd like, but one of us has got to tackle those books!

[*She exits to his study.*]

GARDNER: I'm not up to this.

MAGS: Oh, good, you're staying!

GARDNER: There's a lifetime of work in there....

MAGS: Don't worry, I'll help. Mum and I will be able to pack everything up in no time.

GARDNER: God....

MAGS: It won't be so bad....

GARDNER: I'm just not up to it.

MAGS: We'll all pitch in....

[GARDNER *sighs, speechless. A silence as* FANNY *comes staggering in with an arm load of books which she drops to the floor with a crash.*]

GARDNER: WHAT WAS   MAGS: GOOD GRIEF!
    THAT?!...

FANNY: [*Sheepish.*] Sorry, sorry....
    [*She exits for more.*]

GARDNER: I don't know if I can take this....

MAGS: Moving is awful...I know....

GARDNER: [*Settling back into his pose.*] Ever since Mum began tearing the house apart, I've been having these dreams....I'm a child again back at Sixteen Louisberg Square...and this stream of moving men is carrying furniture into our house...van after van of tables and chairs, sofas and love seats, desks and bureaus...rugs, bathtubs, mirrors, chiming clocks, pianos, iceboxes, china cabinets...but what's amazing is that all of it is familiar.... [FANNY *comes in with another load which she drops on the floor. She exits for more.*] No matter how many items appear, I've seen every one of them before. Since my mother is standing in the midst of it directing traffic, I ask her where it's all coming from, but she doesn't hear me because of the racket...so finally I just scream out..."WHERE IS ALL THIS FURNITURE COMING FROM?"...Just as a moving man is carrying Toots into the room, she looks at me and says, "Why, from the land of Skye!"...The next thing I know, *people* are being carried in along with it.... [FANNY *enters with her next load; drops it and exits.*] People I've never seen before are sitting around our dining-room table. A group of foreigners is going through my books, chattering in a language I've never heard before. A man is playing a Chopin polonaise on Aunt Alice's piano. Several children are taking baths in our tubs from Cotuit....

MAGS: It sounds marvelous.

GARDNER: Well, it isn't marvelous at all because all of these perfect strangers have taken over our things....

[FANNY *enters, hurls down another load and exits.*]

MAGS: How odd....

GARDNER: Well, it *is* odd, but then something even odder happens....

MAGS: [*Sketching away.*] Tell me, tell me!

GARDNER: Well, our beds are carried in. They're all made up with sheets and everything, but instead of all these strange people in them, *we're* in them!...

MAGS: What's so odd about that?...

GARDNER: Well, you and Mum are brought in, both sleeping like angels...Mum snoring away to beat the band....

MAGS: Yes...

[FANNY *enters with another load; lets it fall.*]

GARDNER: But there's no one in mine. It's completely empty, never even been slept in! It's as if I were dead or had never even existed.... [FANNY *exits.*] "HEY...WAIT UP!" I yell to the moving men..."THAT'S MY BED YOU'VE GOT THERE!" But they don't stop; they don't even acknowledge me...."HEY, COME BACK HERE...I WANT TO GET INTO MY BED!" I cry again and I start running after them...down the hall, through the dining room, past the library....Finally I catch up to them and hurl myself right into the center of the pillow. Just as I'm about to land, the bed suddenly vanishes and I go crashing down to the floor like some insect that's been hit by a fly swatter!

FANNY: [*Staggers in with her final load; drops it with a crash and then collapses in her posing chair.*] THAT'S IT FOR ME! I'M DEAD! [*Silence.*] Come on, Mags, how about you doing a little work around here.

MAGS: That's all I've been doing! This is the first free moment you've given me!

FANNY: You should see all the books in there...and papers! There are enough loose papers to sink a ship!

GARDNER: Why is it we're moving, again?...

FANNY: Because life is getting too complicated here.

GARDNER: [*Remembering.*] Oh, yes...

FANNY: And we can't afford it anymore.

GARDNER: That's right, that's right....

FANNY: We don't have the...*income* we used to!

GARDNER: Oh, yes...*income!*

FANNY: [*Assuming her pose again.*] Of course, we have our savings and various trust funds, but I wouldn't dream of touching those!

GARDNER: No, no, you must never dip into capital!

FANNY: I told Daddy I'd be perfectly happy to buy a gun and put a bullet through our heads so we could avoid all this, but he wouldn't hear of it!

MAGS: [*Sketching away.*] No, I shouldn't think so. [*Pause.*]

FANNY: I've always admired people who kill themselves when they get to our stage of life. Well, no one can touch my Uncle Edmond in that department....

MAGS: I know, I know....

FANNY: The day before his seventieth birthday he climbed to the top of the Old North Church and hurled himself facedown into Salem Street! They had to scrape him up with a spatula! God, he was a remarkable man...state senator, president of Harvard....

GARDNER: [*Rises and wanders over to his books.*] Well, I guess I'm going to have to do something about all of these....

FANNY: Come on, Mags, help Daddy! Why don't you start bringing in his papers....

[GARDNER *sits on the floor; picks up a book and soon is engrossed in it.* MAGS *keeps sketching, oblivious; silence.*]

FANNY: [*To* MAGS.] Darling?...HELLO?...God, you two are impossible! Just look at you...heads in the clouds! No one would ever know we've got to be out of here in two days. If it weren't for me, nothing would get done around here.... [*She starts stacking* GARDNER's *books into piles.*] There! That's all the maroon ones!

GARDNER: [*Looks up.*] What do you mean, *maroon* ones?!...

FANNY: All your books that are maroon are in *this* pile...and your books that are green in *that* pile!...I'm trying to bring some order into your life for once. This will make unpacking so much easier.

GARDNER: But, my dear Fanny, it's not the color of a book that distinguishes it, but what's *inside* it!

FANNY: This will be a great help, you'll see. Now what about this awful striped thing? [*She picks up a slim, aged volume.*] Can't it go?...

GARDNER: No!

FANNY: But it's as queer as Dick's hat band! There are no others like it.

GARDNER: Open it and read. Go on...open it!

FANNY: We'll get nowhere at this rate.

GARDNER: I said...READ!

FANNY: Really, Gar, I...

GARDNER: Read the dedication!

FANNY: [*Opens and reads.*] "To Gardner Church, you led the way. With gratitude and affection, Robert Frost."
[*She closes it and hands it to him.*]

GARDNER: It was published the same year as my *Salem Gardens*.

FANNY: [*Picking up a very worn book.*] Well, what about this dreadful thing? It's filthy. [*She blows off a cloud of dust.*]

GARDNER: Please...*please*?!

FANNY: [*Looking through it.*] It's all in French.

GARDNER: [*Snatching it away from her.*] André Malraux gave me that!...

FANNY: I'm just trying to help.

GARDNER: It's a first edition of Baudelaire's *Fleurs du Mal*.

FANNY: [*Giving it back.*] Well, pardon me for living!

GARDNER: Why do you have to drag everything in here in the first place?...

FANNY: Because there's no room in your study. You ought to see the mess in there!...WAKE UP, MAGS, ARE YOU GOING TO PITCH IN OR NOT?!...

GARDNER: I'm not up to this.

FANNY: Well, you'd better be unless you want to be left behind!

MAGS: [*Stops her sketching.*] All right, all right...I just hope you'll give me some more time later this evening.

FANNY: [*To* MAGS.] Since you're young and in the best shape, why don't you bring in the books and I'll cope with the papers. [*She exits to the study.*]

GARDNER: Now just a minute....

FANNY: [*Offstage.*] WE NEED A STEAM SHOVEL FOR THIS!

MAGS: OK, what do you want me to do?

GARDNER: Look, I don't want you messing around with my...

[FANNY *enters with an armful of papers which she drops into an empty carton.*]

GARDNER: HEY, WHAT'S GOING ON HERE?!...

FANNY: I'm packing up your papers. COME ON, MAGS, LET'S GET CRACKING!

[*She exits for more papers.*]

GARDNER: [*Plucks several papers out of the carton.*] What is this?...

MAGS: [*Exits into his study.*] GOOD LORD, WHAT HAVE YOU DONE IN HERE?!...

GARDNER: [*Reading.*] This is my manuscript.

[FANNY *enters with another batch which she tosses on top of the others.*]

GARDNER: What *are* you doing?!...

FANNY: Packing, darling...PACKING!

[*She exits for more.*]

GARDNER: SEE HERE, YOU CAN'T MANHANDLE MY THINGS THIS WAY! [MAGS *enters, staggering under a load of books which she sets down on the floor.*] I PACK MY MANUSCRIPT! I KNOW WHERE EVERYTHING IS!

FANNY: [*Offstage.*] IF IT WERE UP TO YOU, WE'D NEVER GET OUT OF HERE! WE'RE UNDER A TIME LIMIT, GARDNER. KITTY'S PICKING US UP IN TWO DAYS...TWO...DAYS!

[*She enters with a larger batch of papers and heads for the carton.*]

GARDNER: [*Grabbing* FANNY's *wrist.*] NOW, HOLD

IT!...JUST...HOLD IT RIGHT THERE!...

FANNY: OOOOOWWWWWWWW!

GARDNER: *I PACK MY THINGS!*...

FANNY: LET GO, YOU'RE HURTING ME!

GARDNER: THAT'S MY MANUSCRIPT! GIVE IT TO ME!

FANNY: [*Lifting the papers high over her head.*] I'M IN CHARGE OF THIS MOVE, GARDNER! WE'VE GOT TO GET CRACKING!

GARDNER: I said...GIVE IT TO ME!

MAGS: Come on, Mum, let him have it.

[*They struggle.*]

GARDNER: [*Finally wrenches the pages from her.*] LET...ME...HAVE IT!...THAT'S MORE LIKE IT!...

FANNY: [*Soft and weepy.*] You see what he's like?...I try and help with his packing and what does he do?...

GARDNER: [*Rescues the rest of his papers from the carton.*] YOU DON'T JUST THROW EVERYTHING INTO A BOX LIKE A PILE OF GARBAGE! THIS IS A BOOK, FANNY. SOMETHING I'VE BEEN WORKING ON FOR TWO YEARS!... [*Trying to assemble his papers, but only making things worse, dropping them all over the place.*] You show a little respect for my things....You don't just throw them around every which way....It's tricky trying to make sense of poetry; it's much easier to write the stuff...that is, if you've still got it in you.

MAGS: Here, let me help....[*Taking some of the papers.*]

GARDNER: Criticism is tough sledding. You can't just dash off a few images here, a few rhymes there....

MAGS: Do you have these pages numbered in any way?

FANNY: [*Returning to her posing chair.*] HA!

GARDNER: This is just the introduction.

MAGS: I don't see any numbers on these.

GARDNER: [*Exiting to his study.*] The important stuff is in my study....

FANNY: [*To MAGS.*] You don't know the half of it...*not the half*!...

GARDNER: [*Offstage; thumping around.*] HAVE YOU

SEEN THOSE YEATS POEMS I JUST HAD?...

MAGS: [*Reading over several pages.*] What is this?...It doesn't make sense. It's just fragments...pieces of poems.

FANNY: That's it, honey! That's his book. His great critical study! Now that he can't write his own poetry, he's trying to explain other people's. The only problem is, he can't get beyond typing them out. The poor lamb doesn't have the stamina to get beyond the opening stanzas, let alone trying to make sense of them.

GARDNER: [*Thundering back with more papers which keep falling.*] GOD DAMNIT, FANNY, WHAT DID YOU DO IN THERE? I CAN'T FIND ANYTHING!

FANNY: I just took the papers that were on your desk.

GARDNER: Well, the entire beginning is gone. [*He exits.*]

FANNY: I'M TRYING TO HELP YOU, DARLING!

GARDNER: [*Returns with another arm load.*] SEE THAT?...NO SIGN OF CHAPTER ONE OR TWO.... [*He flings it all down to the floor.*]

FANNY: Gardner...PLEASE?!

GARDNER: [*Kicking through the mess.*] I TURN MY BACK FOR ONE MINUTE AND WHAT HAPPENS?...MY ENTIRE STUDY IS TORN APART! [*He exits.*]

MAGS: Oh, Daddy...don't...please...Daddy...*please*?!

GARDNER: [*Returns with a new batch of papers which he tosses up into the air.*] THROWN OUT!...THE BEST PART IS THROWN OUT!...LOST.... [*He starts to exit again.*]

MAGS: [*Reads one of the fragments to steady herself.*] "I have known the inexorable sadness of pencils, Neat in their boxes, dolor of pad and paperweight, All the misery of manilla folders and mucilage..." They're beautiful...just beautiful.

GARDNER: [*Stops.*] Hey, what's that you've got there?

FANNY: It's your manuscript, darling. You see, it's right where you left it.

GARDNER: [*To* MAGS.] Read that again.

MAGS: "I have known the inexorable sadness of pencils,
   Neat in their boxes, dolor of pad and paperweight,
   All the misery of manilla folders and mucilage..."

GARDNER: Well, well, what do you know....

FANNY: [*Hands him several random papers.*] You see...no
   one lost anything. Everything's here, still intact.

GARDNER: [*Reads.*] "I knew a woman, lovely in her bones,
   When small birds sighed, she would sigh back at
      them;
   Ah, when she moved, she moved more ways than
      one:
   The shapes a bright container can contain!..."

FANNY: [*Hands him another.*] And...

GARDNER: [*Reads.*] Ahh...Frost...
   "Some say the world will end in fire,
   Some say ice.
   From what I've tasted of desire
   I hold with those who favor fire."

FANNY: [*Under her breath to* MAGS.] He can't give up
   the words. It's the best he can do. [*Handing him
   another.*] Here you go, here's more.

GARDNER:
   "Farm boys wild to couple
   With anything   with soft-wooded trees
   With mounds of earth   mounds
   Of pinestraw   will keep themselves off
   Animals by legends of their own..."

MAGS: [*Eyes shut.*] Oh, Daddy, I can't bear it...I...

FANNY: Of course no one will ever publish this.

GARDNER: Oh, here's a marvelous one. Listen to this!

   "There came a Wind like a Bugle—
   It quivered through the Grass
   And a Green Chill upon the Heat
   So ominous did pass
   We barred the Windows and the
      Doors
   As from an Emerald Ghost—
   The Doom's electric Moccasin..."
   SHIT, WHERE DID THE REST OF IT GO?...

208

FANNY: Well, don't ask *me*.

GARDNER: It just stopped in mid-air!

FANNY: Then go look for the original.

GARDNER: Good idea, good idea!
[*He exits to his study.*]

FANNY: [*To* MAGS.] He's incontinent now, too. He wets his pants, in case you haven't noticed. [*She starts laughing.*] You're not laughing. Don't you think it's funny? Daddy needs diapers....I don't know about you, but I could use a drink! GAR...WILL YOU GET ME A SPLASH WHILE YOU'RE OUT THERE?...

MAGS: STOP IT!

FANNY: It means we can't go out anymore. I mean, what would people say?...

MAGS: Stop it. Just stop it.

FANNY: My poet laureate can't hold it in! [*She laughs harder.*]

MAGS: That's enough...STOP IT...Mummy...I beg of you...*please stop it!*

GARDNER: [*Enters with a book and indeed a large stain has blossomed on his trousers. He plucks it away from his leg.*] Here we go...I found it....

FANNY: [*Pointing at it.*] See that? See?...He just did it again! [*Goes off into a shower of laughter.*]

MAGS: [*Looks, turns away.*] SHUT...UP!... [*Building to a howl.*] WILL YOU PLEASE JUST...SHUT...UP!

FANNY: [*To* GARDNER.] Hey, what about that drink?

GARDNER: Oh, yes...sorry, sorry...
[*He heads towards the bar.*]

FANNY: Never mind, I'll get it, I'll get it. [*She exits, convulsed; silence.*]

GARDNER: Well, where were we?...

MAGS: [*Near tears.*] Your poem.

GARDNER: Oh, yes...the Dickinson. [*He shuts his eyes, reciting from memory, holding the book against his chest.*]

"There came a Wind like a Bugle—
It quivered through the Grass
And a Green Chill upon the Heat
So ominous did pass

We barred the Windows and the Doors
As from an Emerald Ghost—"
[*Opens the book and starts riffling through it.*] Let's
see now, where's the rest?... [*He finally finds it.*]
Ahhh, here we go!...

FANNY: [*Reenters, drink in hand.*] I'm back! [*Takes one
look at* GARDNER *and bursts out laughing again.*]

MAGS: I don't believe you! How you can laugh at him?!...

FANNY: I'm sorry, I wish I could stop, but there's really
nothing else to do. Look at him...just...look at
him...!
[*This is all simultaneous as* MAGS *gets angrier and
angrier.*]

MAGS: It's so cruel....You're so...incredibly cruel to
him....I mean, YOUR DISDAIN REALLY TAKES
MY BREATH AWAY! YOU'RE IN A CLASS BY
YOURSELF WHEN IT COMES TO HUMILIA-
TION!...

GARDNER: [*Reading.*]
"The Doom's electric Moccasin
That very instant passed—
On a strange Mob of panting Trees
And Fences fled away
And Rivers where the Houses ran
Those looked that lived,—that Day—
The Bell within the steeple wild
The flying tidings told—
How much can come
And much can go,
And yet abide the World!"
[*He shuts the book with a bang, pauses and looks
around the room, confused.*] Now, where was I?...

FANNY: Safe and sound in the middle of the living room
with Mags and me.

GARDNER: But I was looking for something, wasn't I?...

FANNY: Your manuscript.

GARDNER: THAT'S RIGHT! MY MANUSCRIPT! My
manuscript!

FANNY: And here it is all over the floor. See, you're
standing on it.

GARDNER: [*Picks up a few pages and looks at them.*] Why, so I am....

FANNY: Now all we have to do is get it up off the floor and packed neatly into these cartons!

GARDNER: Yes, yes, that's right. Into the cartons.

FANNY: [*Kicks a carton over to him.*] Here, you use this one and I'll start over here.... [*She starts dropping papers into a carton nearby.*] BOMBS AWAY! ...Hey...this is fun!...

GARDNER: [*Picks up his own pile, lifts it high over his head and flings it down into the carton.*] BOMBS AWAY...This *is* fun!...

FANNY: I told you! The whole thing is to figure out a system!

GARDNER: I don't know what I'd do without you, Fan. I thought I'd lost everything.

FANNY: [*Makes dive-bomber noises and machine-gun explosions as she wheels more and more papers into the carton.*] TAKE THAT AND THAT AND THAT!...

GARDNER: [*Joins in the fun, outdoing her with dips, dives and blastings of his own.*] BLAM BLAM BLAM BLAM!...ZZZZZZZZRAAAAAAA FOOM!...BLATTY-DE-BLATTY-DE-BLATTY-DE-KABOOOOO-OOOM!...WHAAAAAAA...DA-DAT-DAT-DAT-DAT...WHEEEEEEEE AAAAAAAAAAAA...FO-OOOOO...

[*THEY get louder and louder as papers fly every which way.*]

FANNY: [*Mimes getting hit with a bomb.*] AEEEE-EEIIIIIIIIIIIII! YOU GOT ME RIGHT IN THE GIZ-ZARD! [*She collapses on the floor and starts going through death throes, having an absolute ball.*]

GARDNER: TAKE THAT AND THAT AND THAT AND THAT... [*A series of explosions follow.*]

MAGS: [*Furious.*] This is how you help him?...THIS IS HOW YOU PACK HIS THINGS?...

FANNY: I keep him company. I get involved...which is a hell of a lot more than you do!

MAGS: [*Wild with rage.*] BUT YOU'RE MAKING A

211

MOCKERY OF HIM.... YOU TREAT HIM LIKE A
CHILD OR SOME DIM-WITTED SERVING BOY.
HE'S JUST AN AMUSEMENT TO YOU!...

FANNY: [*Fatigue has finally overtaken her. She's calm,
almost serene.*]...and to you who see him once a year,
if that...What is he to *you*?...I mean, what do you
give him from yourself that costs you something?...Hmmmmmm?...[*Imitating her.*] "Oh, hi
Daddy, it's great to see you again. How have you
been?...Gee, I love your hair. It's gotten so
...*white*!"...What color do you expect it to get when
he's this age?...I mean, if you care so much how he
looks, why don't you come and see him once in a
while?...But oh, no...you have your paintings to
do and your shows to put on. You just come and see
us when the whim strikes. [*Imitating her.*] "Hey, you
know what would be really great?...To do a portrait
of you! I've always wanted to paint you, you're such
great subjects!"...*Paint* us?!...What about opening
your eyes and really *seeing* us?...Noticing what's
going on around here for a change! It's all over for
Daddy and me. This is it! "Finita la comme-
dia!"...All I'm trying to do is exit with a little flourish; have some fun....What's so terrible about
that?...It can get pretty grim around here, in case
you haven't noticed...Daddy, tap-tap-tapping out his
nonsense all day; me traipsing around to the thrift
shops trying to amuse myself...He never keeps me
company anymore; never takes me out anywhere....I'd put a bullet through my head in a minute, but then who'd look after him?...What do you
think we're moving to the cottage for?...So I can
watch him like a hawk and make sure he doesn't get
lost. Do you think that's anything to look forward
to?...Being Daddy's nursemaid out in the middle of
nowhere? I'd much rather stay here in Boston with
the few friends I have left, but you can't always do
what you want in this world! "L'homme propose, Dieu
dispose!"...If you want to paint us so badly, you
ought to paint us as we really are. There's your pic-

ture!... [*She points to* GARDNER *who's quietly playing with a paper glide.*] Daddy spread out on the floor with all his toys and me hovering over him to make sure he doesn't hurt himself! [*She goes over to him.*] YOO-HOO...GAR?...HELLO?...

GARDNER: [*Looks up at her.*] Oh, hi there, Fan. What's up?

FANNY: How's the packing coming?...

GARDNER: Packing?...

FANNY: Yes, you were packing your manuscript, remember? [*She lifts up a page and lets it fall into a carton.*]

GARDNER: Oh, yes....

FANNY: Here's your picture, Mags. Face over this way...turn your easel over here.... [*She lets a few more papers fall.*] Up, up...and away....

BLACKOUT

Scene 2

The last day. All the books and boxes are gone. The room is completely empty except for MAGS's *backdrop. Late afternoon light dapples the walls; it changes from pale peach to deeper violet. The finished portrait sits on the easel, covered with a cloth.* MAGS *is taking down the backdrop.*

FANNY: [*Offstage; to* GARDNER.] DON'T FORGET TOOTS!

GARDNER: [*Offstage; from another part of the house.*] WHAT'S THAT?...

FANNY: [*Offstage.*] I SAID: DON'T FORGET TOOTS! HIS CAGE IS SITTING IN THE MIDDLE OF YOUR STUDY! [*Silence.*]

FANNY: [*Offstage.*] HELLO?...ARE YOU

GARDNER: [*Offstage.*] I'LL BE RIGHT WITH

213

THERE?...   YOU; I'M JUST
GETTING TOOTS!

GARDNER: [*Offstage.*] WHAT'S THAT? I CAN'T HEAR
YOU?

FANNY: [*Offstage.*] I'M GOING THROUGH THE
ROOMS ONE MORE TIME TO MAKE SURE WE
DIDN'T FORGET ANYTHING....KITTY'S PICK-
ING US UP IN FIFTEEN MINUTES, SO PLEASE
BE READY....SHE'S DROPPING MAGS OFF AT
THE STATION AND THEN IT'S OUT TO ROUTE
3 AND THE CAPE HIGHWAY....

GARDNER: [*Enters, carrying* TOOTS *in his cage.*] Well, this
is it. The big moment has finally come, eh what,
Toots? [*He sees* MAGS.] Oh, hi there, Mags, I didn't
see you....

MAGS: Oh, hi, Daddy, I'm just taking this down.... [*She
does and walks over to* TOOTS.] Oh, Toots, I'll miss
you. [*She makes little chattering noises into his cage.*]

GARDNER: Come on, recite a little Grey's Elegy for Mags
before we go.

MAGS: Yes, Mum said he was really good at it now.

GARDNER: Well, the whole thing is to keep at it every
day. [*Slowly to* TOOTS.]

"The curfew tolls the knell of parting day,
The lowing herd wind slowly o'er the lea..."
Come on, show Mags your stuff!
[*Slower.*]
"The curfew tolls the knell of parting day,
The lowing herd wind slowly o'er the lea..."
[*Silence;* GARDNER *makes little chattering sounds.*]
Come on, Toots, old boy....

MAGS: How does it go?

GARDNER: [*To* MAGS.] "The curfew tolls the knell of
parting day,
The lowing herd wind slowly o'er the lea..."

MAGS: [*Slowly to* TOOTS.] "The curfew tolls for you and
me,
As quietly the herd winds down..."

GARDNER: No, no, it's, "The curfew tolls the knell of parting *day*..."!

MAGS: [*Repeating after him.*] "The curfew tolls the knell of parting day..."

GARDNER: "The lowing herd wind slowly o'er the lea..."

MAGS: [*With a deep breath.*] "The curfew tolls at parting day,
The herd low slowly down the lea...no, *knell*!
They come winding down the *knell*!..."

GARDNER: Listen, Mags...*listen*!

[*A pause.*]

TOOTS: [*Loud and clear with* GARDNER'*s inflection.*] "The curfew tolls the knell of parting day,
The lowing herd wind slowly o'er the lea,
The ploughman homeward plods his weary
way,
And leaves the world to darkness and to me."

MAGS: HE SAID IT....HE SAID IT!...AND IN YOUR VOICE!...OH, DADDY, THAT'S AMAZING!

GARDNER: Well, Toots is very smart, which is more than I can say for a lot of people I know....

MAGS: [*To* TOOTS.] Polly want a cracker? Polly want a cracker?

GARDNER: You can teach a parakeet to say anything; all you need is patience....

MAGS: But *poetry*...that's so hard....

FANNY: [*Enters carrying a suitcase and* GARDNER'*s typewriter in its case. She's dressed in her traveling suit, wearing a hat to match.*] WELL, THERE YOU ARE! I THOUGHT YOU'D DIED!

MAGS: [*To* FANNY.] HE SAID IT! I FINALLY HEARD TOOTS RECITE GREY'S ELEGY. [*She makes silly clucking sounds into the cage.*]

FANNY: Isn't it uncanny how much he sounds like Daddy? Sometimes when I'm alone here with him, I've actually thought he *was* Daddy and started talking to him. Oh, yes, Toots and I have had quite a few meaty conversations together!

[FANNY *wolf-whistles into the cage; then draws back.*

215

GARDNER *covers the cage with a traveling cloth. Silence.*]

FANNY: [*Looking around the room.*] God, the place looks so bare.

MAGS: I still can't believe it ... Cotuit, year round. I wonder if there'll be any phosphorus when you get there?

FANNY: What on earth are you talking about? [*She carries the discarded backdrop out into the hall.*]

MAGS: Remember that summer when the ocean was full of phosphorus?

GARDNER: [*Taking* TOOTS *out into the hall.*] Oh, yes....

MAGS: It was a great mystery where it came from or why it settled in Cotuit. But one evening when Daddy and I were taking a swim, suddenly it was there!

GARDNER: [*Returns.*] I remember.

MAGS: I don't know where Mum was....

FANNY: [*Reentering.*] Probably doing the dishes!

MAGS: [*To* GARDNER.] As you dove into the water, this shower of silvery green sparks erupted all around you. It was incredible! I thought you were turning into a saint or something; but then you told me to jump in too and the same thing happened to me....

GARDNER: Oh, yes, I remember that ... the water smelled all queer.

MAGS: What *is* phosphorus, anyway?

GARDNER: Chemicals, chemicals ...

FANNY: No, it isn't. Phosphorus is a green liquid inside insects. Fireflies have it. When you see sparks in the water it means insects are swimming around....

GARDNER: Where on earth did you get that idea? ...

FANNY: If you're bitten by one of them, it's fatal!

MAGS: ... and the next morning it was still there....

GARDNER: It was the damndest stuff to get off! We'd have to stay in the shower a good ten minutes. It comes from chemical waste, you see....

MAGS: Our bodies looked like mercury as we swam around....

GARDNER: It stained all the towels a strange yellow green.

MAGS: I was in heaven, and so were you for that matter. You'd finished your day's poetry and would turn somersaults like some happy dolphin....

FANNY: Damned dishes...why didn't I see any of this?!...

MAGS: I remember one night in particular.... We sensed the phosphorus was about to desert us; blow off to another town. We were chasing each other under water. At one point I lost you, the brilliance was so intense...but finally your foot appeared...then your leg. I grabbed it!...I remember wishing the moment would hold forever; that we could just be fixed there, laughing and iridescent.... Then I began to get panicky because I knew it would pass; it was passing already. You were slipping from my grasp. The summer was almost over. I'd be going back to art school; you'd be going back to Boston.... Even as I was reaching for you, you were gone. We'd never be like that again.

[*Silence.*]

FANNY: [*Spies* MAGS's *portrait covered on the easel.*] What's that over there? Don't tell me we forgot something!

MAGS: It's your portrait. I finished it.

FANNY: You finished it? How on earth did you manage that?

MAGS: I stayed up all night.

FANNY: You did?...*I* didn't hear you, did you hear her, Gar?...

GARDNER: Not a peep, not a peep!

MAGS: Well, I wanted to get it done before you left. You know, see what you thought. It's not bad, considering...I mean, I did it almost completely from memory. The light was terrible and I was trying to be quiet so I wouldn't wake you. It was hardly an ideal situation....I mean, you weren't the most cooperative models.... [*She suddenly panics and snatches the painting off the easel. She hugs it to her chest and starts dancing around the room with it.*] Oh, God, you're going to hate it! You're going to hate it! How did I ever get into this?...Listen, you don't really want to see it...it's nothing...just a few dabs here and there....It was awfully late when I finished it. The light was really impossible and my eyes were hurting like crazy....Look, why don't we just go out to the sidewalk and wait for Kitty so she doesn't have to honk....

GARDNER: [*Snatches the painting out from under her.*] WOULD YOU JUST SHUT UP A MINUTE AND LET US SEE IT?...

MAGS: [*Laughing and crying.*] But it's nothing, Daddy...*really!*...I've done better with my eyes closed! It was so late I could hardly see anything and then I spilled a whole bottle of thinner into my palette....

GARDNER: [*Sets it down on the easel and stands back to look at it.*] THERE!

MAGS: [*Dancing around them in a panic.*] Listen, it's just a quick sketch....It's still wet....I didn't have enough time....It takes at least forty hours to do a decent portrait....
[*Suddenly it's very quiet as* FANNY *and* GARDNER *stand back to look at it.*]

MAGS: [*More and more beside herself, keeps leaping around the room wrapping her arms around herself, making little whimpering sounds.*] Please don't...no...don't...oh, please!...Come on, don't look....Oh, God, don't...please....
[*An eternity passes as* FANNY *and* GARDNER *gaze at it.*]

GARDNER: Well...

FANNY: Well...[*More silence.*]

FANNY: I think it's perfectly dreadful!   GARDNER: Awfully clever, awfully clever!

FANNY: What on earth did you do to my face?...

GARDNER: I particularly like Mum!

FANNY: Since when do I have purple skin?!...

MAGS: I told you it was nothing, just a silly...

GARDNER: She looks like a million dollars!

FANNY: AND WILL YOU LOOK AT MY HAIR...IT'S BRIGHT ORANGE!

GARDNER: [*Views it from another angle.*] It's really very good!

FANNY: [*Pointing.*] That doesn't look anything like me!

GARDNER: ...first rate!

FANNY: Since when do I have purple skin and bright orange hair?!...

MAGS: [*Trying to snatch it off the easel.*] Listen, you don't have to worry about my feelings...really...I...

GARDNER: [*Blocking her way.*] NOT SO FAST...

FANNY: ...and look at how I'm sitting! I've never sat like that in my life!

GARDNER: [*Moving closer to it.*] Yes, yes, it's awfully clever....

FANNY: I HAVE NO FEET!

GARDNER: The whole thing is quite remarkable!

FANNY: And what happened to my legs, pray tell?...They just vanish below the knees!...At least my dress is presentable. I've always loved that dress.

GARDNER: It sparkles somehow....

FANNY: [*To* GARDNER.] Don't you think it's becoming?

GARDNER: Yes, very becoming, awfully becoming...

FANNY: [*Examining it at closer range.*] Yes, she got the dress very well, how it shows off what's left of my figure....My smile is nice too.

GARDNER: Good and wide....

FANNY: I love how the corners of my mouth turn up....

GARDNER: It's very clever....

FANNY: They're almost quivering....

GARDNER: Good lighting effects!

FANNY: Actually, I look quite...*young*, don't you think?

GARDNER: [*To* MAGS.] You're awfully good with those highlights.

FANNY: [*Looking at it from different angles.*] And *you* look darling!...

GARDNER: Well, I don't know about that....

FANNY: No, you look absolutely darling. Good enough to eat!

219

MAGS: [*In a whisper.*] They like it.... They like it!
[*A silence as* FANNY *and* GARDNER *keep gazing at it.*]

FANNY: You know what it is? The wispy brush strokes make us look like a couple in a French Impressionist painting.

GARDNER: Yes, I see what you mean....

FANNY: ...a Manet or Renoir...

GARDNER: It's very evocative.

FANNY: There's something about the light.... [*They back up to survey it from a distance.*]

FANNY: You know those Renoir café scenes?...

GARDNER: She doesn't lay on the paint with a trowel; it's just touches here and there....

MAGS: They *like* it!...

FANNY: You know the one with the couple dancing?...Not that we're dancing. There's just something similar in the mood...a kind of gaiety, almost....The man has his back to you and he's swinging the woman around....OH, GAR, YOU'VE SEEN IT A MILLION TIMES! IT'S HANGING IN THE MUSEUM OF FINE ARTS!...They're dancing like this....
[*She goes up to him and puts an arm on his shoulders.*]

MAGS: They like it.... They like it!

FANNY: She's got on this wonderful flowered dress with ruffles at the neck and he's holding her like this....That's right...and she's got the most rhapsodic expression on her face....

GARDNER: [*Getting into the spirit of it, takes* FANNY *in his arms and slowly begins to dance around the room.*] Oh, yes...I know the one you mean....They're in a sort of haze...and isn't there a little band playing off to one side?...

FANNY: Yes, that's it!
[*Kitty's horn honks outside.*]

MAGS: [*Is the only one who hears it.*] There's Kitty! [*She's torn and keeps looking towards the door, but finally gives in to their stolen moment.*]

FANNY: ... and there's a man in a dark suit playing the violin and someone's conducting, I think.... And aren't Japanese lanterns strung up?...

[*They pick up speed, dipping and whirling around the room. Strains of a far-away Chopin waltz are heard.*]

GARDNER: Oh, yes! There are all these little lights twinkling in the trees....

FANNY: ... and doesn't the woman have a hat on?... A big red hat?...

GARDNER: ... and lights all over the dancers, too. Everything shimmers with this marvelous glow. Yes, yes... I can see it perfectly! The whole thing is absolutely extraordinary!

[*The lights become dreamy and dappled as they dance around the room.* MAGS *watches them, moved to tears as ...*]

SLOWLY THE CURTAIN FALLS

BARD BOOKS
DISTINGUISHED DRAMA

BENT Martin Sherman	75754-0/$2.50
BROKEN PROMISES: FOUR PLAYS David Henry Hwang	81844-2/$3.95
CHRISTOPHER DURANG EXPLAINS IT ALL FOR YOU Christopher Durang	82636-4/$3.95
FANTASTICKS Jones Schmidt	54007-X/$2.50
FIVE PLAYS BY RONALD RIBMAN Ronald Ribman	65342-7/$4.95
FOUR PLAYS: THE CHILDREN, THE MIDDLE AGES, SCENES FROM AMERICAN LIFE and THE DINING ROOM A. R. Gurney, Jr.	89498-X/$3.95
GAY PLAYS: THE FIRST COLLECTION William H. Hoffman, Ed.	77263-9/$3.95
THE IMPORTANCE OF BEING EARNEST Oscar Wilde	77404-6/$1.95
KEY EXCHANGE Kevin Wade	61119-8/$2.50
MASS APPEAL Bill C. Davis	77396-1/$2.50
OUR TOWN Thornton Wilder	61118-4/$2.25
PETER PAN, OR THE BOY WHO WOULD NOT GROW UP James M. Barrie	57752-6/$2.50
THE RING: FOUR PLAYS FOR CHILDREN Adapted by Philip Caggiano	79434-9/$2.50
THREE PLAYS BY THORNTON WILDER Thornton Wilder	57257-5/$2.50
THREE PLAYS BY TINA HOWE Tina Howe	85001-X/$4.95
UNCOMMON WOMEN AND OTHERS Wendy Wasserstein	80580-4/$2.95
WHOSE LIFE IS IT ANYWAY? Brian Clark	64808-3/$2.95
YOUNG PLAYWRIGHTS FESTIVAL COLLECTION Compiled & Edited by the Foundation of the Dramatists Guild, Inc.	83642-4/$3.95

ATTENTION
THEATRE GROUPS!

Avon Bard plays are available at special quantity discounts for bulk purchases for sales promotions, premiums, fund raising or educational use.

★ ★ ★

For details write or telephone the office of the Director of Special Markets, Avon Books, Dept. FP, 1790 Broadway, New York, New York 10019, 212-399-1357.